The
Christian
Musicians
Devotional

365 Days of
Digging Deeper into Ministry

Marie Wise

Author of
The Christian Band Handbook
ChristianBandHelp.com

Dedication

This book is dedicated to my amazing husband, Mark, who shows me every day what true ministry is about: the love of Jesus.

Special thanks to our Grandma Sue for her daily prayers and financial support. Without your help, this book would not have been possible. We love you and are so grateful that we get to spend eternity with you.

Lastly, I want to thank our parents: Don and Armene, Carol, and Darlene and Jim. You have helped mold Mark and I into the quirky but wonderful couple we are today.

Acknowledgements

Thank you to the many people who have attended my seminars and concerts through the years. You have been a source of constant encouragement to go beyond the industry standards and try new ideas. Special thanks go out to my husband Mark Wise. When I was single I was advised to marry the man who looked most like Jesus. Then I realized my advisors meant that I should marry the man who acted most like Jesus. I was exceptionally blessed to marry Mark, a man who physically looks like many people picture Jesus and has the most Christ-like character I have ever known. This book is a direct result of what we have learned on our journeys both separately and together to become effective ministers of the Gospel.

Special Thanks

A special "Thank You" must be given to Katie Erickson, who expertly edited this book out of selfless service to Christ. She asked for nothing in return and has done so with several Christian ministries. So, please, take a moment and pray that God will grant Katie exceptional favor and blessings as she continues to serve the body of Christ.

Disclaimer

Table of Contents

February

1 Luke 12:15   Life is Not What You Own
2 I Timothy 2:8   Holy and Anointed Hands
3 Hebrews 4:13   Accountable to God
4 Proverbs 3:5-6   God's Dream or Yours?
5 1 Thessalonians 2:3-6   Flattery and Praise
6 Zechariah 4:6   By My Spirit
7 Amos 5:21-24   Just and Righteous Living
8 Psalm 68:24-26   The Procession of God
9 2 Corinthians 2:17   Sincerity and Authority
1 Acts 3:7-8   Culture and God
11 Ephesians 2:12   Designed and Created
12 1 Corinthians 4:12   Weariness and Love
13 Ephesians 6:18   Pray at All Times
14 1 Corinthians 13:13   The Greatest is Love
15 Isaiah 30:1   Directed By the Spirit
16 Ephesians 4:2   Make Allowance for Faults
17 Matthew 4:1   Jesus Was Tempted
18 Psalm 92:1-3   It Is Good
19 Philippians 1:27   Standing Together
20 Genesis 49:23-24   Strengthened by God
21 Romans 13:1-2   Christian Cheaters and Liars
22 Jeremiah 14:22   We Will Wait for Your Help
23 Genesis 50:20   "But God" Positions My Future
24 Philippians 4:12   Know How to Live
25 Acts 18:1-3   God Appointed Co-Workers
26 Ezekiel 34:26   In the Proper Season
27 Proverbs 14:8   Where Are You Going?
28 Hebrews 12:1   Run Without Weights

March

1 Romans 12:18   All That You Can
2 Matthew 6:33-34   God Has It Covered!
3 Isaiah 52:7   What God Hears About You
4 Jeremiah 9:23-24   Boast About God
5 Matthew 28:18-19   Therefore
6 Romans 12:2   Good, Pleasing, & Perfect

11 Ecclesiastes 10:7   Right Side Up Ministry
12 Psalm 55:22   Rest in Following
13 Acts 14:21-22   We Must Suffer Hardships
14 Proverbs 29:11   Venting Anger
15 Job 40:4   God is in Control
16 Psalm 87:7   Tour Guides of Worship
17 Revelation 3:19   You Don't Realize
18 Romans 14:10-13   Comparisons and Judgments
19 Psalm 126:1-3   God Has Done Amazing Things
20 Psalm 126:4-6   Streams Renewing the Desert
21 Matthew 16:24-26   Do What You Wanna Do
22 Revelation 4:10-11   The Elders Worship, Like Us
23 Galatians 5:24-25   The Journey & The Destination
24 2 Chronicles 9:1   Beautiful Things
25 Philippians 24:7d-8   What Are We Working For?
26 Luke 19:26   Excuses and Talents
27 Acts 4:13   Ordinary Men with Jesus
28 Hebrews 12:11-13   But Afterward
29 Isaiah 29:13   Lukewarm Routines
30 Hebrews 10:35-36   Persistent Endurance

May

1 Luke 24:49   God's Power and Work
2 Matthew 26:41   Powered By Prayer
3 Job 38:2-7   Hear From God
4 Mark 6:37-38   Faith vs. Planning
5 Psalm 138:1-3   Backed By His Name
6 Romans 14:19   Relationship Harmonies
7 Philippians 4:2   Because You Belong to Him
8 Colossians 4:6   Attractive Words
9 2 Kings 18:6-7a   Success as a Result
10 Exodus 14:13   Standing Still
11 1 Corinthians 1:26-27   Powerless Foolish Things
12 1 Peter 5:8-9   Hungry Lions
13 Matthew 6:12   Forgive the Church
14 Ruth 2:2   Times of Famine
15 Proverbs 25:28   It's Not Only About Us

19 Matthew 23:5-8   Being Exalted
20 Psalm 144:9   New Songs
21 Jeremiah 10:23   One Step at a Time
22 John 5:17   God Still Works
23 Psalm 52:8-9   Seasons of an Olive Tree
24 Psalm 119:105   Hiking in the Dark
25 Mark 4:37-38   Rest in the Storm
26 1 Samuel 15:22   Submission Vs. Sacrifice
27 Isaiah 26:3   Communication Builds Trust
28 2 Corinthians 4:5   Name Recognition
29 Romans 8:31   Unsuccessful Ministry
30 Proverbs 27:23-24   The Next Generation

July

1 2 Timothy 2:12   Growing Through Hardship
2 Genesis 9:21-23   Love Covers Sin
3 Acts 16:14   The Lord Opens Hearts
4 2 Timothy 2:1-2   Praying for Authorities
5 Luke 8:50   Fear vs. Faith
6 Leviticus 19:18   Battling for Love
7 2 Kings 6:5-6   Borrowed Equipment
8 Isaiah 30:18   Waiting for You
9 2 Chronicles 25:8-9   Bad Business Deals
10 Luke 6:46-48   Saying & Doing
11 Philippians 1:4-5   Praying for Partners
12 Galatians 6:12   A Job Well Done
13 Matthew 7:12   Do Unto Others
14 John 6:3   Band Time
15 2 Samuel 11:2   One Step at a Time
16 Matthew 5:5-8   Unsung Heroes
17 Jeremiah 16:20   The God of Success
18 Exodus 17:14   Merchandise Reminders
19 2 Corinthians 3:5   Qualified?
20 1 John 2:6   What Did Jesus Do?
21 Hosea 11:4   Ropes of Love
22 Joel 1:3   Let Children Tell Children
23 2 Chronicles 23:18   Ready to Sing & Rejoice

October

1   Psalm 23:1-3   Rest Renews
2   Jeremiah 17:7-8   Never Stop Producing Fruit
3   Matthew 25:29   God's Business Manager
4   Revelation 2:9a   God's True Riches
5   Ephesians 5:19   Heart Music
6   Acts 4:29   Boldness or Safety
7   Romans 15:5-6   Doing Life in Harmony
8   2 Corinthians 1:4   Comfort Others
9   Acts 4:20   Can't Stop Talking
10 Psalm 97:10   The Evil Within
11 Zechariah 13:9   The Fire of God
12 Exodus 22:6   The Fires of Destruction
13 John 21:20-22   What About Him?
14 Isaiah 42:8   Our Ministry or God's?
15 James 3:8-9   Made in the Image of God
16 Psalm 27:5-6   Sacrifices with Shouts of Joy
17 Proverbs 20:18   Succeed with Good Counsel
18 1 Chronicles 9:33   No Other Responsibilities
19 Luke 11:5b-8   Shamelessness Gets Results
20 Proverbs 17:17   Friends and Brothers
21 1 Timothy 4:12   Be an Example
22 Galatians 6:9   Doing what is Good
23 Proverbs 27:6   Wounds, Kisses & Truth
24 John 13:14-17   Do As I Have Done
25 Philippians 2:3-4   Take an Interest in Others
26 Psalm 63:5   Songs of Joy in the Wilderness
27 Proverbs 22:1   A Good Reputation
28 Numbers 14:11   Belief and Contempt
29 James 1:5   God's Wisdom and Plan
30 Mark 9:23   Believe for Small Things
31 Luke 24:38-40   Not As Expected

November

1   Psalm 35:18   Thank God Publically
2   Colossians 3:23-24   Working for God
3   Proverbs 26:17   Don't Yank the Dog's Ears
4   Isaiah 12:5   Make His Praise Known
5   Matthew 20:25-27   Servant Leaders
6   Proverbs 2:6   Wisdom, Understanding & Knowledge
7   Zephaniah 3:17   He Rejoices Over You
8   James 4:17   Do This... Don't Do That
9   Isaiah 35:10   Sing With Joy and Gladness
10   1 John 3:16-18   Help New Music Ministers
11   Ecclesiastes 2:4-8   The Value of Musicians
12   Proverbs 26:13   Lions and Laziness
13   Ecclesiastes 4:12   Braided Cords
14   Acts 16:25   Singing and Praying
15   1 Chronicles 15:58   Do Something
16   2 Chronicles 2:13-14   Huram-Abi
17   Matthew 6:5   Quality Creative Work
18   Isaiah 55:8   Thoughts and Ways
19   John 7:2-6   Pursuing Fame
20   Luke 8:5-8   Our Responsibility
21   Philippians 2:14-15   Crooked and Perverse People
22   2 Corinthians 12:9   Covenant Power
23   Jonah 1:3   Running to Tarshish
24   Numbers 20:10   Frustrating People
25   Mark 1:9-11   Dearly Loved
26   1 Samuel 21:10   Fight or Flight
27   Colossians 2:7   Thankful for Opposition
28   Luke 4:18   Effective Ministry
29   1 Thessalonians 2:10   Genuineness
30   Romans 15:2   Build Then Up in the Lord

December

About Marie Wise

I have been working for over 30 years in Christian music ministry and I have pretty much seen it all: the financial successes and those who sacrificed everything, the fake Christians who think they can get ahead in the music industry by starting out in Christian music, and the true Christ followers, the bands that please God and the ones who poorly represent Him. Through it all I constantly encourage Christian musicians to increase the excellence of business in their ministry because the way we handle the business side of ministry demonstrates our integrity. The Bible is very clear that if we want to be entrusted with the true riches of ministry (people) we must do what is right simply because it is right, with our money and our business decisions (Luke 16:11). Sometimes integrity costs us money, but God's blessing has no price tag and He will more than make up for anything our integrity might cost.

The explosion of technology in the music industry provides you with the opportunity to change the world more effectively than any musicians before you. It is my sincere hope that this devotional book helps you stay close to God and make use of every opportunity He provides for you to bring people closer to Jesus.

> *"If you need wisdom –*
> *if you want to know what God wants you to do –*
> *ask Him, and He will gladly tell you.*
> *He will not resent your asking."*
> **James 1:5**

Marie enjoys many creative hobbies including sewing, knitting, and fine art painting. She can often be found painting crazy murals on the walls of her church or planting an edible landscape in her yard. Most of her time is spent working at home with her husband, Mark, who is also a musician and an author.

Preface

Christian musicians are often so busy doing the work of the ministry that we do not take the time to feed ourselves as much as we should. We play late on Saturday and usually either do not attend or sleep through Sunday morning church services, so our churches are not able to feed us as much as we need either. Pastors try to help us and give us the very best advice they can, but they have not lived the life and frequently do not give us the very best answers to our questions. Where do we turn to for help to stay strong spiritually?

The Christian Musicians Devotional was written to help Christian musicians be transformed into Christian music ministers. By increasing our daily diet of Scripture and applying the daily Bible verses specifically to our lives as Christian musicians we can learn to be better ministers. (Yes, that would be the mission statement of this book.)

When I first prayed about writing this book I thought, "How hard can it be? I can spend the first half hour or so writing each day and it should be done in a year." At that point I am pretty sure God chuckled.

The Christian Musicians Devotional took over two years to write and was the most intense, difficult process I have ever been through. It is not that the actual writing was hard. It does not take long to read or write each day's devotions. It is the applying of the principles that was painful and changed me. Every day I started the day saying, "God, what do You want to say to Christian musicians?" and I ended the day saying "Ouch, that hurt. I need to do better, I need to be better." This process changed me and raised the bar for my personal ministry. If the book did that for me, I trust that it will do that for you as well.

So I say, "If growth requires pain, embrace the pain." As Christian music ministers we must continually be growing our faith. It is essential that we are consistently listening to what God is speaking to us and applying it because in the end the only thing that matters is faith expressing itself through love.

Let the journey begin...

Introduction

We are all too often consumed with the breadth of our ministry. But the scope or largeness of our ministry can only be sustained with depth. For example, take the construction of the foundation of a building. When we want to build a one-story ranch house, we could use a slab foundation. It is quick to construct using somewhat shallow perimeter footings and a few inches of poured concrete with a base of sand and gravel underneath. When we want to build a much larger multistory house, we use much deeper perimeter footings to hold the additional weight of the house. But when we want to build a skyscraper, the foundation is quite different because the buildings are expected to resist earthquake, fire, and wind. The extra weight of the large building and the necessity of protecting the large number of occupants cause us to dig down to bedrock before attempting to create the foundation. Then we use large steel footings and beams which are reinforced with rebar for added strength. Skyscraper foundations are often five stories or more deep, while the average house foundation is usually one or two feet deep.

Most of us want our ministries to be as large as skyscrapers. We have all seen what happens when skyscrapers collapse, both actual buildings and large ministries. Frequently the cause of the collapse is a foundation that is not strong enough to support the weight of the structure through the ever-changing conditions around it. If, in this analogy, the skyscraper is our ministry it must be built on the foundation of the strength of our spiritual life, which must be set on the bedrock of Jesus.

This book is designed to help you build a stronger foundation for your ministry through daily devotions. When many people talk about expanding band ministry or going deeper into ministry they discuss topics such as leadership development, expanding your band's fan base and getting signed to a label. But a strong foundation starts with an extremely deep relationship with God. There is no substitute for it. There are no fast tracks and no hacks to get there quickly. Relationship is developed and grown over time consistently spent with another person. It cannot be phoned in or put off and expected to grow. Relationship cannot be completed; it is ever growing, ever changing, and eternal. Therefore, it must be worked on daily, consistently, and with intention.

Success in music ministry depends on us keeping relationship with God as our highest calling and then staying focused on the work He has called us to do. We cannot be so easily distracted by the tasks of music ministry, family, church etc. as to lose sight of the reason we are in music ministry: to bring people closer to Jesus. The reason we do what we do—people—are always more important than the tasks of what we do. Living in God's love and practicing His presence moment by moment is the only way we can experience success as music ministers.

January 1

The Purpose of Devotions

"For the grace of God has been revealed, bringing salvation to all people. And we are instructed to turn from godless living and sinful pleasures. We should live in this evil world with wisdom, righteousness, and devotion to God, while we look forward with hope to that wonderful day when the glory of our great God and Savior, Jesus Christ, will be revealed."

Titus 2:11-13

A New Year brings the hope of a fresh start. We evaluate the past year and make resolutions to help us make changes and improve the upcoming year. There is always the anticipation that this year will be better than last, but there are no guarantees. Life has an odd way of dishing out the unexpected, and it often turns out to be just a little more than we think we can handle.

One of the best and most foundational things we can do to be prepared for whatever the New Year has to offer is to stay strong and consistent in our faith. The only way to do that is to spend time with God regularly. So, we have daily devotions, or a daily time set aside to spend with God. This time is not meant to remind God that we are still here or to show God how much we love Him by our self-discipline. It is meant to remind us about the greatness of God and His love towards us. Our time with God leaves us in a position of greater trust in Him.

Daily time spent with God brings our lives into line with His plan for us. He reveals our sins and shortcomings, and then shows us how to come into line with His plan for our lives and our ministries. The true definition of success is not found in accomplishments or recognition. God's success is simply defined by how closely we followed His plan for our lives and ministries.

Father, I want to follow You more closely this year than last. Reveal Yourself and Your plan to me as I spend time with You. Help me to make this my most successful year ever.

January 2
Success Envy

"Then I observed that most people are motivated to success because they envy their neighbors. But this, too, is meaningless—like chasing the wind."

Ecclesiastes 4:4

Most of us have learned that attempting to "keep up with the Joneses" with the latest and greatest stuff is meaningless. Trying to accumulate the latest technology, the best house, and the newest car will wear us out and leave us in debt. We get it; we have learned to buy what we need or want based on ourselves rather than others. But many of us have not learned to apply this same principle when we look at the success, significance, and impact of other people's lives and ministries compared to ours.

There will always be people that are better known, have larger ministries, put on bigger shows, draw more fans, and attract more attention than us. Just as other musicians will have more and better equipment, they will also seem to be doing more important and impactful ministry. It is easy to envy what God has called someone else to do. It is downright hard not to be jealous when they are especially successful at doing it.

But, look at ministry from God's perspective. How many people do you think will agree to be in a famous band? How many people will accept His call to tour the world? Then consider how many people might agree to stay in their hometown and play in the prisons and jails. How many people would say "Yes" enthusiastically if God told them to play at the local nursing home every weekend? Which "ministers" are more difficult to find, and so are more rare and valuable? God's success is all about the heart—are you being true to what God has called you to be and do?

Father, help me to see my ministry through Your eyes. Show me how to base my success on Your calling and my obedience.

January 3

Everything You Need

"Seek the Kingdom of God above all else, and live righteously, and he will give you everything you need."
                                                              Matthew 6:33

There are only two requirements listed here: (1) seek the kingdom of God above all else, and (2) live righteously. The promise is that if we do, God will give us everything we need. This does not sound complicated. But, in our typical humanness, we make it difficult. We analyze this verse from every angle: from what exactly is defined as "needs" to how righteous we have to live to qualify. Then, there is the ever popular discussion of how do we know if we are seeking the kingdom of God above all else. These are all valid questions. But, perhaps, we need to look at this verse with a different perspective.

We are human. Although we strive to be more perfect, we will never attain it. We will never live 100% righteously or seek the kingdom of God above all else 100% of the time. We cannot earn the right to have all our needs met. So, how can we expect that God will give us everything we need? By grace and faith—the same way we live the rest of our lives.

As Christian music ministers, we are constantly trying to be more righteous, to live more the way God wants, and to put His kingdom first. Hopefully, with each passing day we are doing better in a cycle of repenting and growing. But after we have done all we can do, we trust the work of Jesus on the cross to make up for what we cannot do. So, let us remove the burden of our needs being met based on how "good" we are and the belief that our needs will not be met if we are not "good enough." Instead, let us realize that God provides for us based on how good He is. We will do our best and trust God for the rest.

Father, thank You for providing for my needs while I work towards putting Your kingdom first and living righteously.

January 4

Rock Stars & Divas

"So Jesus called them together and said, 'You know that the rulers in this world lord it over their people, and officials flaunt their authority over those under them. But among you it will be different. Whoever wants to be a leader among you must be your servant, and whoever wants to be first among you must be the slave of everyone else. For even the Son of Man came not to be served but to serve others and to give his life as a ransom for many.'"

Mark 10:42-45

Rock stars and divas: the stereotypes conger an image of big dreams, big lifestyle, and big attitudes. Egos and money rule whenever the divas are around. In the Christian music industry, we would like to believe that there are no rock stars or divas, but experience has proven that to be false. Christians are human and we fall prey to poor attitudes and lifestyles far more often than we would like. It is easy to spot these attitudes in someone else.

But, look in the mirror; do you see a rock star or a diva? Of course not. Really? Look again. Look harder. Imagine your life being replayed as a movie where you are the central character. How do people react around you? How have their lives changed because of being in contact with you? Do they feel special, valued, and loved, when you walk in the room? Who cleans up the messes and takes care of the worst jobs—you or them?

Often, it is the little things that give our rock star attitudes away. Do we help other bands unload their gear? How do we respond to a fan at an inconvenient time? What does our heart say when our set gets cut short? Look in that mirror again and again, frequently and diligently. Be determined to be a music minister, servant, slave, and leader of all.

Father, search my heart and show me attitudes I need to change. I want to represent You well as a music minister.

Expressing Thankfulness

> *"The LORD will comfort Israel again*
> *and have pity on her ruins.*
> *Her desert will blossom like Eden,*
> *her barren wilderness like the garden of the LORD.*
> *Joy and gladness will be found there.*
> *Songs of thanksgiving will fill the air."*
>
> *Isaiah 51:3*

In this prophecy we see that songs of thanksgiving follow joy and gladness. Have you ever noticed that people tend to sing when they are happy? Often, the volume is turned up until the music literally fills the air. It is a natural reaction—part of celebrating and rejoicing. God seems to love it when people sing songs of thanksgiving.

Interestingly, God never describes the music—the genre, decibel level, the look of the musicians, or even the number of people involved. Most often the details are left to the reader's imagination. This would lead us to believe that God is more concerned with the heart of the people being thankful than He is with exactly how it is expressed.

As music ministers, we have the honor of leading people in expressions of thankfulness toward God. We get to write songs and lead the celebration as the people follow. Perhaps we can rejoice in their thankful hearts and allow them the freedom of expressing that thankfulness in their own way. When we focus on the joy and gladness being expressed, we can make room for ways of expressing that do not live up to our personal preferences. We can truly celebrate expressions of thankfulness toward God in the hearts of our brothers and sisters.

Father, thank You for times of gladness and rejoicing. Help me to focus on the hearts of Your people as they express their thankfulness toward You.

January 6
Music in the House

"Meanwhile, the older son was in the fields working. When he returned home, he heard music and dancing in the house."
Luke 15:25

Imagine this son walking towards his home to find a party going on. Not only are there extra people in his house, but there is singing and dancing—obviously something big happened while he was gone. The event must be good because the musicians were invited and are playing lively tunes. He walks a little faster because he is curious. Before he even hits the front door, this son knows something exciting, something wonderful has occurred. Why? He heard the music.

No other artistic medium has the ability to convey emotions as quickly and as far reaching as music. Music sets the mood and tone for celebrations, special moments, and even funerals. It can break up the monotony of our daily routine by inspiring us to remember or feel something related to the lyrics. The sounds are carried through the air to touch and communicate directly with people's hearts. Music has the ability to change our emotions and to open the doors to our hearts and spirits in ways that teaching and preaching will not. This ability carries with it a weighty responsibility for Christian musicians.

Are we using music to bring people closer to Jesus? Or have we wasted some of our best musical efforts on mediocre messages? Are we communicating what God wants people to hear? Is our music having and impact on people and changing the world around us? We need to be constantly striving to become better at using music to communicate God's message so that even those who are just starting out on the path home will hear and know that something good and exciting is happening.

Father, show me how to be the best possible communicator of Your heart and Your love towards people through music.

January 7
I Don't Need You

"But our bodies have many parts, and God has put each part just where he wants it. How strange a body would be if it had only one part! Yes, there are many parts, but only one body. The eye can never say to the hand, 'I don't need you.' The head can't say to the feet, 'I don't need you.'"
1 Corinthians 12:18-21

Relationships between band members are probably the most meaningful, impactful, and difficult relationships that any music ministry will experience. More bands break up and band members leave because of personality conflicts than any other reason. We have learned to tactfully say, "It was because of musical differences." But most often, the root problem is that we could not find a way to love and value each other.

Each person in the band brings different giftings and perspectives. For example, some people are more administrative and want to build systems; others need to meditate and seek a spiritual solution for each decision; still others want to discuss every issue from all sides before attempting to come up with a plan. It is easy to come up with Bible verses to support your point of view, no matter what it is. It is human nature to use these verses as weapons and judge other people by them. We all do it.

In order to walk in love and to grow in our relationships with each other, we must have a change of heart. When we begin to truly appreciate each other's gifts, personalities, and perspectives, we see the advantage of diversity within the band. Face it: no one gets everything right all the time. But, when we act as a team, using all the gifts of each member, we have the opportunity to do far better than we would individually.

Father, show me the gifts You have placed in my band mates. Teach me to value those gifts and love my brothers.

January 8
Helpful Words

"The lips of the godly speak helpful words,
but the mouth of the wicked speaks perverse words."
Proverbs 10:32

It is generally assumed that the primary difference between Christian and secular music is the lyric content. We only have to listen to the radio for a few minutes to know that many secular songs contain lyrics that we do not want replaying in our minds. But is it enough for Christian lyrics to NOT be perverse? Is it enough to NOT be something, or do our lyrics need to BE something else in order to qualify as Christian?

This verse says that our words (our lyrics) should be helpful. While this verse is not the only verse in the Bible about our words, being helpful is certainly one criterion that our lyrics should meet to be considered Christian. Have you read the lyrics to your songs lately? How helpful are they to your audience? Could your lyrics be rewritten to be more helpful?

Have you ever considered what kind of help your target audience needs? A primarily Christian audience may need words that encourage, while a young secular audience might need words that talk about God's love no matter what you have done. Who is the target audience for your music? What are their needs? What lyrics can you write that will be the most helpful? These are all questions that music ministers must continually ask themselves in order to grow as ministers. The most effective lyrics do not only grab the audience's attention or get the most radio airplay. Godly lyrics pierce the heart and draw the listener closer to God, which is the very best help we as music ministers can give to anyone.

Father, inspire me to write lyrics that help people. Show me their needs and teach me how to draw them closer to You by meeting those needs through song lyrics.

Wise Choices and Understanding

"Wise choices will watch over you.
Understanding will keep you safe."
Proverbs 2:11

Being a musician can be very exciting. There is the rush of performing, the adoration of fans, and all the hype of marketing. It is very easy to buy into the image. But often, "buying" into it is exactly what happens. Musicians can sink every dollar they have and borrow more to make their dreams come true, only to find they may have been unrealistic. Homes have been lost, bankruptcy declared, and families broken over less than stellar music careers.

The way to avoid ruining your life over a career in music is to consistently make wise choices. Wisdom, especially when making decisions, must be diligently sought out. Start by getting knowledge about the subject, and then spend time completely understanding that information. Seek wise counselors who have experience in the area and talk to people that know you and your situation. Spend time in the Bible doing word studies about your topic. Meditate on the applicable verses. All the work of seeking out wisdom can be time consuming. Are you willing to do it?

What if the answers are not what you want to hear? So many times we would rather hear, "Do whatever it takes to get the results you want." It is easier to say that we are trusting God when we do something crazy and exciting than when we do something wise and mundane. But what if God is using wisdom to show us that crazy and exciting is not best for us and our ministries? Can we trust God to guide us through wisdom? Can we seek wisdom diligently and then apply it to make wise choices, even when those choices are not what we think we want?

Father, give me wisdom and I will follow You.

January 10
Celebrate with Joyous Praise

"Then Hezekiah ordered that the burnt offering be placed on the altar. As the burnt offering was presented, songs of praise to the LORD were begun, accompanied by the trumpets and other instruments of David, the former king of Israel. The entire assembly worshiped the LORD as the singers sang and the trumpets blew, until all the burnt offerings were finished. Then the king and everyone with him bowed down in worship. King Hezekiah and the officials ordered the Levites to praise the LORD with the psalms written by David and by Asaph the seer. So they offered joyous praise and bowed down in worship."

2 Chronicles 29:27-30

The Temple had been closed, and the people turned from God under the leadership of the previous king. But now Hezekiah is king! The Temple is purified and reopened—the people turned back to God. This is a cause for celebration; who is called upon? The musicians. Admittedly, this is one of our favorite callings: to lead the people in joyous praise and worship.

Musicians have been given an honor far beyond what we have earned. We are absolutely blessed beyond measure to be able to please God by leading the people in praise and worship. It is amazing to think that we can make God happy by singing our praise to Him. It is even more amazing to know that other people and the heavenly hosts join us in that joyful celebration.

Let us never forget or minimize the favor that God granted us when He chose us to lead praise and worship with music. It is humbling. But it also gives us great cause for celebration without any other special occasion. God chose us to lead celebrations that make Him happy!

Father, I am honored by Your favor. I am honored to serve You with my music. As long as I live I will sing praises to You in joyful celebration and lead Your people to do the same.

Stand Strong in Him

"If you think you are standing strong, be careful not to fall."
1 Corinthians 10:12

Being role models comes with the territory of being a Christian musician. Unfortunately, that also means that our lives are held up as examples of Christianity for all to see. Well-meaning fans put us on pedestals, and when we fall our sin affects them. Many have used the excuse that the fans should have been looking at Jesus instead of them, which is true. But, this verse instructs us not to fall, clearly implying that we have a responsibility to live a lifestyle befitting a Christian.

We have all heard about the big names who have committed the big sins and fallen. But, being on the top of a pedestal can be a heady experience even if you have not yet experienced popularity as a musician. Christians admire you for working so hard in the ministry. People want to be like you, not because of your fame but because of your assumed spirituality. It is easy to buy into the hype. The opportunity for egos to grow is directly related to your list of sacrifices and accomplishments in the ministry. Falling is not always about the "big" sins. Falling occurs every time your sin gets in the way of your ministry—a sharp word, a bad attitude, an ego that takes credit for work you did not do—anything that is not Christ-like is a fall.

The most common time to fall is when you feel higher than others, on a pedestal. When you feel strong and are doing well, look out—that drop down can hurt. The higher the pedestal and the less prepared you are to catch yourself, the more damage will be done. So, watch yourself and steady your footing on the solid foundation of Christ and what He has done for you.

Father, cause me to remember that my sacrifices and accomplishments are not my strength. My strength is found in what Jesus did and Your continued involvement in my life.

January 12

Recount the Victories

"Listen to the village musicians
gathered at the watering holes.
They recount the righteous victories of the LORD
and the victories of his villagers in Israel.
Then the people of the LORD
marched down to the city gates."

Judges 5:11

One of the greatest honors bestowed on a Christian musician is to recount the past victories of God acting on behalf of His people. This retelling of the past inspires and encourages all who hear to take action and be victorious in the present and future. We have seen Christians given the courage to fight their battles with the reminder of past victories. We may have even led the songs that provided the inspiration.

Yet, as musicians we often feel worn down by our circumstances. Sometimes, the difficulty of ministry leads us to feel jaded, hopeless, and defeated. Isn't it funny that we, as humans, know how to encourage other people but often forget how to encourage ourselves? The secret is to recount the victories in our own lives and ministries, to encourage ourselves in the Lord. So often, we forget the little victories that helped us get to where we are today. But those "little" victories can continue to be a source of encouragement for the rest of our lives. Remember all the way back to our first performances when we prayed that we could just get through the set without embarrassing ourselves... and we made it. Remember the times when we just wanted to play a show, then one got booked. Or what about the time we had no gas money and somehow we got to the show? Recount what God has done and be encouraged.

Father, help me to remember what You have done in my past and know that You will continue to be involved in my future.

January 13
Solitude in Prayer

"After sending them home, he went up into the hills by himself to pray. Night fell while he was there alone."
Matthew 14:23

Jesus himself needed to pray. This is just one of many verses that talk about Jesus leaving the crowds of people to be alone in prayer. It is interesting to note that He left people, sent them home, and stopped doing ministry, so He could pray alone.

In this age of cell phones, texting, messaging, internet, Wi-fi hotspots, streaming video, television, radio, etc. we may need to do just a little more than leave the room to be alone to pray. Today, the distractions follow us wherever we go. We need to disconnect in order to find solitude. How often do we completely disconnect, become inaccessible to every human being on earth so we can spend uninterrupted time with our heavenly Father? And when we do, how often is that time cut short due to our inability to stay focused?

We want our ministries to explode with the power and love of God. We want people's lives to change and to have an impact on the world around us. But, where does that kind of ministry come from? Solitude in prayer with God. We need to hear from God, to know His plans for us and our ministries, and to understand what we are to do next. There is no hope for us to be successful in His eyes without His guidance.

Better management of social media, connecting with fans before and after the show, engaging the audience during the show, and even praying with people one on one are all good things. But, they are meaningless until we have heard from our Father. The direction, strength and power of our ministries can only come from spending time in solitude in prayer.

Father, I want to have an extraordinary music ministry. Help me to overcome distractions to spend more time with You.

The Quality of Your Words

"Preach the word of God. Be prepared, whether the time is favorable or not. Patiently correct, rebuke, and encourage your people with good teaching."

2 Timothy 4:2

Some people have the gift of gab—talking just comes naturally, so they always have something ready to say. Other people are more reserved, preferring to think about what is being said in a conversation before participating in it. Either way, just having a conversation is not enough.

Christian ministers represent God. We should be speaking God's thoughts on any given topic. But how often are we prepared to do so? Do we know God's thoughts? Good teaching begins with knowing God. The best ways to know God are prayer and studying the Bible. We all know this. We do not do it as well as we should. Knowing God can be frustrating because it is time consuming and requires patience. It is human nature to want to be actively doing the work involved with ministry rather than spending time studying and praying. We want to see progress and growth; we want to be able to demonstrate that our ministry is helping more people than ever, so we tend to focus on tasks.

The quality of our ministry comes from knowing God. Speaking more words does not increase ministry. Speaking God's words does. The world is full of noise; advertisers hawking the next great product, films and books distracting us with stories, politicians' pontificating on world events—the list is endless. People do not need to hear more words. We need to hear quality words, God's words, in our everyday life. Have you taken the time to know God so that you can speak His thoughts in any situation on any topic? Represent God with quality words.

Father, teach me Your thoughts, and show me how to talk to people so that I will represent You well.

January 15
Share the Light

"You are the light of the world—like a city on a hilltop that cannot be hidden. No one lights a lamp and then puts it under a basket. Instead, a lamp is placed on a stand, where it gives light to everyone in the house."

Matthew 5:14-15

Have you ever tried to sleep when someone is reading in the same room? You want to be polite, you roll over and close your eyes but in the end you still know someone is reading. The pages turn, the light seems to be just enough to keep you from a sound slumber, the minutes tick away, and sleep is elusive. But to the person doing the reading, the light is an amazing tool—allowing them to read comfortably in what used to be darkness. They are free to explore whatever topic the book has to offer because the needed light is available. Ah, to be the light that keeps the world from slumber. It's not always welcome, and not always wanted by those that prefer to sleep in pitch black. But, it does the job of illuminating the darkness for readers.

Our ministries can be like the light in a room—welcomed by someone that wants to read, not by people that prefer to stay in darkness. But the light of the love of Jesus in our lives might just be what it takes to get them to wake up and ask about "the book" we are reading. Just like the light, our ministries can seem offensive without ever intending to be so. But since our goal is to illuminate the darkness so people can see, we must not hide or put out the light. Light is needed but not always welcome, so we need to be as warm as light to help people overcome their offense. We must share the light and help others to see the benefits of light.

Father, remind me that people can be offended by the light You offer but I am not to respond with anger. Help me to simply share Your love with anyone willing to receive it.

January 16
Celebrate His Presence

"And the Levites who were musicians—Asaph, Heman, Jeduthun, and all their sons and brothers—were dressed in fine linen robes and stood at the east side of the altar playing cymbals, lyres, and harps. They were joined by 120 priests who were playing trumpets. The trumpeters and singers performed together in unison to praise and give thanks to the LORD. Accompanied by trumpets, cymbals, and other instruments, they raised their voices and praised the LORD with these words:
'He is good! His faithful love endures forever!'
At that moment a thick cloud filled the Temple of the LORD. The priests could not continue their service because of the cloud, for the glorious presence of the LORD filled the Temple of God."

2 Chronicles 5:12-14

This verse is part of the description of the largest celebration in Israel—the celebration of the Ark of the Covenant being brought into the temple Solomon built. A large portion of the celebration was devoted to praise and worship led by priests that were musicians. What an honor—to usher in the very presence of God!

Today, we too can usher in God's presence every time we perform. But our calling is not to usher God's presence into a particular building. Instead, we bring God to the hearts of people. We may not see a cloud but we will see an even greater miracle: change in hearts. Our calling and ministry as Christian musicians is fulfilled when we bring people closer to Jesus through our music, our testimonies and our lives. We are like the musician priests of the Old Testament, but our Temple is not a building, it is a heart.

Father, help me to stay focused on bringing people closer to You. I will celebrate Your presence in our hearts!

January 17
Real Power

"But you will receive power when the Holy Spirit comes upon you. And you will be my witnesses, telling people about me everywhere—in Jerusalem, throughout Judea, in Samaria, and to the ends of the earth."

Acts 1:8

The early church of the New Testament did not have all the tools we have available to us today. There were no sound systems, electric instruments, microphones, computers, screens, air-conditioned buildings, vans to transport the equipment and people, etc. But, they were effective—people were added to their numbers daily. What did they have that made them able to impact the world so much that we still feel their influence today? They had power given through the Holy Spirit.

So often, we get caught up in our tools. We make sure all the equipment gets to where it needs to be and is working properly on time. We practice, we write new music, we record, and we sound check. We pay attention to the business of our ministry so we can afford to do the ministry. We post and tweet, inviting fans to the shows. The to-do list is endless. We should do all these things and more to build extraordinary music ministries.

But, in the end, the power to bring people closer to Jesus comes from the Holy Spirit. All our words and works are dead and meaningless without His power. His power can cut quickly to a person's heart and change their lives forever. His presence is more important than all the methods or equipment available. His power to change lives is what our ministry is all about.

The Holy Spirit's power working through us is what our ministry needs to be effective. Everything else is secondary. In all our activities and tasks, let's not forget who and what is most important.

Father, thank You for sending the Holy Spirit. Work through my ministry today with the power that changes lives.

January 18
Care for Each Other

"This makes for harmony among the members, so that all the members care for each other. If one part suffers, all the parts suffer with it, and if one part is honored, all the parts are glad."

1 Corinthians 12:25-26

Relationships between band members can be volatile. Differences of opinion on almost every subject including lyric contents, music styles, ministry techniques, business ethics, and priorities for spending band money can threaten to rip apart the closest friends and partners. Long "discussions" frequently occur as a result of our differences. Interestingly enough, the suffering or honoring of one band member can be a uniting influence on the band. This seems to be contradictory behavior.

When band members truly care for each other, we feel free to "battle it out" amongst ourselves. Relationships are strong, so we are not threatened by difference of opinion. We keep talking until we come to the best decision. But when an outside force threatens one of us, we tend to band together in defense of our brother. There is no discussion, no differences. We do whatever it takes. Likewise, when one of us receives acknowledgement for an achievement, we are there to rejoice. We sit in the front row and are first in line with congratulations. These reactions are healthy demonstrations that we are living out brotherly love. We demonstrate our care by our actions.

Love in action is not always without conflict. How can you tell if you truly care for your band mates? Look at your actions within your relationships for signs of love. Are you free to share your opinions without risking friendships? Are you there in times of trouble and rejoicing? Do you protect your brother at all costs? If so, you may be experiencing real love.

Father, I want my band mates to know I care deeply for them. Show me what I can do to better demonstrate my love.

Missing Wisdom

> *"For whoever finds me finds life*
> *and receives favor from the LORD.*
> *But those who miss me injure themselves.*
> *All who hate me love death."*
>
> Proverbs 8:35-36

In context, this verse is about the value of wisdom. Everyone wants to be wise; everyone wants a successful life. But, many people like to try the shortcut of being crafty and shrewd. Still others value getting education and knowledge but just do not seem to be able to apply it practically in life. In a sense, they learn to love shrewdness or learning but hate wisdom. We think of them as foolish.

However, most people do not hate wisdom; they just do not make time to seek it out. We make what we consider to be the best decisions we can in the moment, we may even ask a few people for their advice. But, we do not truly invest the time it takes to do everything we can to seek out true Godly wisdom. Look what happens: we injure ourselves when we miss wisdom. Of course, that is not what we say happened. In ministry we often cry "persecution," or "the devil's attack" when we actually brought the injury upon ourselves through lack of wisdom.

Wisdom does not protect us from every calamity. For sure, we can be persecuted or attacked. Sometimes we simply reap the consequences of living in a fallen world. But much of the time our misfortunes are caused by missing wisdom. Let us be honest with ourselves when this happens and learn from our mistakes. More importantly, take the time to diligently seek wisdom and apply it to our lives and our ministries.

Father, change my heart to value Your wisdom more than quick decisions, exciting prospects, and my time. Show me how to receive Your favor by finding wisdom.

January 20
Running the Right Race

"Don't you realize that in a race everyone runs, but only one person gets the prize? So run to win! All athletes are disciplined in their training. They do it to win a prize that will fade away, but we do it for an eternal prize."
1 Corinthians 9:24-25

Secular bands work hard. Many bar bands learn hundreds of cover tunes and play for 8 hours a night. They practice several nights a week and invest most of their personal money into the band. They sacrifice their families and their careers. For the most part, they get paid in free beer. They do all this for a shot at a record deal, fame, and fortune—hollow, fleeting rewards.

Christian music ministers are running their race for a much more important prize. The stakes are much higher. But, are we running to win? Some would say that because we are not willing to sacrifice our relationships and families that we are losers. Others would say that we are automatically disqualified from the race because our primary reason for living is not a record label deal. But Christian musicians are running a completely different race! Our goals and reasons for playing music put us on a different course.

The race we are running is to be obedient and please God first, above all else. We are winners if we accomplish that. For us, it is not a matter of fame, fortune, or label deals. We focus all our energy, all our strength on pleasing God. Laziness has no part in our training. We practice self discipline and sacrifice more than many secular musicians. But we apply all our efforts towards living the way God has laid out for us. Our ministries and music are not the goal of our lives; they are a tool for accomplishing what God has called us to be.

Father, help me to stop comparing my success to secular musicians. Show me how to run to win Your prize.

January 21
Worthless Things

*"Turn my eyes from worthless things,
and give me life through your word."*
                                                    Psalm 119:37

What are worthless things? The "big" sins come to mind immediately, but there are far more treacherous worthless things that are not always sin. Anything that comes between us and God is worthless: the cares of this world, the deceitfulness of riches, or wasting time on pointless endeavors. Musicians often have a flexible schedule, with small amounts of time free in between events. Do you spend that time getting close to God?

We know what we should do, but when it comes down to doing it we seem gravitate towards worthless things. We try to motivate ourselves by remembering that people are going to hell. We picture what hell must be like, and we vow to do better. We fail. So, we try to motivate ourselves with the rewards we will gain in heaven. Fail. We even try to picture what it would be like to meet Jesus face to face and see His disappointment in us. It may work for a while, yet we go back to choosing pointless things. The passion of all that Jesus did on earth for us will evoke an emotional response, but emotions do not last and we find ourselves once again focusing on worthless things. It seems to be human nature to choose poorly.

We cannot consistently turn our own eyes from worthless things. But, God can. Notice that this verse does not say "I will turn my eyes from worthless things." God must do the work in us. He can stir up a longing in us for His word; as we yield to it we will experience His kind of life. But, this is not a prayer for the faint hearted. Are you willing to allow God to turn you from worthless things?

Father, HELP! Change me so that I will experience the life that comes from Your word. Turn my eyes toward You.

January 22
I Will Hold You Up

"Don't be afraid, for I am with you.
Don't be discouraged, for I am your God.
I will strengthen you and help you.
I will hold you up with my victorious right hand."
                                            Isaiah 41:10

Musicians live a risky life. We regularly travel without enough money, counting on the money we will make to get us to the next show. Often, venues and promoters do not live up to their promises, not understanding how if affects our ministries. We break down in the middle of nowhere, our merchandise orders get sent to the wrong place, and our families have to live without us coming home at the end of each day. It is easy to become overwhelmed and discouraged, and at times afraid.

This verse is a promise made to Israel, who is referred to as God's servant. It is also made to Jacob whom God says He chose, and to Abraham whom God calls His friend (see verse 8). Are we not all those things and the spiritual descendants of Israel, Judah, and Abraham? This promise is also for us.

When the circumstances of music ministry become overwhelming, remember what God has promised—to strengthen us and to hold us up. Look at all that God has already done for us. Will He not honor His word now? Of course He will. Jesus went through the humiliation and pain of crucifixion for us. Will He do nothing now? No. The Father gave up His only Son to have relationship with us. Would He abandon us now? No. The Holy Spirit was given to comfort and counsel us. Will He only do that once in a while for a few people? No. God honors His word. He honors His promises. When things look bad, pause and remember what God has already done to build trust in what He will do.

Father, instead of being overwhelmed by my circumstances, I am overwhelmed by what You have done and will do for me.

January 23
Sinking

"'Yes, come,' Jesus said. So Peter went over the side of the boat and walked on the water toward Jesus. But when he saw the strong wind and the waves, he was terrified and began to sink. 'Save me, Lord!' he shouted. Jesus immediately reached out and grabbed him. 'You have so little faith,' Jesus said. 'Why did you doubt me?'"

Matthew 14:29-31

Starting out in music ministry is an exciting time. Jesus says, "Yes, come," when we are called into music ministry and we begin to do it. Generally, we do not really know what we are getting into so it is easy to have faith. But once we have been around the block a few times, we realize what a daunting task music ministry can be. We look at the improbability of success, see all the work it will take, understand that we will probably struggle financially, and realize that not everyone we have to work with has pure motives. Often, we look at all the problems, the waves, become afraid and start to sink.

Sinking is not all bad. Think about it—in order to sink you must have first gotten out of the boat. Most people prefer to stay in their comfort zone, so they will never sink. We experience doubt because we first had enough faith to start! Sinking times are when we call out to Jesus to save us; some of our best praying times. Jesus is always faithful to reach out and grab us, which in turn causes the little faith we already had to grow. It is not a comfortable process, so most people will not do it. Look at Peter: everyone else stayed dry and safe in the boat, but he got wet and risked his life. The result is that Peter was the only person besides Jesus who walked on water that day. Jesus was faithful to reach out and grab Peter when he needed help. Peter acted on his little faith and his faith grew. We must be willing to do the same—to try, fail, grow and try again.

Father, I do not want to be comfortable—grow my faith.

January 24
Distracted

"Her sister, Mary, sat at the Lord's feet, listening to what he taught. But Martha was distracted by the big dinner she was preparing. She came to Jesus and said, 'Lord, doesn't it seem unfair to you that my sister just sits here while I do all the work? Tell her to come and help me.' But the Lord said to her, 'My dear Martha, you are worried and upset over all these details! There is only one thing worth being concerned about. Mary has discovered it, and it will not be taken away from her.'"

Luke 10:39-41

Martha and Mary, the worker and the listener: we are all familiar with stories of these two sisters throughout the Gospels. Jesus loved them and they were dedicated to Him. In this instance, Martha wanted to cook a big dinner for Jesus and His disciples. There is nothing wrong with cooking or a big dinner, and nothing wrong with serving Jesus. But, Martha got into trouble when she became distracted with the work.

We have all been there—too much work to do, too little time. It is easy to start looking around at our band mates and decide that they are not doing their fair share. It is easy to start a mental conversation about how we carry the band, or think, "Where would they be without me?" As soon as we start to walk down those paths, we are distracted. At that point we are not in communion with God. We cannot hear Him clearly.

Could Mary have carried on with the work and listened to what Jesus was saying? Probably. Christian music ministers strive to work and listen. This is not a matter of balance, alternating between the two. We need to simultaneously do both. Doing our work while listening to God is having fellowship with Him. This fellowship enables us to have a powerful, effective ministry.

Father, show me how to avoid being distracted by the work of the ministry. Talk to me as I seek to do my work with You.

January 25
What Do You Want?

"Guard your heart above all else,
for it determines the course of your life."
Proverbs 4:23

What do you want? Be careful with the answer to that question. It is not, "What do you think you're supposed to want?" The answer may be found in what you think about when you are free to think about anything. Do you picture yourself on the big stage as the headliner? Do you dream of what you will purchase with the money you will be paid after you are successful? Do you fantasize about releasing multiple projects that dominate the radio airwaves or touring extensively? What do you want?

It is difficult for Christian musicians to keep focused because of all the trappings of the music industry. What is a goal to secular musicians is just a tool for Christian music ministers. We want souls in heaven. We want lives changed. We want to bring people closer Jesus. Money, radio airplay, big shows, publicity, touring, etc. are tools to help us connect with people.

Guarding our heart requires us to continually remind ourselves that we are in the music business for people. We can easily fall into the temptation of seeking fame in the name of finding significance in ministry. But God knows our true heart, our true motivations. Are we in ministry because above all else we love people? When we dream do we dream of souls in heaven?

Our focus on bringing people closer to Jesus will change the course of our life. It may cost us fame and fortune. We may never play the big stage. We may never even be able to make a living from our music. We could end up playing in obscure places like prisons, nursing homes, or homeless shelters. But, if we guard our hearts we will get what we want.

Father, pierce my heart with a desire to bring people closer to You. Cause me to love people more than the music.

January 26
Running with Endurance

"Dear brothers and sisters, when troubles come your way, consider it an opportunity for great joy. For you know that when your faith is tested, your endurance has a chance to grow. So let it grow, for when your endurance is fully developed, you will be perfect and complete, needing nothing."

James 1:2-4

No one is happy when the band's van breaks down, no one rejoices when merchandise is stolen, and certainly no one likes it when a band member quits the band. When things go wrong, we are given the opportunity to test ourselves. Do we lash out? Or do we allow ourselves to grow stronger in endurance?

Unfortunately, there is not a way to increase endurance except by enduring. Wouldn't it be great if a long distance runner could take a pill and be able to run longer and farther? It does not work that way. Runners have to run more and longer to increase their endurance. They have to break through the wall of wherever they stopped last time in order to get farther this time. We must do the same to increase our own endurance.

Runners can choose when they want to increase their endurance by deciding to run farther at almost any time. In life, however, we cannot decide to endure more until a circumstance comes across our path that requires more endurance. We have to wait for the opportunity. This is why we can consider troubles a joy—they are opportunities to increase endurance.

Certainly, no one finds working through the pain of endurance to be fun. The fun comes in the pride of accomplishment after you have endured. We can be joyful when we are enduring because we know we will be able to look back and say, "We did it—we made it... we got through... we endured."

Father, when troubles come remind me to look at them as an opportunity to grow in endurance, to become stronger in You.

January 27
Listening and Understanding

"Spouting off before listening to the facts
is both shameful and foolish."

Proverbs 18:13

Answering before listening is a common problem we all face from time to time. It is foolish and damaging to our relationships. When we answer before we have listened, we have devalued the speaker by communicating that what we have to say is more important than what they have to say. We have also inferred that we are somehow smarter or know more than the speaker. Is this a good way to communicate? Of course not. Nothing will be solved by insulting the people you are talking to.

Band members spend so much time with each other that we begin to speak in abbreviated communication, based on previous conversations. In effect we are communicating, "Remember that time when..." and both people have the same frame of reference to work from. We do not need to go over the entire conversation again. The abbreviations save time and are especially helpful during set up and tear down at gigs. But, as we spend more and more time together, we start to assume we understand each other all the time. Then someone blows up.

Making time to truly listen and understand each other is critical in bands. As St. Francis of Assisi said, "Seek first to understand, then to be understood." Spouting off in anger to someone who is blowing up only stokes their anger. Long standing relationships have ended in this kind of communication. A wise music minister will diffuse the situation by listening and seeking to understand before responding. Value what your band mate has to say and the anger will subside. Friends will remain friends when both friends seek to understand each other.

Father, cause me to desire to understand my band mates.
Help me set aside what I want to say until I understand them.

January 28

Pause and Remember

"Let the godly sing for joy to the LORD;
it is fitting for the pure to praise him.
Praise the LORD with melodies on the lyre;
make music for him on the ten-stringed harp.
Sing a new song of praise to him;
play skillfully on the harp, and sing with joy.
For the word of the LORD holds true,
and we can trust everything he does.
He loves whatever is just and good;
the unfailing love of the LORD fills the earth."

Psalm 33:1-5

Do we need reasons to sing for joy to the Lord? Look at the list of reasons given in this psalm: the word of the Lord holds true, we can trust everything God does, He loves what is just and good, His love is unfailing, and His love fills the earth. So we sing to the Lord because we are godly and it is fitting to do so.

As we perform the same set over and over, sometimes we lose our enthusiasm. We lose sight of the real reasons we sing. It is easy to fall into the trap of going through the motions without actually praising God from our hearts. During those times we need to pause and reflect on God and His love for us; to become overwhelmed once again with the God we fell in love with.

The distractions of each gig can keep us from experiencing the love of God in the moment we are performing. There is so much to get right: getting to the gig, unloading, set up, sound check, eating, and greeting fans can take our focus off of God before we even start to perform. So, before we walk on stage each night, let's take a moment to pause and remember why we sing.

Father, I know I am supposed to worship every time I play.
Remind me to pause and remember so I really am worshiping.

January 29
Faith and Good Deeds

"Now someone may argue, 'Some people have faith; others have good deeds.' But I say, 'How can you show me your faith if you don't have good deeds? I will show you my faith by my good deeds.'"

James 2:18

Faith and good deeds go hand in hand. How are you exercising and growing your faith as a Christian music minister? Look at your good deeds.

What are good deeds? Is it a good deed to perform your music on stage? Maybe, a little. But, you receive and enormous amount of benefit from doing so—people clap, they buy your music, and you gain fans. This process boosts your self esteem and ego. You get to express your artistic side. It costs you little.

What about really ministering to the people you meet before and after the gig? Now you have to go over and above what comes natural to do. It costs you time that you may have otherwise spent relaxing, and it takes you out of your comfort zone. You have to reach out rather than waiting for people to come to you. You have to humbly ask to help them when you are tired. You have to meet their needs when your own needs have not been met. That sound much more like faith in action.

Do your good deeds extend to the other bands you play with? Many bands view joint shows as a competition. But, do you demonstrate your faith by helping them? Do you load and unload their equipment in addition to your own gear? Do you help them get on and off stage? Do you loan them any pieces of your equipment they have forgotten? Do you do all this for bands you do not like, or who are vulgar? Are you standoffish, or do you get out of your comfort zone and demonstrate your faith? Show your faith by your actions, and people will notice.

Father, I want to represent You well. Show me new ways to stretch my faith by doing good deeds.

January 30
How Would Jesus Live Your Life?

"But now you must be holy in everything you do, just as God who chose you is holy. For the Scriptures say, 'You must be holy because I am holy.'"

1 Peter 1:15-16

In this verse, the word holiness means separated from sin and consecrated or devoted to God. Holiness results in right living. Judging by the number of verses that talk about living holy lives, personal holiness seems to be extremely important to God. God expects us to live holy lives because we are His children, His examples on earth, and He is holy.

Are you living a holy life? Are you living like Jesus would live if He were physically present on earth today? Take a moment and imagine Jesus living your life. Imagine Jesus as a member of your band. What would He do differently? What things would He do the same? Remember the things the Bible says Jesus did in ministry when He walked on earth. Are you doing those things? Where can you do better, to grow in holiness? Is your band a good representation of Jesus' ministry when He walked the earth? Where can you act more like Jesus?

Ultimately, none of us can live rightly all the time, we sin. None of us can be holy on our own; we are not good enough. We must receive holiness by God's grace. But grace does not give us an excuse to continue to walk in sin. We must be striving to be better, to grow in righteousness and holiness. We can live more rightly, more holy today than we did in the past. We are holy because God makes us holy as His children. We can grow in holiness as we continue to devote ourselves to God and His ways.

Father, I see many areas that I need to grow in holiness. Thank You for Your grace. Help me grow in right living.

January 31
I Can't... I'm Too...

"'O Sovereign LORD,' I said, 'I can't speak for you! I'm too young!' The LORD replied, 'Don't say, 'I'm too young,' for you must go wherever I send you and say whatever I tell you. And don't be afraid of the people, for I will be with you and will protect you. I, the LORD, have spoken.'"

Jeremiah 1:6-8

God called Jeremiah to be a prophet. His response: "I can't, I'm too young." Whenever God calls us to do something our first reaction is usually to see all of our shortcomings and faults. The reasons why we can't are often overwhelming to the point that we wonder if God is talking to the wrong person.

In the verses just prior to these, God tells Jeremiah that He has known him since he was in his Mother's womb. God knew way ahead of time what Jeremiah's talents and gifts were. He knew Jeremiah's personality and weak areas. God knows what it takes to be a prophet. God knew if Jeremiah would make a good prophet or not, before He called him to speak.

God may not be calling us to be prophets. But He is calling us to be something—in our case, Christian music ministers. Yet, we so often say, I can't because I'm too _____. We fill in the blank with whatever talent or gift we think is needed at the moment. "I'm too old to be touring," "too fat to be on stage," "my voice isn't good enough," "I don't know how to manage a business," etc. are just excuses we make. The truth is we make the excuses because we are looking at ourselves rather than God. We do not see ourselves through God's eyes. God knew us before He asked us to do anything. He knows what it will take to get the job done. He knows if we will make good music ministers before He asks us.

Father, I say "Yes" when you call me to do anything. If you will show me how, I will do whatever You ask.

February 1
Life Is Not What You Own

*"Then he said, 'Beware! Guard against every kind of greed.
Life is not measured by how much you own.'"*

Luke 12:15

Christian music ministers give up a larger paycheck to do their ministry. We often take lesser paying jobs that free us up on the weekends and we consistently turn down overtime to play a gig. Some of us get to the point of working only as a musician, taking a huge pay cut to do so. Generally, Christian musicians are not as wealthy as we could be if we put our undivided effort into a secular job. Those choices affect how we and our families live.

Sometimes, it is hard to continue to make the sacrifices necessary to be a Christian music minister. We see that other people have more stuff and other musicians have better equipment. But, just as life is not defined by how much you have, the quality of your ministry is not measured by the quality and abundance of your gear. There will always be someone who has more and better equipment than you do. The key is to use what you have to do your ministry to the best of your ability.

Fulfillment in life and ministry comes after contentment. We can miss the satisfaction that comes with doing our ministry by constantly looking toward getting more. Of course, we want to do better and often that requires better gear. We should keep up with new technology and have a prioritized plan for new equipment purchase. But, a constant yearning and attention given to better equipment can rob us from the satisfaction of the ministry we are doing right now. Greed can be subtle; it can start out as a well-intentioned desire to be better at our ministries. But it can quickly turn into envy, then greed without us noticing. Are you content? Are you fulfilled? If not, check for greed.

Father, I want to do Your ministry well and live a fulfilled life. Help me to keep greed in check as I purchase equipment.

February 2
Holy and Anointed Hands

"In every place of worship, I want men to pray with holy hands lifted up to God, free from anger and controversy."
1 Timothy 2:8

Whose hands are more anointed than that of a musician? We use our hands to play the instruments that lead people in the worship that opens hearts to prayer. Often, we feel that the Holy Spirit takes over and plays through us. We like to think that holiness is a prerequisite for anointing. So, we avoid looking honestly at our lives because we experience God's anointing so frequently. But holiness is not a prerequisite for anointing. We cannot assume that we are holy because we feel anointed.

God can anoint anything or anyone to do whatever needs to be done to fulfill His purposes. For example: a talking donkey, an adulterer, a prostitute, a liar. Anointing is simply being given the power to accomplish God's will. It is not necessarily wanted, earned, or deserved. So, an anointed musician is not always holy.

Holiness requires action on our part. Holiness starts with repentance—changing our hearts and actions from sin, accepting God's forgiveness, and moving forward to become more Christ-like. It is not always about the sins we do not do; holiness also encompasses what we do, think, and strive to become.

Anger and controversy, while not necessarily sins in themselves, can be symptoms of a thought life or goals that are out of line with God's way of life. We can use times of anger and controversy as a trigger to cause us to reexamine ourselves. Are we walking in holiness in the area we are angry in? If not, correct the problem and humbly move on to be the most effective kind of musician possible—a musician with anointed AND holy hands.

Father, thank You for anointing me to play music. Show me areas in my life that I can work on holiness. I want to be a holy and anointed musician for Your use.

February 3

Accountable to God

"Nothing in all creation is hidden from God. Everything is naked and exposed before his eyes, and he is the one to whom we are accountable."

Hebrews 4:13

Have you ever had someone say, "If you were really a Christian you would..." or "You are not really a Christian band because..."? Our lives and our ministries are constantly being judged by people who do not know us. These people may have become familiar with our music online and attended multiple concerts; they may even be co-workers such as promoters or agents. But, they do not know us; they do not know our hearts.

While some people may know us better than others, only God truly knows who we are. This is both freeing and scary. Think about who God is: King of Kings, owner of the cattle on a thousand hills, creator of the universe. Now consider that this is the One who not only knows you best, but gets to judge you based on what He knows—now that's the fear of God!

We do not have to be condemned by people judging our lives and ministries. We may want to do a heart check to see if there is any truth in what they say as God often places people in our lives to correct a problem. We do have to be concerned with what God thinks about us. We are accountable for both our lives and our ministry to God.

It is wise to have life coaches and ministry counselors. We should learn from each other. But at the end of time, when we stand before God, He is not going to ask "so and so" what they thought about us or our ministries. God probably will not even ask if we did what our advisors told us to do. He is going to hold us accountable for our heart's attitudes and our actions; and He has seen them all!

Father, help me to focus on pleasing You. Teach me how to humbly respond to other people that I must please You first.

February 4
God's Dream or Yours?

> *"Trust in the LORD with all your heart;*
> *do not depend on your own understanding.*
> *Seek his will in all you do,*
> *and he will show you which path to take."*
> **Proverbs 3:5-6**

God has not called most Christian musicians to be in one of the top ten Christian bands. Is that your dream? The reality is that it might not happen. You need to ask, "Am I living the dream God has for me?" Living God's dream creates an amazing life. Living your own dream will always be less than what you could have had and done, no matter how successful you appear.

Most Christian musicians are in a Christian band for a period of time and then transition to something else: a worship leader, playing on a worship team, youth group leader, pastor, or careers outside ministry. Some people view this as failure. But, what if God's plan for your life included being in a less than famous Christian band? What if you need that experience to help prepare you for the future? What if you did exactly what God wanted you to do with the band? Would you consider the band to be a success?

Do not allow disappointment with the amount of ministry, fame or income your band experiences to direct your path. Those disappointments can be divine intervention to point you towards success. Bring your disappointment to God, seek His plan, and when you find it—follow it with all your heart.

The definition of a successful Christian band is not the band that is the most famous, sells the most music, or even wins the most people to the Lord. The definition of a successful Christian band is the band that most closely follows the path God shows them to take.

Father, reveal your dream for my life so I may follow it.

February 5

Flattery and Praise

"Never once did we try to win you with flattery, as you well know. And God is our witness that we were not pretending to be your friends just to get your money! As for human praise, we have never sought it from you or anyone else."

1 Thessalonians 2:3-6

Christian bands are constantly flattered by fans. Some of it is genuine and some is said to gain attention from band members. Unfortunately some Christian bands also flatter their fans in the hope that they will purchase merchandise or donate to the band's ministry. We have seen those bands; the ones that gush all over their fans, get their photos taken and sign all the autographs but as soon as possible they are gone. There is no praying with people, listening to their stories, or truly caring about them in any way. Their goal is simply to develop a fan base to make a living doing Christian music. Don't be that band.

Seek to please God. To win God's praise you must love people. "'And you must love the Lord your God with all your heart, all your soul, all your mind, and all your strength.' The second is equally important: 'Love your neighbor as yourself.' No other commandment is greater than these." (Mark 12:30-31)

Christian musicians so often get caught up doing all the things it takes to make their ministries successful that they no longer do the work of the ministry. They may be famous and even popular but they are only musicians, not music ministers. God's way is to focus on loving Him and then loving people. Loving people is inconvenient, messy, and at times even disturbing. Loving people will cause you to get behind schedule, forget to do some tasks, lose your reputation, or lose money. But God has a way of working it all out. He praises you when you love people.

Father, help me keep my love for people alive in the midst of the craziness of trying to be a successful Christian band.

February 6
By My Spirit

"Then he said to me, 'This is what the LORD says to Zerubbabel: It is not by force nor by strength, but by my Spirit, says the LORD of Heaven's Armies.'"

Zechariah 4:6

A certain amount of administration and organization must be done to run a successful music ministry. But doing all the right tasks does not necessarily make a successful music ministry. We can apply all the techniques that other bands have used to become successful. Those techniques can help us gain a measure of notoriety, fame, and popularity. Although good techniques, fame and popularity can help a band look successful; only God's Spirit can actually accomplish the ministry.

Success is God's Spirit working through us and our music ministry to bring people closer to Jesus. God's Spirit is not dependant on our efforts. His work will be accomplished with or without us. We are the ones who are privileged to be able to participate in His work.

Picture a child helping her mother bake cookies. In the end the cookies are going to be baked with or without the child's help. But most children are extremely happy when Mom lets them participate by stirring and measuring, sometimes licking the spoon. But, ultimately, Mom is responsible to see that the cookies are baked correctly.

We are God's children, privileged to help in His ministry and excited to be part of what He is doing in the world around us. But let us never inflate or esteem the importance of our tasks, our participation in His work. It is not our efforts and work that brings people closer to Jesus; we are honored to participate in the work He is doing—the work of His Spirit.

Father, open my eyes to see the work of Your Spirit so I may better participate in Your ministry.

February 7
Just and Righteous Living

"I hate all your show and pretense—
the hypocrisy of your religious festivals and solemn
assemblies.
I will not accept your burnt offerings and grain offerings.
I won't even notice all your choice peace offerings.
Away with your noisy hymns of praise!
I will not listen to the music of your harps.
Instead, I want to see a mighty flood of justice,
an endless river of righteous living."

Amos 5:21-24

God enjoys a good party—celebration and praise give Him cause to delight in us. He loves to see us sacrifice and give our best to Him. Although He enjoys these things, they are not always pleasing to Him. What He desires from us before sacrifice and praise is justice and right living.

We have all heard of Christian band members living a far less than holy life. Often, in our humanness, we make excuses for ourselves to do so. If we continue along this path of hypocrisy, there will come a point when God will not listen to our praises and sacrifices. Our Christian music can become offensive to God because our lives do not line up with His way of living.

Are you living rightly? Do other people see your life as an example of right living? Do you treat other people justly? Do other people come to you because they know you are fair and honest? If you want to please God and have your praise and sacrifices bring God pleasure, you need to take a close look at your life. Bring whatever does not line up with His way of living back in line. Living justly and rightly is more important than creating excellent music when it comes to pleasing our Father.

Father, show me areas in my life that You want me to change. I want to please You above all else.

February 8
The Procession of God

"Your procession has come into view, O God—
the procession of my God and King as he goes into
the sanctuary.
Singers are in front, musicians behind;
between them are young women playing tambourines.
Praise God, all you people of Israel;
praise the LORD, the source of Israel's life."

Psalm 68:24-26

Picture this in your mind: the procession of God, just as if you were watching a parade march by. The singers go by first, calling the crowd to sing along, followed by the young women playing tambourines, getting the crowd to clap and dance, and then the musicians march past as the crowd claps and cheers, bringing even more excitement to the whole event. The crowd eagerly anticipates the arrival of God.

Music prepares the way as God enters His sanctuary. The sanctuary of the Old Testament was made of some very expensive physical building materials: special colored fabrics, gold, acacia wood, etc. The sanctuary of the New Testament is much more valuable: individual people. When God enters into those sanctuaries, lives are changed forever.

Today's Christian musicians prepare the way for God to work in people's hearts. We help create the excitement and anticipation of God working in their lives, which builds their faith. Faith leads to changed lives. People who used to be discouraged and living their own way now are full of joy, walking in God's ways. That is the kind of procession other people notice. That is the procession of God.

Father, thank You for giving me the privilege of leading Your procession, a procession of people who love You.

February 9
Sincerity and Authority

"You see, we are not like the many hucksters who preach for personal profit. We preach the word of God with sincerity and with Christ's authority, knowing that God is watching us."
2 Corinthians 2:17

There are people in ministry who are very sincere, yet they are sincerely wrong. How can this happen? Sometimes it is a lack of correct information, which can easily be corrected. But most of the time it is a lack of desire to seek out and know the truth. Most of the time, people who are sincerely wrong are more concerned with their own feelings and opinions than they are with God's thoughts on any given matter. They may seem to be expressing spiritual views but are building their own kingdoms rather than God's. Their personal profit may not be money, although that is the motivation for some. Their profit may come in the form of popularity, respect, or recognition from others.

When we know God is watching and we have a healthy fear of God, we cannot help but come under Christ's authority. We desire His truth more than our own opinions. We spend time seeking out God's thoughts and learning His ways in both prayer and Bible reading. We allow His truth to change our opinions. Then, we line up our actions accordingly. This is what it is to come under Christ's authority. When we do this, we can be both sincere and right.

Christian music ministers preach with that same authority when our lives have been brought under Christ's authority. We may not always have the most popular message, because God's opinions are not based on what other people want to hear. But, do we want to please our fans, ourselves, or God? The authority of Christ comes after obedience to Christ.

Father, show me where I preach my own opinions instead of Yours. Help me to desire Your ways above popularity.

February 10
Culture and God

"Then Peter took the lame man by the right hand and helped him up. And as he did, the man's feet and ankles were instantly healed and strengthened. He jumped up, stood on his feet, and began to walk! Then, walking, leaping, and praising God, he went into the Temple with them."

Acts 3:7-8

Certain behaviors are expected in specific places. Leaping and praising God was not normal behavior in the Temple. It probably was not received well by some of the leaders. But, it did attract attention because it was an emotionally honest response to what God had done.

Each music genre and venue has expectations for behavior; some of us clap along with the songs, others jump up and down, while still others stare in quiet enjoyment. Part of our job as music ministers is to engage people using the culture they are most comfortable with. Often this causes us to change our behavior to match theirs. But sometimes, using culture to engage people stifles our response to God. In an effort to blend in with culture we forget that God requires us to stand up and stand out. When we express ourselves in an emotionally honest way because of what God has done, people notice.

Standing out from the crowd draws attention. Because of this man's expression, Peter was able to preach to a crowd that was already curious about what had happened. People heard about Jesus because one man expressed his emotions for what God had done in an honest but culturally unusual way. We do not always have to fit in to social norms. We do have to love God with our whole heart and be willing to express that love.

Father, help me to clearly see the difference between using the culture to draw people to You and allowing the culture to stifle the expression of my love for You.

February 11

Designed and Created

"For we are God's masterpiece. He has created us anew in Christ Jesus, so we can do the good things he planned for us long ago."

Ephesians 2:12

Do you believe that God planned for you to live here and now? He chose the date of your birth; it was not a random accident. He planned for you to be alive at this time, this place in all of history because He has good things for you to do. Yes, He even planned what those good things would be. In all of that planning He designed you to be His masterpiece—perfectly designed, built, and equipped to accomplish those tasks.

We often hear that people who are successful in their careers are those with the most education and experience. In our society, college degrees give people greater credibility in their fields. Certainly, education is a benefit. But education is not nearly as important as being specifically designed and created to do certain tasks. For example, a hammer cannot saw a piece of wood with a nice clean cut, no matter which brand, which kind of handle, or the high quality with which it has been manufactured. Only a saw cuts wood in a nice straight line. But, imagine that same saw trying to pound a nail.

God created you to be a music minister. Not many people have that same design, so you are unusual and that is a good thing. Since you have been designed and created to do specific work, you can trust in your Creator to have made you correctly and well. We do not have to hope that our past experience or our education will have prepared us for our ministry. We can simply believe that God planned our good work and created us as His masterpiece to do that work. We can trust that God has planned and created us to be exactly what is needed today.

Father, thank You for designing and creating me to do the good work You have planned for me to do. Help me do it well.

February 12
Weariness and Love

"We work wearily with our own hands to earn our living. We bless those who curse us. We are patient with those who abuse us."

1 Corinthians 4:12

Most Christian music ministers work a day job to make ends meet. For most of us, we would rather be doing ministry full time but the ministry does not pay enough to live on or provide for our families. Unfortunately, the jobs available with flexible enough hours to allow us to do our ministry do not usually pay well either. This is the harsh reality of music ministry. We sacrifice our careers and our paychecks to do ministry. Most of us have accepted that, and although we wish it were otherwise, we have tried to order our lives accordingly.

Life gets especially difficult when people who should be blessing us—those inside the church—do not understand. They can be harsh with judgments and criticisms. We are often looked down upon whenever we do not live up to their expectations of a 9-to-5 lifestyle or volunteering at church. Yet, God wants us to bless them and be patient with them, even while we have to work another job to support our ministry.

It is no wonder we get weary. We work secular jobs, and we bless and are patient with the church before we even begin to fulfill our mission of bringing people closer to Jesus through our music. In our weariness we will probably not always get it right, and not always act in love. But through our weariness we grow and mature in the love of Christ.

We are in good company. It is an honor to serve in the same way as such prestigious men as the apostles! It is humbling to know that God has not set us up to fail—He believes in us as much as He did in the apostles. We can do this because of Him!

Father, give me the strength to grow in Your love. Hold me up through my weariness.

February 13

Pray at All Times

"Pray in the Spirit at all times and on every occasion. Stay alert and be persistent in your prayers for all believers everywhere."

Ephesians 6:18

People are inconvenient. They show up at the worst times, wanting more than we have to give. How many times have you had someone want your attention during set up and sound check? How often are you ready to walk to the door after a long night's gig only to be stopped by yet another person who wants some of your time? People are relentless; they do not stop just because you are sick or exhausted.

God knows all about people. Yet, He says pray for them "at all times" and "on every occasion." He even goes on to say, "Stay alert"—be watching for more opportunities to pray for people; and even, "be persistent"—pray constantly for people. These terms do not imply that we should pray only when someone asks us. They do not allow for time off from praying because we are busy or sick. They do not give us room to let someone else pray because they are better at it or less busy.

Christian music ministers need to offer to pray with each person we talk to, whenever possible. We do not do it only after we have developed an overwhelming love for each person; that is just not realistic. We do not pray only when people see us, as part of our ministry. We do not do it because we feel like it or because it is easy. We do it simply because God asks us to. What if our normal conversations ended with, "How can I pray for you today?" What if each fan received not only an autograph but also an unhurried, heartfelt, sincere prayer? What do you think God would do with a ministry and a person like that?

Father, change my heart. Constantly remind me that praying with people is more important than anything else on my agenda in any given moment.

February 14
The Greatest is Love

"Three things will last forever—faith, hope, and love—and the greatest of these is love."

1 Corinthians 13:13

The love chapter on Valentine's Day is a natural. We think about the people who are most special to us and go out of our way try to do something nice for them. It is important to honor our loved ones. But this chapter was not written for Valentine's Day, weddings, and anniversaries only. It was written to guide our lives and our ministries.

In our lives and our ministries, love trumps everything. In our efforts to get ahead, be successful, and do our ministries well we often forget this. Our ministries will eventually come to a close. Even the best ministries do not last through eternity. What does this mean in light of love? Your ministry is not greater or more important than love. Your ministry should be built on love.

If we have to treat someone unlovingly in order to get ahead in the ministry, fall behind. If the success or failure of our ministry depends on acting without love to one person, shut it down. If our ministry's reputation will be destroyed because we love undesirable people, let it be destroyed. Most often, the choices are not that extreme. But the way we handle situations is affected by our willingness to put love ahead of our ministries. How much farther would you go to demonstrate love to one person if the reputation and success of your ministry was not important? Would you walk the extra mile with a disreputable person if getting ahead in your career was unimportant?

Jesus never compromised love for ministry. His ministry is love. We can do the same if we stay focused on loving God and loving people above all else. There is no reason for our careers, our ministries, or even our lives to exist without love. In the end, there are three things that remain... and the greatest is love.

Father, teach me how to truly love above all else.

February 15
Directed By the Spirit

> *"'What sorrow awaits my rebellious children,'*
> *says the LORD.*
> *'You make plans that are contrary to mine.*
> *You make alliances not directed by my Spirit,*
> *thus piling up your sins.'"*
>
> *Isaiah 30:1*

At this point in time, the Israelites were doing what was logical—making alliances with Egypt. This seemed like a great idea politically because it would ensure the safety of Israel. Financially, it was a wonderful plan to build strong ties to Egypt because Egypt was rich. So, doing business with Egypt would make the Israelites prosperous. But God did not see it that way. He knew that in the end Egypt would slowly enslave the Israelites. God's people would lose not only what they already had but their freedom as well. Nevertheless, God's long term plan for His people was not thwarted. In His mercy, God eventually rescued them, but imagine all the Israelites' had to endure in the meantime. What pain and misery could they have avoided if they had consulted with God first?

Christian music ministers want to believe that we follow God. Most of the time, we are following His calling to be music ministers. But are we doing our ministry the way God has planned for us? All too often we implement a plan that has worked for someone else, without consulting God first. We try to sign with certain labels, use specific technology, and buy certain equipment, etc. because it works for another ministry. While it is certainly a good idea to get recommendations from other people and ministries, let us not forget to give utmost importance to the greatest recommendation—God's plan. Check with Him first.

Father, I want to do my ministry Your way. Caution me in my spirit whenever I take steps that are not Your best. Remind me constantly to consult with You above anyone else.

February 16
Make Allowance for Faults

"Always be humble and gentle. Be patient with each other, making allowance for each other's faults because of your love."
Ephesians 4:2

Band members develop a community that is so close-knit that it becomes family. Spending hours trapped in a van together, songwriting in the practice space, and recording in small studios creates a camaraderie that cannot be found in many other circumstances. We learn more about and experience more of each other than many spouses. As the saying goes, "iron sharpens iron." Eventually we start cutting on each other.

We all agree that no one is perfect. But, when that band member does that same annoying thing again or falls into the same temptation yet another time, our love can fall by the wayside. The actions are made all the worse because we know each other so well—we know just how often the bad behavior happens and just how much it affects our music and ministry. Irritation is bound to surface. We can and should talk about it, again. We can and should try to work it out, one more time. But in the end, there is a very good chance that the band member will do the same thing yet another time. How frustrating is that? How can we overcome our irritation?

We can humbly accept that we are no better than the offending band member; we have habits that are just as annoying to someone else. In this humility we can treat the band member as gently and patiently as we would want to be treated when our behavior is wrong. We can make allowances for faults, knowing that it might be a long time before they change, because of our great love for each other. There are few relationships that get to practice this kind of love. Treasure these people and this time.

Father, help me to make allowances for the faults I see in my band mates because of my love for them.

February 17

Jesus Was Tempted

"Then Jesus was led by the Spirit into the wilderness to be tempted there by the devil."

Matthew 4:1

Christian musicians are frequently music missionaries—going to places other Christians normally would not go. These places are often far more unseemly than we would prefer, but the lost are there so we go there too. So, why do Christian music ministers feel guilty? Often, it is because the church tells us that we should not put ourselves in a position to be tempted; we should not go get the lost, but they should come to church to find Jesus. Is that what Jesus did? No. When we resist temptation and still feel guilty, the guilt is false guilt.

Being tempted and giving in to temptation are two very different things. Jesus was tempted in the desert, when no one else was around to influence Him. If Satan was bold enough to tempt Jesus, of course he will tempt us. Being holy does not stop temptation, if so Jesus would not have been tempted. Separating yourself from the unrighteous actions of other people will not stop temptation; otherwise Jesus would not have been tempted in the desert. Jesus did not stop Satan from tempting Him. We cannot stop the evil one from tempting us. Loving Jesus more does not make us immune from temptation. Temptation will come no matter who we are, where we are, or what we do. The evil one is relentless.

What we can do is to resist temptation. Being tempted is not a sin; it comes with being human. Giving in to the temptation is sin. We have the ability to choose and God provides us with the power through His Holy Spirit to act on our good choices. So, stay strong, put on the full armor of God, resist temptation, and do not allow yourself to feel guilty because you are tempted.

Father, remind me that I am like Jesus when I am tempted and that, like Jesus, I have the power to resist.

February 18
It Is Good

"It is good to give thanks to the LORD,
to sing praises to the Most High.
It is good to proclaim your unfailing love in the morning,
your faithfulness in the evening,
accompanied by the ten-stringed harp
and the melody of the lyre."

Psalm 92:1-3

Much of our life focuses on correcting the negative or the bad. We are constantly striving to improve ourselves and the circumstances we live in, always learning from the failures of the past, moving forward and progressing, working towards a better future. All the striving can leave us feeling inadequate.

Once in a while it is nice to be told that what we are doing is good, not just good enough but good. In these verses the King of kings, Commander of Heaven's armies is telling us that we do good when we give thanks, sing praise, and proclaim His love. We do not have to press forward to be better, or strive for perfection when we do these things. We can simply rest in the knowledge that what we are doing is good and pleasing to God.

God is more interested in the condition of our hearts in worship than He is in our musical expertise. We are all going to hit wrong notes and mess up intros and solos from time to time. We all can be more skilled at playing our instruments. We can all improve, and we will as we continue to practice and grow. But when God sees us giving thanks, singing His praises, and proclaiming His love, what He sees is good. In His eyes, what we are doing is good because it expresses our hearts to Him. At that point, it is not about us or how skillful we are at our instruments. It is about loving God, and loving God is good.

Father, help me to stay focused on You, especially when I feel my music is inadequate to lead Your people in worship.

February 19
Standing Together

"Above all, you must live as citizens of heaven, conducting yourselves in a manner worthy of the Good News about Christ. Then, whether I come and see you again or only hear about you, I will know that you are standing together with one spirit and one purpose, fighting together for the faith, which is the Good News."

Philippians 1:27

We hear many sermons about personal lifestyles: right living in each of our own lives. Certainly, this is part of what this verse considers to be "living as citizens of heaven" and "living in a manner worth of the Good News." But that is only the first part of the verse. The second part says "then." In other words "if" you are living as citizens of heaven, "then" I will know that you are standing together. We do not hear much about standing together in unity being a result of living rightly. Yet, one definitely does follow the other, especially in a Christian band.

In order for the band to be able to stand together and fight the good fight in unity, each member of the band must be committed to living Godly lives. Sins such as selfishness, controlling attitudes, and laziness must be cast aside to fight together for the faith. As soon as those sins surface, there is division within the band. Is your band having problems with division? Look at personal sin as the possible root of the problem.

Conflict is not always a sign of impending division. There will be conflicts whenever people get together to accomplish anything. Healthy conflict causes us to reexamine our viewpoints and grow together. The ability to resolve conflicts while leaving relationships intact is a sign of mature Christian living; it is the result of both parties being committed to living as citizens of heaven, in a manner worthy of the Good News.

Father, teach my band to resolve conflicts while leaving our relationships intact. Reveal my sin so I may repent.

Strengthened by God

"Archers attacked him savagely;
they shot at him and harassed him.
But his bow remained taut,
and his arms were strengthened
by the hands of the Mighty One of Jacob,
by the Shepherd, the Rock of Israel."
Genesis 49:23-24

Jacob is on his death bed, telling each of his sons their future. When he gets to Joseph he says Joseph is like the foal of a wild donkey in spring. We tend to overlook this verse, because it does not mean much to our society which is based on industry and technology. But the analogy means that Joseph was a blessing and a treasure, much like a new baby in a family. Yet, these verses that follow say that he was attacked by archers. He was not attacked because he did anything wrong, but he was attacked because of who he was.

We are attacked just like Joseph. We are tempted by Satan and wounded by other people. These attacks do not necessarily come because we have done anything wrong. Often, they come because of who we are, God's favored children. But look at what God does for Joseph. He does not take the attacks away or smite the attackers. Instead, He strengthens Joseph's arms with His own hands. The picture here is of God's hands being laid upon Joseph's arms, like a father teaching his small son to shoot a bow. The power of God Himself was given to Joseph to withstand the attacks and accomplish all that God had for him to do. What God did for Joseph, He will do for us. When we are attacked we can ask and expect our Father to guide and strengthen us. He will give us the power to accomplish His work.

Father, it hurts to be attacked. Thank You for your strength to go beyond the hurt and accomplish Your will in my life.

February 21

Christian Cheaters and Liars

"Everyone must submit to governing authorities. For all authority comes from God, and those in positions of authority have been placed there by God. So anyone who rebels against authority is rebelling against what God has instituted, and they will be punished."

Romans 13:1-2

Tax season is here. This is the time of year when many Christians and Christian ministries become liars. We cheat on our taxes, either because we do not want to know the correct way to do them or because we disagree with our government. When it comes to taxes, our government does not allow ignorance of the law or disagreement with the law as an excuse. Either way, in God's eyes, cheating and lying on our taxes is intentional rebellion. Christian music ministers are no exception. In fact, because so much of our ministry is handled with cash and since we are artists and not accountants by nature, we are some of the biggest, most consistent Christian cheaters and liars. How can we possibly get upset when God does not bless our ministries financially when we have not followed His principles? God's blessing is worth far more than any extra expense in taxes and tax preparation we may have to pay.

We do not have to pay more than we actually owe. We do not have to agree with everything our government does or how they spend our tax money. The point is not our government or our money. The point is to acknowledge God's placing of our government in authority over us and so obeying that authority. We do not obey because our government is so wonderful; we obey simply because God asks us to. Filing our taxes correctly brings our heart into the same obedience Christ had when He went to the cross for us.

Father, change my hearts attitude about taxes. I will demonstrate my obedience and then ask for Your blessing.

February 22
We Will Wait for Your Help

"Can any of the worthless foreign gods send us rain?
Does it fall from the sky by itself?
No, you are the one, O LORD our God!
Only you can do such things.
So we will wait for you to help us."
Jeremiah 14:22

There comes a time in the life of every ministry when no one can solve the problem at hand, and we simply do not have the resources or experience to fix it. God is going to have to do something or the enemy will win. This is not the time to panic. This is the time to remember who God is, how much He loves us, and wait for His help. It sounds so simple when we see it written out in black and white print, doesn't it?

"Wait" is a four letter word. It is not popular because no one likes to do it. When our car breaks down we have to call for a tow truck and wait. Those minutes seem like some of the longest minutes of our lives. There is nothing we can do but sit and watch everyone else drive by. Waiting. We know the truck will come, but we still have to wait for the help.

Sometimes circumstances happen that we cannot fix. We know God will help us and we will get through it. But the time of waiting can be extremely uncomfortable. Why does God make us wait? He certainly has the ability to fix everything right away. Perhaps waiting has some benefit to us. When we wait we cease from our everyday business. Our minds and hearts are freed from the demands of the now to refocus on what is truly important. As we continue to wait, believing that God will help us, our faith is stretched and grown. When we are done waiting, we have a fresh experience with God's love and provision from which to draw strength. Waiting may not be popular, but it is good for us.

Father, help me see the benefits of waiting for You to help.

February 23

"But God" Positions My Future

"You intended to harm me, but God intended it all for good. He brought me to this position so I could save the lives of many people."

Genesis 50:20

Joseph's brothers sold him into slavery and told his father that Joseph was dead. Unforgiveable, until we consider the words "but God." How would Joseph's life have been different if his brothers had not betrayed him? Would he have lived out a safe life as a farmer or shepherd? Life may have been easier, but he probably would not have ended up in God's book of heroes. Understanding "but God" allows us to move from unforgivable to compassion. "But God" allows God's plan to unfold in our lives regardless of how other people treat us.

As musicians we often feel betrayed or taken advantage of by people on the business side of our music. Concert promoters don't pay enough or advertise our shows well. Labels offer contracts slanted firmly in their direction. Everyone wants to help our ministries—for a price. Often, people don't do what they say they will do and still want to get paid. It never ends. Money is tight and we have calling to fulfill... "But God."

Although God does not approve of people harming us, He often uses their actions to position us. Unfortunately, we cannot see the whole picture in the midst of betrayal and hurt. Sometimes it takes years for God's plan to be revealed. Yet we MUST trust that there is a plan both for us personally and for our ministries. God positions us now for His plan for our future. Positioning can be painful. Forgiving is difficult. Compassion towards the offenders is almost inconceivable. "But God..."

Father, help me to remember today that You are in control of my future. No one can stop Your plans for me, but You can use people to position me. Remind me to trust my future to You so that I can have compassion and love in the present.

February 24
Know How to Live

"I know how to live on almost nothing or with everything. I have learned the secret of living in every situation, whether it is with a full stomach or empty, with plenty or little."
Philippians 4:12

Most Christian musicians know full well how to live on almost nothing. We usually say that we are not sure we know how to live with everything, but we sure would like to try. In this context we are referring to the income that provides the things we need and want. Of course, this is part of what Paul meant. But when he says "I know how to live..." was he only referring to his income? Probably not. Our western way of thinking puts more emphasis on what we have in life than what Paul probably means. We may get a more complete picture if we said, "I know how to live a full and fulfilled life."

Life for Paul was primarily about his ministry, not what he had or what he wanted. Reread the verse with that thought in mind: "I know how to live (to be fulfilled in ministry, to do the work of my ministry well, to reach people for Jesus) on almost nothing or everything." To Paul, that is knowing how to live!

Musicians need equipment. But all too often Christian music ministers focus far too much on getting the new equipment we need rather than doing as much ministry as we can do with the gear we already have. We justify it by saying that "we can reach more people" or "raise the quality of our ministry." But, in the end, we spend more time planning and contemplating the new gear than we do helping the hurting and praying for the lost. The focus needs to remain on the ministry and the people, not the equipment. Equipment is only a tool; it does not lead to knowing how to live a full life. Choose to live in fullness.

Father, I want the fullness of ministry You have planned for me. I trust You to provide whatever I need to live.

February 25

God Appointed Co-Workers

"Then Paul left Athens and went to Corinth. There he became acquainted with a Jew named Aquila, born in Pontus, who had recently arrived from Italy with his wife, Priscilla. They had left Italy when Claudius Caesar deported all Jews from Rome. Paul lived and worked with them, for they were tentmakers just as he was."

Acts 18:1-3

Some relationships are so important to our ministries that God specifically arranges and appoints them. In this case, Paul arrived in Corinth just after Priscilla and Aquila. All three "happened" to be tentmakers so they not only worked together but lived together, probably working out of their home. Priscilla and Aquila were with Paul in Corinth, Ephesus, and Rome, where believers met in their home. They maintained a relationship for many years after they first met in Corinth. Later Paul calls them his co-workers in the ministry.

Band members can be some of the most influential people in our lives. Often, band members remain lifelong friends even after the band breaks up. What may seem like an ordinary way to meet a potential new band member could be God orchestrating a relationship that will affect the rest of your life; treasures given to help you grow personally and in ministry. But, these relationships take work and communication. Can you imagine living and working with Paul 24/7? He was not known for going along with the crowd or being mild-mannered, probably not the ideal roommate, and definitely difficult to work with in ministry. But also consider the benefits Priscilla and Aquila received—being friends with the apostle Paul! Your band mates are your co-workers in ministry; treasure them and treat them as Priscilla and Aquila treated Paul.

Father, show me how to demonstrate love for my band mates. Remind me that You placed them in my life for a reason.

February 26
In the Proper Season

"I will bless my people and their homes around my holy hill. And in the proper season I will send the showers they need. There will be showers of blessing."

Ezekiel 34:26

It is not always a good time for rain. Too much rain during the planting season delays planting. Too much rain during the harvest will leave crops rotting in the fields. Not enough rain during the growing season leaves the crops stunted. Even houseplants have problems when they are over or under watered.

Just as too many rain showers can destroy crops, too many blessings could ruin our lives. Consider the lottery winners who are bankrupt a few short years after winning. Even good blessings given at the wrong time can make the rest of our lives difficult. Children who have been given whatever they want often struggle years later with laziness and entitlement. But our Father knows when to send us rain and exactly how much is best. We are guaranteed showers of blessing because He is such a good Father. Those showers may not happen when we want or provide as much rain as we want, but they will be exactly what we need, when we need it. His blessings will always be for our good.

What happens when we pray and the showers of blessing do not come? Do we seek to attain what we want using our own means? Do we stomp our feet in rebellion like little children? Or do we trust that God will give us what we ask for, or else He will give us something better? Ministries and ministers are not immune from the "I wants." Most often we justify it by pointing out the more or higher quality ministry we could do if we just had whatever. But God has seasons for blessing that are best for us. He knows how to give us what is good in the proper season.

Father, help me to see Your blessing and Your plan when I don't get what I want when I want it.

February 27
Where Are You Going?

"The prudent understand where they are going, but fools deceive themselves."

Proverbs 14:8

Effective ministries have a clear destination, or mission. Decisions about what the ministry will do then become much easier to make because they are proactively based on lining up to the mission rather than reacting to each situation. Reacting to the situations life can throw at you is not the best way to lead a ministry. When we react we end up changing course constantly to avoid problems and temptations. The ministry flounders for lack of clear mission and vision. Reacting and avoiding is like driving and choosing only the best traffic conditions; you may drive for a very long time but never actually arrive at your destination.

Does your music ministry have a clear destination or mission? Has that mission been given by God and discovered through relationship with Him in prayer? If so, do you regularly hold up your mission as the standard when making decisions about your band? When we do these things, we lay a solid foundation for accomplishing what God has for us in ministry.

God is a God of order and administration. He does have a plan for us and for our ministries. The gift of administration is no less spiritual than any other gift as long as we follow the Spirit's leading, just like any other gift. So, it is reasonable to expect that while God probably will not lay out every detail of the plan for our lives to us, He will give us the direction we are to head. As we seek Him daily, He will provide course corrections and adjustments, but they will always be the best way to get us to our destination, not a random course change. This mission will keep us going in the right direction to the correct destination.

Father, refine my ministry's mission. Show us the way to stay on track with all that You have for us to accomplish. Remind us that it is not easy to stay on mission, but it is effective.

February 28
Run Without Weights

"Therefore, since we are surrounded by such a huge crowd of witnesses to the life of faith, let us strip off every weight that slows us down, especially the sin that so easily trips us up. And let us run with endurance the race God has set before us."
Hebrews 12:1

When athletes train, they often use weights to add resistance to their movements. This resistance makes it much more difficult and tends to slow them down. But when they actually compete, athletes remove all the weights. It makes their movements easy compared to using the weights. Weights are not sin. They can be a useful tool for training. They can also be detrimental if we use them when we should be running the race.

What are the weights in your life? Look at things that are good but not necessarily God's best for you. Some common weights are: busyness (doing too much, more than what God has given you to do), fellowship (spending too much time with family and friends and not enough time with God), and musicianship (practicing our instruments more than doing our ministries).

What are the weights in your ministry? Common music ministry weights are the same as personal weights. In fact, this is an area where your ministry is usually a magnification of your personal life. Is your band accomplishing the ministry God has called you to do? If the band is too busy to focus on doing its ministry, spends too much time in fellowship, or practices extensively without playing out, the root of the problem is probably found in your personal life.

The most effective Christian music ministers and ministries run with endurance and speed because they do not have weights to slow them down. They win, just like the huge crowd of witnesses that have gone before them.

Father, show me my weights and how to get rid of them.

All That You Can

"Do all that you can to live in peace with everyone."
Romans 12:18

How far will you go to make things right with a family member or band mate? How about a friend or close ministry partner such as your manager or booking agent? Should you go the extra mile to make things right with people who are not that close to you, say a fan or the tech support guy for your web site host? What about the people who have gone out of their way to take advantage of or hurt you and your ministry?

Most of us will go much farther to make things right with the people closest to us and ignore difficult situations when they involve people we do not know well. But this way of deciding when to work through tough relationships is not scriptural. Doing all that we can or walking away should not be based on how close we are to a person. It should be based on the other person's willingness to keep trying to make the relationship right.

This is not to say that we need to keep trying and allow the other person to willfully continue to hurt us. Sometimes we must simply walk away. At that point we lay the person at the feet of Jesus and pray for them. We cannot hold on to anger or hate. But, we can forgive both ourselves and the other person and use the relationship as a learning tool for ourselves so that we can do better in the next relationship.

So, how do we determine what is "all that we can"? Let love be your guide. We do not need to be right, we do not need to invest all our emotional strength, and we do not need to prove our point. We do need to prove our love. We simply need to do our very best to work out every relationship, knowing that it will require time and that not every relationship will work out.

Father, I want to live at peace with everyone. Give me wisdom to handle tough relationship situations with love.

God Has It Covered!

"Seek the Kingdom of God above all else, and live righteously, and he will give you everything you need. So don't worry about tomorrow, for tomorrow will bring its own worries. Today's trouble is enough for today."

Matthew 6:33-34

We lose sleep all too often worrying about our ministry and money. The contract negotiations, which merchandise designs will sell, equipment purchases and repairs, copyrights; the list of details we can worry about is endless. There is far too much on most music ministers' plates because there are so many aspects of music ministry. If we get any one of them wrong, it costs us money and impacts the effectiveness of our ministry.

The trick is to get all the tasks involved with music ministry done correctly while not worrying. The way to do this is found in this verse: (1) seek the kingdom of God first, (2) live righteously, and (3) take each day one day at a time. These three priorities permeate our Christian walk. We seek the kingdom first by placing the highest priority on spending time with God alone in prayer, seeking His guidance for our lives and ministries. Then, we live rightly by doing what He says both in the Bible and from what we hear in prayer. When we have done these two steps, it becomes much easier to take one day at a time without worrying. When we have given God control over our day and allowed Him to prioritize the day, we can sleep through the night without worry.

Self-discipline is required to spend each day seeking the Kingdom first, living rightly, and taking one day at a time. There will always be a battle in our minds to worry about the potential problems of tomorrow. But God has our tomorrows covered!

Father, help me to live each day knowing that You are in control of all the inner workings of my life and my ministry.

March 3
What God Hears About You

> *"How beautiful on the mountains*
> *are the feet of the messenger who brings good news,*
> *the good news of peace and salvation,*
> *the news that the God of Israel reigns!"*
>
> *Isaiah 52:7*

The messenger in this verse was a runner who ran from the battlefield to the king to let him know how the battle was going. Obviously, the king was happy to hear that his plans were being implemented and he was winning. He would then make plans to honor the heroes and celebrate his victory. The king was not so happy when his army was not doing what he said and he was losing. He would either send a message back to the battlefield to change his strategy or plan to live with defeat.

So, what is your King hearing about you and your music ministry? Are you on the battlefield, implementing His plan? If so, you can be sure His messengers are telling Him good things about you. We want God to know that we are working to advance His kingdom. He loves to hear about it because when we do His work, peace and salvation are the result. He wins the battle and the world is shown once again that our God reigns.

If you are on the battlefield but have not been implementing His plan correctly, ask for the changes and implement them right away. You are in a battle and your enemy is attacking—you do not have time to beat yourself up; your enemy is more than happy to do that for you. Simply stop doing things your way and start doing what the King says.

Remember that you cannot always see how the battle is going when you are in the midst of it. But your King is high on a hill; He can see the whole battle. Follow His plan for victory.

Father, I want the world to know that You reign as a result of my ministry. Bring peace and salvation as I follow Your plan.

March 4
Boast About Knowing God

"This is what the LORD says:
  'Don't let the wise boast in their wisdom,
  or the powerful boast in their power,
  or the rich boast in their riches.
But those who wish to boast should boast in this alone:
  that they truly know me
  and understand that I am the LORD
  who demonstrates unfailing love
  and who brings justice and righteousness to the earth,
and that I delight in these things.
I, the LORD, have spoken!'"

                                        Jeremiah 9:23-24

Most Christian musicians do not boast about being rich or powerful, because we're not. But we do have a tendency to boast about, or at least find pride in, our musical abilities and successes. Somehow, we find it rewarding to play more shows, or have better equipment, or be more skilled on our instruments, or have a more interesting website, etc. than other bands or musicians. Although we may not always speak these comparisons out loud, we gauge our success in ministry by comparing ourselves to other music ministers, especially those who we feel are in direct competition with us.

In these verses God is clearly saying that our musical acumen or even our success in ministry is not what we are to boast about. How would we rate if we compared ourselves by discerning who knows God best? Who knows the most about His love, justice, and righteousness? Who knows best what God delights in? If you would win that competition, boast about it. If not, you have some spiritual work to do.

Father, help me to know You better. Show me what is important to You, so it can be important to me.

March 5
Therefore

"Jesus came and told his disciples, 'I have been given all authority in heaven and on earth. Therefore, go and make disciples of all the nations, baptizing them in the name of the Father and the Son and the Holy Spirit.'"

Matthew 28:18-19

Christian bands often engage people from cultures that are not well represented in a typical Sunday morning church service. We are missionaries within our own country, speaking the language of music. Like most missionaries, we pay the price of living a different lifestyle than the average American. Most of us do not make as much money as we could if pursued a secular career. Many of us have put off long term commitments such as education, relationships, and home purchases in order to continue our ministries. The personal cost is high and people often look down on us for not living up to their expectations.

The word "therefore" is pivotal in the above verses. It means "because of" or "so." "Therefore" is connecting the idea of making disciples with Jesus being given all authority. In other words, we can go and make disciples because Jesus has been given all authority. Or, Jesus has been given all authority, so go make disciples. Because Jesus has all authority, we have been enabled to go make disciples. We do not have to fear that we will not be well-equipped; we do not have to worry about lack of provisions. We are ambassadors of the King. We do not have to please people that claim to be kings and set themselves in judgment over us. We only have to please our King, who is King above all other kings. When we represent and are obedient to our King, we walk under His authority. We are equipped and able to do everything He asks, including making disciples.

Father, I serve at Your bidding. I represent You as I do my ministry and I walk under your authority and provision.

March 6
Good, Pleasing, & Perfect

"Don't copy the behavior and customs of this world, but let God transform you into a new person by changing the way you think. Then you will learn to know God's will for you, which is good and pleasing and perfect."

Romans 12:2

The Christian music industry has a certain way of doing things, a plan that many musicians have historically followed. This plan has led to the success of several Christian musicians and the failure of others. Those that have failed are often thought of as not good enough to be professional musicians. This way of doing Christian music is patterned after the secular music industry; contracts and royalties are virtually the same. It is set up to sell music with the main goal of making money. Is this the plan you should follow?

Doing things the Nashville way is very controversial now in Christian music. The other path both secular and Christian musicians take is to stay an indie. Indies keep control of their projects and pay all the up front costs themselves. The power of technology has made it possible to record and distribute music effectively without a label. But, you have to have up front cash and might not make it back. Is this the plan you should follow?

Indie vs. label is just one example of behaviors and customs of the world. Both customs are worldly and may or may not be the right choice for your music ministry. The challenge of this verse is to set aside all worldly customs and find out what God thinks. What will work for you might be wrong for another band. But, God knows which is which and when the best timing is for each band. Your ministry will be good and pleasing and perfect to Him when you follow His plan.

Father, help me set aside my worldly thinking. Show me how You think and what Your plan is for my ministry.

March 7

Strength from the Lord

"But those who trust in the LORD will find new strength.
They will soar high on wings like eagles.
They will run and not grow weary.
They will walk and not faint."

Isaiah 40:31

There is a supernatural strength and energy available when we are doing God's work. Christian music ministers often experience this strength without realizing it. We have come to rely on God's strength and energy to get us through the weird hours and inconsistent sleep schedules. We perform when we are sick and when we are hungry; we play when it is time, not when it is convenient for us.

Have you ever been tired or sick prior to a show? You show up to play the gig regardless of how you feel. Then, you walk on stage and feel fine. That is God's supernatural strength enabling you to do your ministry. You experience this energy because you trusted God enough to show up to the gig when you did not feel well. Sometimes God allows us to go back to not feeling well immediately after the performance to demonstrate a gentle reminder that He provided the strength. Other times, we leave the show feeling better than when we arrived as a testimony to His power in our lives.

Most of us have experienced this so frequently that we have come to see it as normal. On one hand it is a sign of maturity that we have come to rely on God so readily. But on the other, have we come to take God's working in our lives for granted? Pause for a moment and consider all the times you have been given energy and strength to do your music ministry; be in awe of your God who cares about the details of your life.

Father, thank You for giving me the strength to soar like an eagle while serving You.

More Precious Than God

"Looking at the man, Jesus felt genuine love for him. 'There is still one thing you haven't done,' he told him. 'Go and sell all your possessions and give the money to the poor, and you will have treasure in heaven. Then come, follow me.'"

Mark 10:21

This man was a good man; he had done everything commanded by the law. Jesus loved him. The challenge given by Jesus was to give up the one thing he held more precious than God. We read this story and say, of course, obviously he should easily have given up his wealth. But, like all parables, the story is meant to cause us to look at ourselves.

Christian music ministers often struggle with the same challenge as the man in the story. Would we give up anything that is most precious to us? The real question is, "What do we have that is more precious to us than our relationship with God?" Would we lay down our ministries if they kept us from God? Would we perform on the smallest, most obscure stages to avoid the pitfalls of fame? Most of us would say, "Yes." But do we do it in our daily lives? Have you ever walked on stage without spending time with your Savior first? Have you ever signed autographs without praying for your fans? Have you ever purchased equipment with money you knew God wanted you to spend elsewhere? Unfortunately, most of us can say "yes" to these kinds of questions as well. We are not so different from the man in this story.

Thank God that He loves us. His love sees through all our faults. His love covered our sins. We will strive to grow and do better at keeping our love for God first and above all else. At times, we will fail. But His love will always call us back.

Father, show me everything I have put ahead of You. Help me to keep my relationship with You first every day.

March 9

Refuge in the Lord

*"It is better to take refuge in the LORD
than to trust in people."*

Psalm 118:8

Trust is consistently broken in business and in ministry. Unfortunately, most people can be trusted whenever the situation works out to their best interest. Keeping the trust of another person is only tested when the situation will cost them something personally to do so. In today's world, most people do not value integrity more than their personal gain. So, trust is easily broken. We tend to expect more from our brothers and sisters in Christ, which makes it all the more devastating when Christians do not keep their word or honor their contracts. The Christian music ministry is not exempt from this phenomenon. Most Christian leaders and musicians will agree that they have been hurt more from inside the church than from the world.

So, what do we do when we are hurt by someone we trusted in ministry? Do we strike back? Do we become defensive? Do we withhold our trust to anyone else? No. We take refuge in the Lord. Taking refuge means to run to a place of safety, protection from danger, and shelter from trouble. Taking refuge does not have anything to do with being good enough to deserve refuge or earning it. Especially in times of trouble, refuge is given freely. Once we are in the place of refuge we are safe. From that place of safety we can call to others to join us and extend help to the hurting. When we have taken refuge in the Lord we can risk trusting people because we know the Lord will keep us safe. People will break our trust, and they will hurt us. But God provides refuge, safety, protection, and shelter.

Father, teach me how to live daily in Your refuge. Remind me to be trustworthy and show me what to do when I break trust with another person. Help me bring people to Your refuge.

Self Discipline

"I discipline my body like an athlete, training it to do what it should. Otherwise, I fear that after preaching to others I myself might be disqualified."
                                          1 Corinthians 9:27

What does our body or our flesh like to do? What would our lives look like if we were ruled by our bodies? We definitely would not be modeling the Christian lifestyle to those around us. Our minds control what our body does. We tell it when to eat and sleep for example. We make decisions every day regarding what our bodies will and will not do, as well as when it will do whatever we choose. What happens when we make poor choices or neglect to choose at all? Our bodies eventually show it. This verse is talking about our minds controlling and making wise choices about our own bodies with self-discipline.

A daily routine is not the same as self-discipline. Most people use their daily routine as a tool to help with self-discipline. For example, they get up in time to prepare to go to work, eat breakfast in the allotted time, take specified breaks throughout the day, come home after work and eat dinner, etc. Their days are defined by consistent work schedules so self-discipline is somewhat easy. But musicians do not have daily routines. Each day has tasks that must be done, but the hours and schedule vary widely between the days. So, our self-discipline becomes all the more important. We know it is right to do certain things each day: spend time with God, eat healthy, rest and exercise, etc. But, as our days get hectic or as our emotions vary, choosing to do those things consistently becomes difficult. Nevertheless, those consistent wise choices keep us strong physically, mentally, and spiritually.

Father, show me where I need to apply more self-discipline and help me to consistently do it.

Safety in Integrity

"People with integrity walk safely,
but those who follow crooked paths will slip and fall."
Proverbs 10:9

Integrity is a noun that is often defined as honesty, but it encompasses more than simply telling the truth. Integrity means that we make decisions and live by sound morals and ethics. It also includes the concept of being preserved in perfect condition, whole and undiminished. In short, integrity means consistently doing what is right simply because it is right, regardless of who is watching or how much it may cost you.

Do you have integrity? Does your ministry walk in integrity? Often, a lack of integrity will show up in how we handle money. For example, do you declare all your band income on your income taxes? Does the band collect and pay sales taxes? Do you pay the people you hire fairly, even when band money is tight? Does your spouse agree with the amount of money you spend on the band? Does the band honor its contracts even when it will cost more money than you anticipated to do so?

Integrity, or a lack thereof, affects our relationships with people. A lack of integrity destroys trust. Consistently practicing integrity causes people to respect and trust you and your ministry. When people see that you did the right thing in any situation, even when it cost you, they will know that you will do the right thing for them as well. Make no mistake; people are watching you and your ministry more closely than they let on.

Most importantly, integrity affects our relationship with God. He says in this verse that we will walk safely when we choose integrity. Do we trust Him in that promise, even though it may cost us in the short term?

Father, I trust You with every aspect of my life and my ministry. Show me where I need to increase my integrity.

March 12
With All Your Heart

"In all that he did in the service of the Temple of God and in his efforts to follow God's laws and commands, Hezekiah sought his God wholeheartedly. As a result, he was very successful."

2 Chronicles 31:21

Many of the Old Testament kings of Israel died young and/or failed miserably, but Hezekiah was not one of them. He brought the nation back to serving God, and God prospered not only Hezekiah but the entire nation. It is interesting to note that Hezekiah did not prosper because he did everything perfectly, or because he worked longer hours than any king before him. He prospered simply because he sought God with his whole heart.

Pursuing God with your whole heart is not the same as pursuing the success of your ministry with your whole heart. It is likely that most of the kings before Hezekiah wanted to be successful and sought to expand and prosper their kingdom. Notice that Hezekiah's success was the result of pursuing God. Of course, we want to be diligent and do our ministries with excellence. But that diligence must be secondary to seeking to know the character of God, what He thinks, and what He wants accomplished in the world. When we know God we can line up our actions and goals to His plans.

The result of the wholehearted pursuit of God is that we will be following God's plan, doing the best tasks to get us where God wants us to be. Can you imagine striving for weeks and working diligently, only to discover all your long hours were wasted because the end result wasn't what you needed? Pursuing God wholeheartedly as your top and first priority will completely avoid this trap. When we seek God with our whole heart the rest of our lives, including our ministries, are made successful by God.

Father, my success in ministry means nothing without knowing You. Show me more of who You are.

March 13
Music & Culture

"When you hear the sound of the horn, flute, zither, lyre, harp, pipes, and other musical instruments, bow to the ground to worship King Nebuchadnezzar's gold statue. Anyone who refuses to obey will immediately be thrown into a blazing furnace."

Daniel 3:5-6

Every culture has expectations of what people are supposed to do when they hear music. In this case people were supposed to worship a gold statue, as ordered by the king. Today we are not expected to worship a statue, but there are expectations of culture associated with music and its genres that are often reflected in how we dress, how we move, and even how we speak. Unfortunately, some very negative behaviors that have devastating, long term repercussions can be part of these expectations. Music ministers try to use the music to engage the people in the culture and call them to the Lord. We have learned that there comes a point when, like Daniel and his friends, we must simply refuse to bow down to the expectations of people and culture. But, many of our fans do not know how or believe that they should stand up to the expectations of their culture.

Imagine living in a world where you do everything the king tells you to do regardless of whether it is right or wrong. That was Daniel's world and the world of many of our fans. In Daniel's world, the disobedient were murdered; in our world the nonconformists are subject to ridicule, bullying, or even completely shunned—the social equivalent to being killed. Many of our fans live under constant social pressure that they are not even aware of because it has been part of their whole lives. Pray for them to see your example and understand why you are asking them to take a stand against their king and their culture.

Father, work in the hearts of my fans and open their eyes. Use me and my music within their culture to call them to You.

March 14
Dividing By Being Right

"Make every effort to keep yourselves united in the Spirit, binding yourselves together with peace. For there is one body and one Spirit, just as you have been called to one glorious hope for the future. There is one Lord, one faith, one baptism, and one God and Father, who is over all and in all and living through all."

Ephesians 4:3-6

What divides band members? Usually it is not our faith or commitment to advancing God's Kingdom. We are all certain of the essential, absolute truths. Most often we are divided because we allow differences of opinion to turn into the need to be right. We think the band should do or believe a certain thing and another person sees it differently. It is not the actual differences of opinion that cause the division. People can get along just fine and accomplish their goals without always being 100% in agreement with each other. Division comes when we cannot allow each other to think differently, when we must be right and everyone else must go along with what we think is right.

Working together as band will absolutely require compromise. Often, things will not get accomplished as efficiently or as well as you could have done them yourself. Other times you might be surprised; something may turn out better than if you had done it yourself. In the end it is not the tasks, the decisions, or even the results that matter most. What God says is most important is unity and peace with your brothers.

"Make every effort" means that sometimes you will have to allow your brothers to make decisions that you believe will impact you negatively. It is more important to be bound together as a band than to always be the smartest person in the room. If you insist on causing division by always being right, eventually you will be alone in that room.

Father, give me a strong desire to be bound together in unity.

March 15
Example of Love

"I have loved you even as the Father has loved me. Remain in my love."

John 15:9

Jesus loves us exactly the same way that His Father loves Him. He is our example of the Father's love. In turn, we are the example of God's love to the world. Being an example of God's love is why we are music ministers—we use music to connect with people and bring them closer to Jesus. Music is the tool; love is the message. Loving our fans the same way that Jesus loves them is our calling.

Consider how God loves us, through all our humanness and inconsistencies. He loves us beyond what we can understand and certainly more than what we deserve! While we cannot model this love perfectly to other people, we are supposed to be growing in love and becoming better at showing it each day. So, how's your love life? Are you an example of God's love?

Fans can be more than annoying; expecting attention at inappropriate times, in inappropriate ways, and willing to do almost anything to get it from us. Jesus faced similar issues with his followers while on earth. He knows what He is asking us to do. Yet, He still asks us to be an example of His love just as he was an example of His Fathers love. Has the Father ever turned you away? Has He ever said that He doesn't have time for you right now? Has He ever caused you to feel unimportant? No, He never has done any of those things. Instead, He has always had an open door policy—if you make the time, He will be there to talk. He listens intently and has withheld nothing from you. His love is safe and consistent, no matter what we do. Are we treating our fans the same way? Remain in His love.

Father, give me a heart of love towards my fans. Cause me to want to demonstrate Your love to them more than focusing on any other tasks I need to do in any given moment.

March 16
Eager to Help the Poor

"Their only suggestion was that we keep on helping the poor, which I have always been eager to do."

Galatians 2:10

Paul went back to the counsel at Jerusalem after converting to Christianity and preaching to the Gentiles. The counsel confirmed that he was doing the work God called him to do and doing it well. We would all love to be able to have that kind of confirmation in our ministries. Interestingly, the counsels' only suggestion was that Paul continue to help the poor. This itinerant preacher, who was once well off but now was living off donations from his churches, was expected to help the poor.

Christian music ministers are often poor by American standards. We usually take lesser paying jobs in an effort to keep a flexible schedule to do our ministry, and our equipment plus travelling is expensive. Almost none of us would consider ourselves to be rich. Most of us pay into our own ministries just to keep them going. Yet, if we went to the counsel at Jerusalem they would undoubtedly ask us to help the poor too. All of us probably have more than Paul did when he went to the counsel.

But, helping the poor does not always mean more financial sacrifice on our part. When we get to the point where we do not have anything left after honoring our word by paying our debts, we cannot give money to the poor. We can help the poor by raising money for them. We can play fundraising concerts to benefit the poor. We can buy and sell goods produced by missionaries at our merchandise table. We can partner with organizations that support the poor and represent them at our concerts. There are many, many ideas and ways that we can use our ministries to help the poor even when we have no cash ourselves. The important thing is that we actually do something!

Father, show me how to help the poor with my ministry.

March 17
Are You Ready to Sacrifice?

"So if you are presenting a sacrifice at the altar in the Temple and you suddenly remember that someone has something against you, leave your sacrifice there at the altar. Go and be reconciled to that person. Then come and offer your sacrifice to God."

Matthew 5:23-24

Being a Christian music minister requires sacrifice of time and money. We willingly give as part of our ministry calling. But God does not want our sacrifices until we have been reconciled to everyone. This verse does not allow us to pick and choose who we feel we need to reconcile with: not just members of our band, other Christians, or family members. The verse uses the word "someone" meaning anyone and everyone. We are not ready to do the work of our ministries until we have been reconciled with everyone we know!

Conflicts are going to happen between you and someone. It's not a matter of if, it's a matter of when and how we will handle the conflicts. The Bible is very clear that any offense, whether you have committed it or it has been committed against you, should be addressed privately and immediately. Go directly to the person and resolve the issue; don't wait, don't tell other people about it first. We all experience friction in relationships and we know what we are supposed to do, but we don't often actually do it. Somehow our ministry seems more urgent and important than one conflict with someone else. Perhaps if we would be more willing to address conflict if we considered that all our ministry and sacrifices for our ministry are not acceptable to God until after we have resolved offenses. He wants us to drop whatever we are doing and go be reconciled.

Father, help me to see the importance of being reconciled before working on my ministry. Give me no rest until I do it.

March 18

Finish the Work

"But my life is worth nothing to me unless I use it for finishing the work assigned me by the Lord Jesus—the work of telling others the Good News about the wonderful grace of God."
Acts 20:24

Musicians love expressing ourselves through the creative process of performing, recording, and songwriting. The primary difference between secular musicians and Christian music ministers is that secular musicians use music to make a living, while Christian ministers use that creativity as a tool to bring people closer to Jesus. Ministers may or may not ever be able to make a living from the music. What separates us is not the tasks we need to do to accomplish our goals, but our calling—the endgame of completing the work assigned to us by Jesus. Everything we do is guided by that assignment.

Christian music ministers have to master all the tools that a secular musician uses to connect with the audience. Then we have to go farther and master ministry tools as well. We have much more to learn and do than our secular counterparts. We work harder and longer than most people will ever know. We are motivated to do it all because we know that the eternal lives of people are at stake. Our work is not finished until every last fan or potential fan has been touched with the love of God.

We do not give our lives for the music; we give our lives to populate heaven. If necessary, we will lay down the music. But, we will never give up loving people to Jesus. Ideally, this is what is happening when a band member leaves the band or a Christian band breaks up. God is simply continuing our assignment using different tools. We finish our assignments for the glory of God and the love of His people.

Father, show me how to best finish the work You have assigned me. Give me courage and strength as I continue on.

March 19
Sheep Are Led

"The gatekeeper opens the gate for him, and the sheep recognize his voice and come to him. He calls his own sheep by name and leads them out. After he has gathered his own flock, he walks ahead of them, and they follow him because they know his voice."

John 10:3-4

Herding sheep is very different than herding cattle. As we have often seen in Western movies, cattle are driven but sheep are led. Sheep follow after their shepherd. The Bible frequently refers to God's people as sheep and to their leaders as shepherds. Jesus, of course, is the head shepherd with earthly spiritual leaders functioning as shepherds under Him, guiding the sheep to follow Jesus. To many of our fans, that makes us shepherds, possibly the only shepherd they know.

Most Christian music ministers do not have the calling of being a pastor. But we are called upon to lead people and we cannot lead any farther than we have already gone. We must be ahead of the sheep in order to lead them; otherwise we are alongside or behind them in a position of attempting to drive sheep like cattle. When we lead the people in worship, we must already be worshipping. When we lead people to grow closer to Jesus we must already be growing closer ourselves. When we teach people a truth about God we must have already let that truth change our hearts. Otherwise we will become frustrated as we attempt to push people rather than lead them. In our frustration we will not remain in the love of Jesus; we may even strike out at the sheep. The loving earthly shepherd realizes his responsibility to be constantly growing closer to and more like the heavenly Shepherd. As earthly shepherds, we are determined to lead the fans under our care closer to Jesus by following Him.

Father, give me discernment to know when a fan needs my leadership. Teach me how to become a leader to Your people.

March 20
Be Satisfied

"Don't love money; be satisfied with what you have. For God has said, 'I will never fail you. I will never abandon you.'"
Hebrews 13:5

The gospel is free but it takes money to get it to them. We need money to do our ministry; equipment and travelling is expensive. Part of our job as Christian music ministers is to raise and manage the funds we need to do our ministry. But, even after we have done all we know to do, we often still do not have the funds we need to do all the ministry we want to do. It is difficult to be content with what we have when our lack affects our ministry. It is difficult to turn down gigs because we cannot afford to play them. Eventually it becomes really hard not to envy bands that have been given more ministry opportunities simply because they have more money available to them.

The secret to being content with the amount of money we have to do ministry is to understand that God's love for us is based on Whose we are, not on how much we accomplish. We are only responsible to do the best we can do with what resources we have been given. If we can only play 10 shows a year and use all our resources to do them as excellently as possible, we know that God is pleased with us. If we have the resources to play 200 shows but only play 20, we might be in trouble. In the end, we have to believe that God guides us through our finances—both the abundance and the lack. A lack of money does not mean that God has failed or left us. It does not mean we have failed God. A lack or abundance of money simply calls us to prayer for discernment about God's guidance for our ministry. When we trust God to use our finances as a way to guide us, we can be content with what we have and focus on using all we have wisely.

Father, don't let me get ahead or fall behind in Your plan for my ministry. I know You will provide what I need as I need it.

I Don't Want To Do That

"He went on a little farther and bowed with his face to the ground, praying, 'My Father! If it is possible, let this cup of suffering be taken away from me. Yet I want your will to be done, not mine.'"

Matthew 26:39

There are parts to every career and ministry that are not fun or easy. Even if we love doing almost all of our work, there is always a small percentage that we just do not want to do. Sometime we simply need to practice some self-discipline to get those jobs done. Other times what we need to do is so difficult that it takes more than the courage and discipline we have to accomplish the task. During those times our only hope to accomplish the ministry God calls us to do is prayer.

Our natural tendency is to avoid situations that make us uncomfortable or are difficult. Our flesh does not want to die and we are usually in no hurry to force it to do so. But Jesus faced his crucifixion head on. How? He settled the matter ahead of time, in prayer. Look at the process of His prayer: He withdrew from all His friends to a private place, alone with His Father. He did not rely on other people to pray for Him nor did He rely on group prayers. Then, He fell on His face, humbled, abandoning all illusion of self sufficiency. In this single act He acknowledged the supremacy of the Father, the creator of the universe. He petitioned Abba, His Father, as a son asking as family. He did not ask as a servant or slave without rights, but relied on a relationship full of affection and love. He asked three times, persistent at presenting His request but always asking, not telling. Finally, He submitted to the will of God. In the end, we know that the Father answered Jesus' prayer by giving Him everything He needed to do the most difficult task ever.

Father, remind me to follow Jesus' example when I come upon a task that I do not want to do. I know You will help me.

Who is in Control?

> *"Teach me to do your will,*
>   *for you are my God.*
> *May your gracious Spirit lead me forward*
>   *on a firm footing."*
>   *Psalm 143:10*

Following God's plan and doing His will is the only way to be 100% sure that your future and the future of your ministry will be secure and good. So, why is it that we tend to play at being God ourselves? Why do we take the responsibility upon ourselves to do things in our own strength? Why do we try to change the people around us? Why do we seek to control our own future? These are all symptoms of a life not fully surrendered to God.

We can only do God's will after we have acknowledged that He is God and surrendered to His authority in our lives. Think just for a moment about who God is: the creator of the universe, the commander of the angel army, the King of kings, the Savior of the world. There are many titles ascribed to Him in the Bible. Perhaps it is summed up best in, "I am the alpha and the omega." He is God. Now consider that you belong to Him. Is there anyone else you would rather belong to? Is there anyone else you would surrender control of your life to? Of course not. It is much easier to lay down our will, our wants, and our desires after we have thought about the sovereignty of God.

We do not have to try to be a junior Holy Spirit by controlling people and situations around us. We simply have to follow the Holy Spirit's leading in our lives. The responsibility for other people, our future, changing circumstances, etc. rests on the Spirit, not us. He is God, we are not. We are doing God's will as we follow the Spirit so we will walk in a secure future.

Father, I release control of my life and my ministry to You. Teach me to follow Your plan by following Your Holy Spirit.

March 23
It Pays to be Humble

"For those who exalt themselves will be humbled, and those who humble themselves will be exalted."
Luke 14:11

The entertainment industry provides many opportunities to be exalted. The audience claps and fans clamor for our attention. Sure, some people are less than encouraging and we might not always be paid much, but for the most part we can usually count on at least a few people to boost our egos. It is nice to be appreciated. It is difficult to remain humble as a Christian music minister. Although the quality of our music does not depend on our humility, the quality of our ministry does.

In an era of more musicians than gigs, bookers are no longer simply hiring quality musicians. They are hiring musicians who connect with the audience, who provide a memorable experience that will impact lives. The age of the stereotype of the prideful stadium rock star kept at arm's length is over. Today bookers are looking for the musician who has a genuine love for connecting with people by sharing music. It is almost impossible to share or connect if we are walking in pride, exalting ourselves or looking to be exalted. True love will keep us humble.

What is the opposite of pride? It is not humility. Humility is the result of the opposite of pride, which is love. The love of Christ towards us teaches us proper perspective—our need for redemption because of our sin. This perspective results in our humility. Our humility enables us to genuinely share the love of Christ with other people. Christ's love for us motivating our love for them causes us to connect in our mutual need for redemption. When this connection is experienced through music we become dynamic, engaging music ministers who impact lives.

Father, remind me of my need for Your love so I may stay humble. I want to be genuine in sharing Your love using music.

The Rewards of Discipline

"Endure suffering along with me, as a good soldier of Christ Jesus. Soldiers don't get tied up in the affairs of civilian life, for then they cannot please the officer who enlisted them. And athletes cannot win the prize unless they follow the rules. And hardworking farmers should be the first to enjoy the fruit of their labor."

2 Timothy 2:3-6

Musicians are often stereotyped as being lazy partiers, bent on having a good time above all else. Unfortunately, this stereotype is projected on to Christian music ministers by uninformed people. Even more unfortunate are the younger Christian musicians that buy into the lie of the easy life/career of music ministry. Christian music ministers have an unusual lifestyle, but we work much harder than most people realize. A successful Christian music ministry requires the creativity of an artist mixed with the discipline of a soldier. We hype the creative aspects of our ministries because that is what attracts fans. We tend to underplay the discipline involved, because hard work is simply not fun or marketable. But is this a fair representation of a Christian lifestyle to our fans and, more importantly, those who would follow us in ministry?

Soldiers, athletes, and farmers are rewarded for their hard work with promotions, prizes, and an abundance of crops. The rewards and the lifestyle are easily seen by people who know and would model their lives after them. But if people looked at music ministers, would they mistakenly see people being rewarded for a lazy, irresponsible lifestyle? Part of our ministry is to inspire and train future music ministers. Perhaps we need a little less hype and a lot more authenticity in our Christian music ministry so we too can say, "Endure suffering along with me".

Father, show me how to let other people see that I represent You in my life and my ministry.

March 25

Rooted in Love

"I pray that from his glorious, unlimited resources he will empower you with inner strength through his Spirit. Then Christ will make his home in your hearts as you trust in him. Your roots will grow down into God's love and keep you strong."

Ephesians 3:16-17

Roots are not seen, but without a strong root system plants and trees do not flourish. Weak, shallow roots produce weak plants that bear small fruit, if they have any fruit at all. Most gardeners spend quite a bit of time making the soil a perfect environment to grow strong roots because they know it will create a much larger harvest.

We cannot expect a large harvest if our own roots are not strong. It is very difficult to sustain consistent ministry when we are not rooted in the love of Christ. Like plants, we will produce very small fruit, if any, when we try to do the ministry from our own strength. The key for Christian music ministers to grow large fruit is to minister from a position of being rooted with deep, strong roots in God's love. We gain our inner strength from God's Spirit pouring out His love into our hearts, just as plants gain strength from water and fertilizer. When we have taken the time to consistently soak up the water and nutrition of the love of God, we build strong roots that are able to trust Him. From this place of strength we are able to do the work of the ministry—consistently loving other people closer to Jesus.

Time spent soaking up the love of God and developing trust in God is time well spent. This investment benefits not only yourself, but the people around you. When you and your ministry are firmly rooted in God's love, you are able to consistently minister from a position of strength.

Father, empower me with inner strength from Your Spirit. Fill me with Your love daily so I can pass it along to other people.

March 26
Love God, Love Each Other

"I know all the things you do. I have seen your hard work and your patient endurance. I know you don't tolerate evil people. You have examined the claims of those who say they are apostles but are not. You have discovered they are liars. You have patiently suffered for me without quitting. But I have this complaint against you. You don't love me or each other as you did at first!"

Revelation 2:2-4

The church at Ephesus had gotten everything right... almost. In their quest for doing good deeds they had grown hard. The tasks had become more important than their relationships with God and with each other. Can you imagine people that only spend time with and talk to each other when they are working together? Unfortunately, many of us do not have to imagine this scenario because we live it. We all know people who only call when they want us to help them out. It hurts to be used, especially by someone we love and respect. It hurts even more when they were too busy doing ministry to spend time with us.

When we started out in music ministry we were excited about our new adventure. We talked with everyone we could about what we were hoping to accomplish. Some people responded back with help, advice, and even money. So, when we needed help again it was natural to go back to those same people. But in between the times we needed help, did we have any kind of interaction with those people? If not, we may be guilty of not loving them as much as we did at first; we might have crossed the line into using people. True ministry means to love God and love each other. Ministry tasks are meant only to facilitate the love. Unfortunately, because we are human, we must constantly be reexamining our lives to keep these priorities.

Father, please constantly remind me of Your priorities for ministry. Help me to consistently show Your love to people.

March 27
Wonderful Results

"Confess your sins to each other and pray for each other so that you may be healed. The earnest prayer of a righteous person has great power and produces wonderful results."
James 5:16

One of the greatest things we can do for our fans is to pray with and for them. But, often, in the chaos that ensues after a show, the one-on-one ministry of prayer is forgotten or somehow deemed inappropriate for the situation. If we were secular musicians, the most important tasks after a show would be to build our fan base by signing autographs and selling merchandise. But as Christian music ministers, the most important task we have to do after the show is the same as any other time—to love people closer to Jesus. We hope to see lives changed as a result of our ministry and music. Those wonderful results must first be birthed in prayer.

We are not righteous people because we are so good, but because God has given us the righteousness of Jesus through the work of the cross. We might be the only righteous people many of our fans meet on any given day. We might be their best hope to experience the love of Christ. We might be their only opportunity to have someone pray with them today. If we do not take the opportunity to do so, they may not experience powerful, wonderful results. When we look for opportunities to pray with our fans we create moments that have the potential to change their lives forever. That is what being a Christian music minister all is about. This wonderful, powerful, life-changing result starts with praying together. Remember your calling, and do the work of your ministry: pray for and with your fans at every show.

Father, impress on me at each show the importance of praying for and with the fans. I pray for my fans right now. Draw them closer to You today. Show them Your love.

Humility Comes Before Honor

"If you reject discipline, you only harm yourself;
  but if you listen to correction, you grow in understanding.
Fear of the LORD teaches wisdom;
  humility precedes honor."

Psalm 15:32-33

Humility is the surrender of every part of our lives and our soul to God. To walk humbly, we must cast off our assessments of ourselves, whether they are positive or negative, and take on Christ-likeness. Jesus Christ is honored; when we are like Him we are also honored. This is why humility comes before honor. The more we take on Jesus' nature the more we are honored. This theology sounds simple enough but walking it out is extremely difficult because it is a process. The process usually involves challenging circumstances and correction before we can even see an area where we are not like Christ. During that time, we should not look at our trials and assume that God is punishing us. In fact, He is correcting and training us to be Christ-like. When He takes the effort to train us, He is demonstrating that He loves us.

Christian music ministers are often corrected and trained by God because we are spiritual leaders. God desires us to be able to go higher and deeper into ministry, which requires us to be extremely Christ-like. We can expect to experience times of correction, discipline and discomfort as we continue to grow in humility. So, we can take heart when we feel God's hand of correction and discipline. It should come as no surprise to us. Our Father is expressing His love and confidence in us. He is showing us where to humble ourselves and become more Christ-like so that He can raise us up in honor.

Father, change me to see that Your discipline and correction is love. Work with me to become more Christ-like today.

March 29

When We Are Not Chosen

"David also ordered the Levite leaders to appoint a choir of Levites who were singers and musicians to sing joyful songs to the accompaniment of harps, lyres, and cymbals."
                                        1 Chronicles 15:16

The Ark was coming to the Temple! This was a big deal, a once in a lifetime opportunity. Every Levite who could carry a tune wanted to be in the choir. But what happened to those that did not get chosen to sing with the choir? Why weren't they chosen? Perhaps they were not talented enough, or maybe they did not know the right Levite leader. It could have been that some of them just did not have the right look to be in the limelight of the parade. In the end, the results were the same—they were not chosen to be a musician in the parade for the Ark.

Being rejected as a musician by the powers that be is not a new thing. The emotions that go along with it have not changed either. Unfortunately, we cannot control the decisions people make to choose or not to choose us for a position in music ministry. What we can control is our response to their decision. The Levites who were not chosen could have become introverted, perhaps even going to their chambers to write new music. But they would have missed the historic event by giving in to their emotions. They could have taxed the patience of the head Levites by continually begging to be added to the musicians. Or they could have moved past their disappointment and gone ahead with doing their ministry in whatever way they could. Maybe they sang from the crowd that ran alongside the big parade and encouraged others to sing along too. Perhaps they found another opportunity to help that did not involve music at all. The best of them chose to serve God regardless of their appointed positions.

Father, remind me that it is not about my position in the music ministry. It's all about serving You however I can.

March 30
Servants Listen

And the LORD came and called as before, 'Samuel! Samuel!'
And Samuel replied, 'Speak, your servant is listening.'"

1 Samuel 3:10

We hear from God in different ways at different times. Sometimes he speaks as a still small voice in our spirits; other times He speaks through His word. The method God uses to communicate to us at any given time is not the most important thing. What is important is that we are listening. Our ministries must be built on hearing what God wants us to do and then doing it. We can learn and apply all the tools of the trade needed to be successful musicians. We may even become well known in this world. But all the attention and notoriety this world has to offer is meaningless if we are not doing God's plan for our lives and ministry. The only way we can be sure we are doing His plan is to listen for His instructions before we take any actions.

If a master had a servant who worked extremely hard all day, wouldn't he be pleased? Not necessarily. If the servant had been instructed to do one thing but worked hard at another, the master would be angry at the servant's disobedience. Or, if a servant had risen early, decided on his own to build on a project and worked hard at all day the master would be frustrated with the servant's pride in not getting instruction. Both the master and the servant would be upset at the waste of time when the project had to be dismantled because it was put in the wrong place or had been done before the necessary foundation was built. We become like those servants when we do not take the time to listen or do what we are instructed. God has a plan for our ministries. It is up to us to stop and listen to the instructions before we begin to implement any plan. When we do, we will be successful in God's eyes.

Father, speak to me—I am listening.

March 31
Don't Hide Love

"Can anything ever separate us from Christ's love? Does it mean he no longer loves us if we have trouble or calamity, or are persecuted, or hungry, or destitute, or in danger, or threatened with death? (As the Scriptures say, 'For your sake we are killed every day; we are being slaughtered like sheep.') No, despite all these things, overwhelming victory is ours through Christ, who loved us."

Romans 8:35-37

Ministry is hard. In fact, our enemy tries to make the circumstances of our life as confusing and difficult as possible so that we will feel separated from the love of God. Our enemy wants us to keep our light hidden under a bushel basket. So, he will do anything to keep us afraid and embarrassed, wanting to hide. Have you told all your friends about something God wants you to do, but it just has not worked out that way? Are you embarrassed and want to hide because of it? Guess who probably orchestrated that? Hint: NOT GOD. Did you try to do something extraordinary for God and now you are in worse condition that before? Would you love to hide out until things get better? Guess whose plan that is? Have you completely embarrassed yourself on stage? Do you feel guilty because you represented God poorly? Do you want to hide until people forget about it? Guess where that shame came from.

Our enemy will do anything to make us feel separated from God's love. Praise God that His love is not conditional upon our performance or our circumstances. We receive His victory in ministry the same way we received salvation—through His love and grace. Our shortfalls and difficult circumstances become a visible example the message of God's love when we do not hide.

Father, thank You for Your love. Help me to see how Your love triumphs over any of my circumstances.

April 1

The Biggest Fool

"Then he told them a story: 'A rich man had a fertile farm that produced fine crops. He said to himself, 'What should I do? I don't have room for all my crops.' Then he said, 'I know! I'll tear down my barns and build bigger ones. Then I'll have room enough to store all my wheat and other goods. And I'll sit back and say to myself, 'My friend, you have enough stored away for years to come. Now take it easy! Eat, drink, and be merry!' But God said to him, 'You fool! You will die this very night. Then who will get everything you worked for?' Yes, a person is a fool to store up earthly wealth but not have a rich relationship with God."

Luke 12:16-21

No Christian music minister would make this mistake. We generally do not have enough money to store up, let alone set aside enough to have a long retirement. What we do work on and value is our music and ministry. Our limited amount of time is a greater resource than this rich man's crops. We use time to pursue our creative endeavors and to do the work of the ministry. But that time is limited, so we choose to spend time doing the things we think are the most important. We value time and what it produces if we manage it well: great music ministry.

Successful ministry can be deceptive because success feeds our self worth. Fans build up our self image, and the rush of being in the limelight on stage can cause us to forget who we are there to serve. We must constantly be guarding our hearts.

The question needs to be asked: Who is the greatest fool: the man who works to attain wealth and doesn't get to keep it or the man who works to attain great ministry and doesn't have a rich relationship with God?

Father, show me how to use my time so that I can serve You in music ministry and have a rich relationship with You.

Pray Until You Pray

"Devote yourselves to prayer with an alert mind and a thankful heart."

Colossians 4:2

"Pray until you pray" is one of the rules Dr. Moody Stuart applied to his personal prayer life. Dr. Moody Stuart was a missionary and prayer warrior out of Scotland in the 1800's. What he meant by the saying is that the amount of time you spend in prayer does not matter nearly as much as connecting with God.

Some days it may take a very long time to get in the right frame of mind to pray effectively. Even though we may say words of prayer, we are thinking about all the distractions of life as well as the tasks of ministry. We have prayed but not spent time with God in prayer. If we say something like, "I am going to pray one half hour each day," we can easily meet our goal without ever touching the heart of God. That kind of praying will not lead to an effective or successful music ministry.

Previous generations used to call the process of praying until you connect with the heart of God "praying through." It takes much more mental discipline to pray through, to set aside our distractions and thoughts and to focus solely on God, than it does to merely spend a certain amount of time in prayer. We may spend the first thirty minutes of prayer wrestling with our own minds to focus on God. The last ten minutes of praying, after our hearts and minds are settled, may mean more to us than the previous half hour. But, praying through or praying until you pray is effective. Do you want a dynamic, extraordinary ministry that is filled with the power of God? Touch God's heart in prayer first. We cannot dare to do any less if we expect to be victorious in our lives and ministries.

Father, I do not always want to pray through. Forgive me. Teach me how to settle my mind, rise above my distractions, and truly communicate with You. I want to know Your heart.

April 3
Suffering to Learn Obedience

"Even though Jesus was God's Son, he learned obedience from the things he suffered."

Hebrews 5:8

Jesus undoubtedly suffered. Unfortunately, some people act like Jesus suffered so that we should never have to experience any kind of discomfort or suffering. Most Christian music ministers understand that the work Jesus did on the cross does not make us immune from suffering. But, in the back of our minds, many of us think that we should get a pass on some personal suffering because we have devoted our lives to ministry. We say we know that we will probably have to go through more difficult times because we are in ministry, but we expect that suffering to be ministry difficulties. A part of our heart is disappointed when we experience personal suffering. Perhaps our disappointment is not caused as much by our personal discomfort in the situation as it is by not truly understanding that, like Jesus, we learn obedience through suffering. Struggles cause us to become more Christ-like and obedient to His call on our lives. Disappointments, hardships, and trials teach us to rely on God and His love in every circumstance, stretching our faith beyond what it had been able to stretch before. These are things that as Christian leaders we want and desperately need.

Suffering is difficult whenever it comes and in whatever form it takes. We are not always going to respond well, especially at its onset. But Jesus experienced the ultimate suffering, so we know He understands what we are going through. He is sympathetic towards us and He walks with us along the difficult path. We can find strength in His companionship. Suffering is proof that He is building us into the kind of Christian leader He has called us to be. We want to be obedient like Jesus.

Father, help me to see suffering as Your hand at work in my life. Cause me to grow into the music minister You desire.

April 4

Complaining Will Change Your Future

"Their voices rose in a great chorus of protest against Moses and Aaron. 'If only we had died in Egypt, or even here in the wilderness!' they complained."

Numbers 14:2

The scouts came back with the report—there were giants in the land. The Israelites would not be able to just walk in and take over; there would be a struggle to succeed. No one wanted to hear that. They had been through so much already; escaping from slavery and walking through the wilderness. God was with them and they had seen His miracles. Now they expected the easy life, not having to work and fight for what appeared to be an unwinnable battle. Silly Israelites! But wait... do they sound a little like Christian musicians who expect God to make them famous and their ministries well known?

When God did not act on the Israelites' behalf as they expected, the Israelites complained. When their complaining grew so great in their hearts as to turn into rebellion, what did they get? Forty years wandering in the desert. Their complaining did not change God's mind to work in the way they wanted. Their complaining did change their own hearts to the point that God could no longer bless them. Have you ever wondered what God would have done if the Israelites had listened to the two spies with the good report? What if they had responded to God by saying, "God, You know that we are tired and broken from our past lives. But we will work towards doing Your will as long as You are for us"? Music ministry can be exhausting; it can sap our relationships and finances. But, what will God do on our behalf if we simply stop complaining and work towards doing His will?

Father, I pledge today to stop complaining. Change my heart and empower my efforts as I seek to do Your will.

April 5
Priceless Treasure

"Myrrh, aloes, and cassia perfume your robes.
In ivory palaces the music of strings entertains you."
Psalm 45:8

Myrrh, aloe, and cassia perfume were precious items usually only found in palaces. They were extremely valuable. Notice what is listed with them—music! Why is music so valuable? Because it inspires us and inspiration is priceless.

Music touches our emotions and opens us up to receive ideas and concepts that are not part of our day-to-day lives. We remember how emotions felt and attach that feeling to an experience, a moment in time. That moment has the ability to inspire us, change our hearts and minds forever. For example, think of your favorite song. Why is it your favorite? What memory does it bring back? How has that experience changed you? Music is powerful. The notes, chords, and beats can calm us down or make us excited; within just a few songs we can be moved from melancholy to joy. Music can affect our emotional state to the point that we change how we feel in a matter of moments. And when our feelings are ready, our hearts and minds open up to receive the message of the lyrics. The message of the lyrics is what makes Christian music more valuable than any other kind of music. It is an effective tool that can be used to bring people closer to Jesus when they otherwise might not be willing to hear about Him. The change is not always instantaneous, but the memory is not easily forgotten. The memory that is attached to the feelings and experience of your music can inspire a life to change forever. Thank God that He has given us priceless treasure in such an effective ministry tool. Rejoice in your priceless gift! Make music and change the world for Him!

Father, thank You for the priceless gift you have given me in music. Remind me of its value even when others do not see it.

April 6
One Sinner

"Or suppose a woman has ten silver coins and loses one. Won't she light a lamp and sweep the entire house and search carefully until she finds it? And when she finds it, she will call in her friends and neighbors and say, 'Rejoice with me because I have found my lost coin.' In the same way, there is joy in the presence of God's angels when even one sinner repents."

Luke 15:8-10

Have you ever watched little kids at someone else's birthday party? They just do not understand why some other kid is getting presents and gets to blow out the candles. Sometimes they pout or cry and even have a temper tantrum. But in the end they do not get the gifts and candles. It is a rare child who can truly be happy celebrating another child's birthday. Yet, isn't that what God asks us to do?

There is a party in heaven and we are invited, but the party is not about us. What is our reaction when someone comes to know Jesus more personally as a result of our ministry? Some of us mentally pat ourselves on the back, others use "our" results as a marketing tool, still other sulk because we are not "playing the big stage" so we could see better results. In our hearts, some of us are jealous of the attention the "sinner" gets after we have done all the work; we expect honor and respect for us and our ministry. Would any of us openly admit to any of this? No, but we would not be human if those feelings did not come at us from time to time. When those thoughts come, let us remember that we are not little children. We are already joint heirs with Christ, the inheritors of all He has. Our goal is to become like Him, laboring and rejoicing whenever His kingdom is advanced.

Father, help me to seek out every lost silver coin and rejoice in true humility, knowing that we have already been given the greatest gift. I want to have pure joy at heaven's party.

April 7

The Promises of God

> *"Remember your promise to me;*
> *it is my only hope.*
> *Your promise revives me;*
> *it comforts me in all my troubles."*
> Psalm 119:49-50

God's promises are better than money in the bank. We can absolutely count on Him to fulfill them. We can trust His promises, find comfort in them, and be revived by remembering what He has said. But our hearts do not always believe in them. We feel that we have been let down in the past and we know other people who feel that way too. Some of those people have even left the church and their faith because of it. So, what is wrong? Why don't all of God's promises come true?

The fact is that all of God's promises do come true, every single one of them. The problem is with us. We are often not very good at determining which things are actually promised by God and which things are paradigms we have been taught, what we hope is true, or we expect to happen based on our own experiences and preference for timing. We have a tendency to take what we hear and twist it to our own liking. The problem gets worse when we, as Christian leaders, communicate those expectations as promises of God. Then, we not only stumble ourselves but cause others to stumble with us.

Christian leaders have a responsibility to trust in God's promises and to continually be growing in that trust. It is our privilege to share that growth experience with people around us, to help them grow. But, we also have a responsibility to be growing in discernment and deeper knowledge of God. With God's discernment we can learn what He has really promised, and stand unwavering and uncompromising on those promises.

Father, show me where I misunderstand what You have promised. Give me the courage to stand on what You say.

April 8
Local, Regional, or National

"Sensible people keep their eyes glued on wisdom,
but a fool's eyes wander to the ends of the earth."
Proverbs 17:24

Most musicians believe that the natural progression is to start out local, move to regional, and then, if you are good enough, go national. National bands certainly have a huge platform from which to share their ministry. There is notoriety and a certain amount of credibility that comes with being large. But God has not called most Christian musicians to a national band. Most of us are called to work locally, and some of us to work regionally. But, being a local or regional band does not make us less of a musician or minister. In fact, staying "small" has big advantages when it comes to both business and ministry.

Local bands can hear from God and change quickly. National acts must first consider and consult all the people with which they have signed contracts. Local bands get to know their fans usually by name, and live out their lives with them. National acts rarely know their fans and can usually only demonstrate their faith to fans by talking about it on stage. National artists bear the burden of providing financially for their families and all the people who work for them. They must make decisions taking into account how the finances will affect everyone. Local bands are much freer to take the risks of playing gigs and making music that national bands cannot afford. Perhaps the biggest advantage local bands have is that they are able to spend time with their families. National and even regional bands are often on the road for weeks at a time. It is not necessarily right for every band to try to become a national act. Stay where God has called you in order to reach your full potential impact for Jesus!

Father, show me where I need to be and what I need to do. Help me to see the value in my calling, no matter what it is.

April 9
Fighting the Lord's Battles

"One day Saul said to David, 'I am ready to give you my older daughter, Merab, as your wife. But first you must prove yourself to be a real warrior by fighting the LORD's battles.' For Saul thought, 'I'll send him out against the Philistines and let them kill him rather than doing it myself.'"

1 Samuel 18:17

In this verse we see Saul acting deceitfully towards David. This comes as no surprise given Saul's jealousy and their relationship. David responds humbly by saying that he was not worthy of becoming a part of Saul's family. Yet, just a few verses later Saul makes almost the same offer to David, and David accepts. Was David aware of Saul's intentions? Quite probably, since court intrigues were common. In the end, what mattered to David was discerning God's battle and fighting it.

Christian music ministers are asked to fight for many things such as laws regulating music licensing, causes that need to raise money, or taking sides in a quarrel. When we are asked to go into battle, our first question needs to be, "Is it God's battle?" The motivations of the people sending us into battle may be deceitful, the battle itself will surely be messy, and we may be hurt. But if it is God's battle, we know we are fighting on the right side. If it is not God's battle, why should we waste our time and risk being wounded to fight, no matter how seemingly great the rewards? God's battles accomplish God's plans. David knew this; he was successful in life because he brought his life into line with God's plans. David fought for God's causes regardless of the rewards or consequences. At times life was very difficult, but as long as he fought for God David was eventually victorious. He reaped God's rewards.

Father, give me discernment to choose carefully what I fight for. I don't want to be involved in battles that are not Yours.

April 10
Meet Me After the Show

"By this time they were nearing Emmaus and the end of their journey. Jesus acted as if he were going on, but they begged him, 'Stay the night with us, since it is getting late.' So he went home with them. As they sat down to eat, he took the bread and blessed it. Then he broke it and gave it to them. Suddenly, their eyes were opened, and they recognized him. And at that moment he disappeared! They said to each other, 'Didn't our hearts burn within us as he talked with us on the road and explained the Scriptures to us?' And within the hour they were on their way back to Jerusalem. There they found the eleven disciples and the others who had gathered with them."

Luke 24:28-33

These verses begin with the disciples being at the end of their day's journey. It was late and they had been walking quite a while. They were tired. This sounds like musicians when they get off stage. We have worked all day and are tired. We have just expended a huge amount of energy and strength on the performance. But look at these disciples just a couple short verses later; within the hour they were walking back to Jerusalem. What happened to these tired men? In between the two trips, the two times of physical exhaustion, they spent time with Jesus. They got excited about Him and what He was doing.

After the show when it's time to meet the fans, the band has a great opportunity for ministry. Establishing relationships with fans is an extremely important part of band ministry. But often we are too exhausted to handle the conversations well. How can we do the work of the ministry when we are still focused on our set? Perhaps the secret is to take a break from music, our labor, and spend a few moments with Jesus to get excited about what He is about to do through us with our fans.

Father, meet me after the show. Inspire and energize me.

April 11
Right Side Up Ministry

"I have even seen servants riding horseback like princes—and princes walking like servants!"

Ecclesiastes 10:7

The way of the world is upside down. Foolish people frequently prosper while good hardworking people with common sense barely get by. In business, profitability defines success. Qualities such as integrity and fairness often go unrewarded and will cost the business money. Yet, even as Christian music ministers we tend to look up to successful business people. Take for example the way we act when a famous Nashville type agent or manager walks into the room during a gig. There may be hundreds of other people in the room, but as soon as we are aware of their presence, our focus shifts. In that moment we may miss the opportunity to change someone's life for eternity in favor of trying to make an impression on a person that we may or may not do business with in the future.

How do we choose who to talk to in our limited time after a show? Do we choose the fan who flatters us the most? The concert promoter that pays us? The pastor? Do we talk to the fan that has something in common with us like video games? Do we spend most of our time talking to members from the other Christian bands? Are we actively recruiting potential donors by seeking out those who look like they have money? Or, are we looking at people through the eyes of God? Both servants and princes alike have a need for Him. People who have material wealth need our ministry just as much as those who do not. We cannot judge who we spend ministry time with based on looks, position, or their potential to somehow benefit our ministry in the future. We must be led by God's Spirit to see past the deceitfulness of this world and directly into the hearts of people.

Father, teach me to see people the way You see them. Lead me to speak to those who need Your ministry the most.

April 12
Rest in Following

"Give your burdens to the LORD,
and he will take care of you.
He will not permit the godly to slip and fall."
Psalm 55:22

We want our ministries to be successful, to bring as many people as possible closer to Jesus. In order to accomplish this level of success there are many tasks and circumstances that need to be worked out. We must consistently keep an eye on what needs to be done at what time and be learning how to do it all well. But it is very easy to cross the line of doing our ministries well and anxiously caring about the myriad of details. We must take care of the things we are responsible for, but there are some things only God can do; those are His responsibilities. When we worry or become anxious about our ministries we begin to carry our burdens and therein lay the seeds of sin. Do we think we are wiser than God or that He will forget something? Do we feel we must attain or achieve something He will withhold or is unwilling to do? Are we willing to grasp for those things in our own wisdom and strength? How far will we go to get what we think we need to be successful?

Successful ministries demand that we seek out and follow the direction of God closely. In this following, we can find rest from worry and anxious care. God wants our ministry to be more impactful, more successful than we ourselves do. God also knows the best way to get the job done. He may ask much of us, but He will never leave us without His trustworthy leadership. We may not see, we may not understand, and we may not want to do as He asks; nevertheless, we must seek His guidance and follow Him. The success of our ministry depends on it.

Father, I rest my ministry in Your hands. Give me direction
each day so I can follow Your plan for this ministry's success.

April 13

We Must Suffer Hardship

"After preaching the Good News in Derbe and making many disciples, Paul and Barnabas returned to Lystra, Iconium, and Antioch of Pisidia, where they strengthened the believers. They encouraged them to continue in the faith, reminding them that we must suffer many hardships to enter the Kingdom of God."

Acts 14:21-22

Why would Paul and Barnabas feel compelled to return to a church to encourage them to continue in the faith? Why would the church need to be reminded that they must suffer hardships? We are all human, and in our humanness we want the easy life. Our flesh constantly cries out for a break from the disciplines of our faith. We see what people who do not act so diligently on their faith have acquired and we want their easier life. We want our ministry too; our flesh would simply prefer it to be easier.

Hardships come with a deep walk in the Lord. Often those who walk closest to God seem like they are afflicted with a more difficult life; look at the Old Testament prophets as examples. Hardships are not punishment for doing something wrong. Some of the hardship is designed by God to train and strengthen us; some of it is orchestrated by our enemy in the hope that we will give in. If he can wear us down, if we will give in just a little, our lives might get easier but our ministries will be diminished. So, do not be discouraged by hardships. They will come. They were expected by the apostles and the early church; they should be expected by us today. If we want to go deeper into ministry and to walk closer to God, we can expect both more attacks from our enemy and more training and discipline from God. Be strong. Continue in the faith!

Father, help me to change my thinking about hardships and see them as training. Strengthen me through each hardship as I grow closer to You.

April 14
Venting Anger

"Fools vent their anger, but the wise quietly hold it back."
Proverbs 29:11

Christian musicians have many reasons to be angry. We are often treated as commodities more than as human beings. The need for our services is not reflected in the amount we are paid, and the industry is set up so that most of us must fail. The majority of us cannot make any kind of a living from our ministry, so our families suffer as we attempt to work day jobs. There is quite a bit of pressure on us. Then, when we finally get to a gig and someone doesn't do what he promised to do and we look bad. It's enough to make us want to scream. Unfortunately, sometimes we do, and not always at the right person either.

Notice that this verse does not say, "Fools express their anger." Being angry at times is part of life and ministry. The trick is to express anger correctly: at the right time, to the right person, for the right purpose, and to the right degree. This kind of purposeful expression leads to correction and healing rather than the hurt feelings that occur when anger is vented. Holding anger in until the appropriate time and place to purposefully express it is healthy. Holding anger in forever is not. Buried anger will eventually come out in destructive forms such as severed relationships, aggression, headaches, ulcers, or depression.

Being a Christian music minister provides many opportunities for us to be angry and frustrated. Most people have no idea of the personal cost involved; they only see the glamour of it all. So when we vent our anger, it is seen as arrogant diva-type behavior. We must learn the self discipline to walk carefully and express anger appropriately with the purpose of bringing people closer to Jesus.

Father, show me where I have expressed anger poorly in the past. Teach me how I can express anger better in the future.

April 15
God is in Control

*"I am nothing—how could I ever find the answers?
I will cover my mouth with my hand."*

Job 40:4

This is Job's response to God after all his friends have attempted to provide answers regarding his situation, after Job himself has questioned God, and after God has revealed the truth. Why was Job's life the way it was? Why was there so much suffering? Even yet today, Bible scholars have differences of opinion without one definitive answer except that God was in control. How often are we like Job? We question why we did not get the record deal, or the solo, or the awards and recognition. We don't understand why people treat us and our ministries the way they do. Why should our families have to pay the price for our ministry because we don't get paid what we are worth? Why should we have to pay such a high price to do the ministry we are called to do, while other ministers live in luxury?

Unfortunately, there is no one definitive answer except that as in Job's situation, God is in control. We can question, we can ask our friends, and hire advisors. We can struggle with the "why" of it all. But in the end, often the only answer is that God has chosen to do it this way. He is not our servant who must do everything the way we want. He is not our employee who must explain everything He is doing. He is the God that we have chosen to obey. He is our Father who loves us and knows what is best for us, even when we do not understand. So sometimes, after all the wrestling is done, we simply must shut our mouths, accept that we do not understand, and let God be God. In His time, He will shape us and our ministries into what He wants them to be, and He will do it however He chooses.

Father, I don't understand why I am in this situation. But, I accept that You love me and are in control; that is enough.

April 16
Tour Guides of Worship

"The people will play flutes and sing,
'The source of my life springs from Jerusalem!'"
Psalm 87:7

Celebration of our Christian faith comes in many forms, but most often in musical worship. We sing and play instruments to express the joy of having a Savior who is the source of our life. Then, the quiet hush comes over the people as God overwhelms us with His presence. It is here that we actually experience relationship with God. This relationship experience is the source of our life; it is what sets Christianity apart from so many other world religions. Using the Jerusalem metaphor, we could say that it is not enough to know that there is a Jerusalem, but we must go visit the city and experience all that it has to offer. We cannot take in all the sights, smells, and sounds in one moment or even one day. We cannot truly know Jerusalem if we rush about doing our business. We must take time to pause and breathe the air, see the grandeur, and the notice the minute details. So it is with the presence of God in worship. Experiencing the source of our life should not be hurried along, rushed, or cut short.

As we lead the people in worship, let us be sensitive to take in all that God has to offer. Let us understand that worship is not only an expression of adoration from the people to our Creator. It is also an experience of the love given from our Creator to the people. This true relationship is the source of our life, our Jerusalem. Our job as worship leaders is simply to lead the people into worship, like a tour guide of the city, as we experience God together. Just like anyone who has taken a guided tour of a city, the people should come away filled with a deeper knowledge and appreciation of God.

Father, show me Your timing as I lead worship. Teach me how to lead the people under Your direction in every moment.

April 17
You Don't Realize

"I correct and discipline everyone I love. So be diligent and turn from your indifference."
Revelation 3:19

This verse was written to the church at Laodicea; the church of the lukewarm, about to be spit out. We know the story, and we have heard the sermons. Certainly we are not lukewarm because we are so busy working in music ministry. But to the Laodicean church God said in an earlier verse, "You don't realize that you are wretched and miserable and poor." How could they not realize that? Their condition sounds pretty severe yet somehow they don't realize. Could that be happening to us?

One certain way to check our level of indifference is to look at how we treat other people. Do we walk by people with needs because we are busy doing our music ministry? Do we even notice there is a need? Is your ministry more about the music or about the people? After a show are you more interested in selling CDs or talking to as many fans as possible? When was the last time you interrupted what you were doing to pray with someone? When was the last time you stopped doing something important that would expand your music ministry to spend time to listen and pray with someone?

If our love-o-meter is not so good, we need to make changes right away. In fact, God has probably already been disciplining us, trying to get those changes to occur. We must pay attention. If we are experiencing a higher than normal level of discipline we may need to work on loving people more than on expanding our music ministry. Indifference to the thing God cares most about (people) is a sure way to have our ministry spit out of His mouth. We need to be red hot ministers in red hot ministries, full of love for God and His people in order to change the world.

Father, please continue to discipline me until I am the kind person in the ministry that brings people closer to You.

April 18

Comparisons and Judgments

"So why do you condemn another believer? Why do you look down on another believer? Remember, we will all stand before the judgment seat of God. For the Scriptures say, 'As surely as I live,' says the LORD, 'every knee will bend to me, and every tongue will confess and give praise to God.' Yes, each of us will give a personal account to God. So let's stop condemning each other. Decide instead to live in such a way that you will not cause another believer to stumble and fall."
Romans 14:10-13

Every music ministry is different. Some of us are called to exhort Christians, others to reach the unsaved. Some ministries are most effective by being signed to a label; others are best off by remaining independent. Some of us preach from the stage, others let the example of our lives do the talking. Some of us perform nationally, while many of us stay local. But, why do we insist upon comparing ourselves and our ministries to each other? Are not our different callings and ministry goals ordained by God? Why do we judge other musicians and ministries based on what we have been called to do? Are we really that shallow as to accept the secular definition of success in our music as the standard we should strive for and judge others by? Is there really only one right way to do God's ministry?

Rather, let us rejoice in our differences knowing that all of God's work is being done. Let us be the ones to lead by example; to encourage our fellow music ministers to be the very best at their ministries. Let us live holy lives that are an example to our fans and other secular bands as well as to every other Christian music minister we meet.

Father, remind me that my ministry is not going to reach every person. Stir up a love in me for the variety of music ministers and ministries You have called.

April 19

God Has Done Amazing Things

"When the LORD brought back his exiles to Jerusalem,
it was like a dream!
We were filled with laughter,
and we sang for joy.
And the other nations said,
'What amazing things the LORD has done for them.'
Yes, the LORD has done amazing things for us!
What joy!"

Psalm 126:1-3

Christian musicians tend to be more aware of our feelings than most people—it is a part of us that we need to be great musicians. Unfortunately, the acute awareness of feelings also comes with a downside. Too often we are prone to depression and despair, especially when circumstances do not go our way long term. As the music industry has shifted from the label way of doing business to musicians connecting directly with fans, many of us have focused on what has been lost. Label contracts are simply not being offered to new bands as much as they were in the past. Performance fees, advances, and tour support are pretty much nonexistent for new bands. Many of us who were focused on getting signed have either quit or fallen into despair.

They key to getting past an unfortunate situation is to focus on what God has done. Yes, the Israelites were slaves in Egypt. They could have spent their time talking and pondering how things could have been for them if they had not been slaves. After all, God could have given them Egypt! Instead this psalm focuses on what God has done to bring them out of slavery. In the case of musicians, we have regained control of our ministries! We are free to do whatever God has for us to do, however and whenever He wants. God's provision of freedom for us and our ministries is worth thinking and talking about!

Father, thank You for the freedom You have given musicians.

April 20

Streams Renewing the Desert

"Restore our fortunes, LORD,
as streams renew the desert.
Those who plant in tears
will harvest with shouts of joy.
They weep as they go to plant their seed,
but they sing as they return with the harvest."
Psalm 126:4-6

In this second half of the psalm we read yesterday, we see the request of the Israelites after they had focused on what God had already done for them. They felt like and were literally desert nomads, no homes, no way to grow or get food, or provide a stable future for their families. Their cry was simply for a way to make a good living. This sounds like many Christian musicians.

We need the streams that renew the desert so we can plant and harvest. But, just as the Nile River does not look like the streams the Israelites found in the Promised Land, the old streams of income for musicians do not look like the new streams. Do we lament that we no longer live on the banks of the Nile, or do we learn how to build wells, plant, and harvest along the new streams? Yes, it is difficult. The Israelites no longer had the power and storehouses of Egypt to back them up. They planted in tears. It is reasonable to expect that we too will experience difficulties as we attempt to grow our ministries. But like the Israelites, we can expect a harvest. We can look forward to a time of joy and singing because God will have answered our request. We must do the hard work, but we can persevere with joy if we remember what He has already done. He has not brought us this far to fail now.

Father, never before in the history of music has technology been so favorable towards musicians. Help me to learn to make use of every opportunity to bring people closer to You.

April 21
Do What You Wanna Do

"Then Jesus said to his disciples, 'If any of you wants to be my follower, you must turn from your selfish ways, take up your cross, and follow me. If you try to hang on to your life, you will lose it. But if you give up your life for my sake, you will save it. And what do you benefit if you gain the whole world but lose your own soul? Is anything worth more than your soul?'"

Matthew 16:24-26

The sad truth is that most people spend their lives doing what they want to do. For some it means taking the path of least resistance while others need the challenge of a fight. Many Christians, even ministers, have found a way to do exactly what they want to do and spiritualize their actions as justification. Nevertheless, there is a significant difference between being a music minister because it is what you want to do and being a music minister because it is what God wants you to do. Sometimes we have the pleasure of doing both at the same time. Other times we are not so sure we want to be a music minister, but we know that God wants us to follow Him along this path. This way is more difficult but ultimately fulfilling.

The danger lies in when God either calls us to switch to something else or never wanted us to be a music minister at all. Are we committed enough in following Him to change? Would you stop being a music minister to go be a janitor in a school if He asked? Are we more committed to our current calling and ministry than we are to following Christ wherever He leads? The act of simply following Jesus keeps us humble. After all, we are simply being obedient. When the stage lights go down and the applause is over, ask yourself, "Did I just perform out of obedience to my calling from Jesus or did I just gratify my flesh?"

Father, I choose to follow You wherever You lead, even if it is not a gratifying position. I choose You over any ministry.

April 22
The Elders Worship, Like Us

"the twenty-four elders fall down and worship the one sitting on the throne (the one who lives forever and ever). And they lay their crowns before the throne and say,

> *'You are worthy, O Lord our God,*
> *to receive glory and honor and power.*
> *For you created all things,*
> *and they exist because you created what you pleased.'"*

Revelation 4:10-11

The elders in the throne room of God must be extremely important beings. They are elders, above the angels but below Jesus in heavenly hierarchy. Yet, look what they do—worship! It would seem that worshipping God is their most important, if not only, task. These elders do not come and go from the throne room, being dispatched to do other tasks, as are other heavenly beings. They stay before the face of God, constantly in worship. There is not one or two or three of them either—there are 24, which in Biblical numerology means "the priesthood!" The fact that God created these high-ranking beings primarily to worship says quite a bit about the importance of worship to God. Our calling as Christian music ministers and worship leaders must be extremely important to Him as well. It is a high honor, not something to be taken lightly or executed poorly. The world may not see it and often even the church may not acknowledge it, but God has given us the same calling as the elders in His throne room—to stand before His face and worship Him. We are called to be a part of the priesthood that worships. Let us strive to live up to that honor and truly worship God with the awe, reverence, admiration, and highest quality music that He so deserves.

Father, I am honored to be chosen as a priestly worshipper. Show me how to worship You in ways that most please You.

April 23
The Journey & The Destination

"Those who belong to Christ Jesus have nailed the passions and desires of their sinful nature to his cross and crucified them there. Since we are living by the Spirit, let us follow the Spirit's leading in every part of our lives."

Galatians 5:24-25

The old rules of the music industry do not work anymore. The new "rules" or ways of doing things that are guaranteed to work well have not quite been established. While this is an exciting time of change for the way musicians do their ministries, it is often difficult to determine what each of our ministries should look like and which steps will get us there.

However, ministry success is guaranteed when we follow God's plan. Wouldn't it be nice if God would give us that plan written down in outline form so we could implement it? But, most of the time discovering God's plan for our lives and ministries is a process. He seems to be just as concerned with the journey as he is with the destination or outcome. We start by laying down what we want and our definition of success. We set aside fame, fortune, and the secular musician's lifestyle in favor of discipline and servanthood. Then the real journey begins as we seek God's face for instruction and leadership. Setting aside the flesh and intentionally, consistently seeking God's plan is the beginning of living by the Spirit, which is like choosing the destination for your journey. But the daily clarity, the most difficult part of the process, comes from following the Spirit's leading moment by moment. He guides us during confusing times, leading us in what, when, and how to do things. As Christian music ministers, we need that guidance now more than ever.

Father, give me ears that hear what You have planned for each day. Give me a spirit that is alertly waiting for Your instruction. Give me a heart that longs to do Your will.

April 24
Beautiful Things

"The king used the sandalwood to make steps for the Temple of the LORD and the royal palace, and to construct lyres and harps for the musicians. Never before had such beautiful things been seen in Judah."

2 Chronicles 9:11

Sandalwood is a slow growing tree that produces a heavy, yellow, fine-grained wood. The distinctiveness of this wood comes not only in its strength and exceptional beauty but also in its fragrance, which lasts for decades. This wood has been prized for centuries. So, why use the best of the best to make instruments? God is worthy of the very best—the most beautiful and holy.

How do you look to God? Are you beautiful? Most of us would say, "NO!" because we see all our sin, faults, and imperfections. Yet, because God sees us through Jesus, we are more valuable and more beautiful than His most beautiful instruments in the temple. If He used the very best sandalwood to create the instruments for musicians to play in His temple, imagine what He must think of the musicians!

Did you know that fragrance is often associated with prayer and being in God's presence? Think about the symbolism of instruments made out of wood with a fragrance that lasts for decades. The musicians did not have to burn incense to get a sweet smell; they just had to play their instruments. Can God really be inferring that our music has the ability to impact the world for decades?

Let's not sell ourselves, our music, and our ministry short. God sees musicians as valuable and beautiful. "Never before has such beautiful things been seen in Judah."

Father, thank You for the way you see me, as valuable and beautiful. Help me to see myself the same way. Remind me to cherish my music and ministry as much as You do.

April 25

What Are We Working For?

"When he appeared in human form,
he humbled himself in obedience to God
and died a criminal's death on a cross."
Philippians 2:7b-8

The idea that God promises to bless us with physical wealth and/or raise our ministries up to be significant (which we assume involves a level of notoriety) if we are living the way God wants is a uniquely western concept. In most parts of the world, it is generally accepted that we will experience more hardship and often severe punishment if we choose to follow Christ.

God has obviously given some Christian music ministers a national platform for their ministries. He has even provided a way to earn a living through music for some musicians. When God raises a ministry to the national level, it is for His benefit as part of His plan to change the world. Sure, we would all like to be that person with that ministry. But what if, like Jesus, God's plan for us is to die painfully, our reputations tarnished, not yet seeing the fruit of our ministry? What if His plan involves ministering to small crowds in obscurity for the rest of our lives? Are we delighted to work God's plan for our lives and ministry no matter what that plan is? Do we find joy in simple obedience?

Jesus experienced times of great difficulty in His ministry on earth; the crowds were not always large and happy to see Him. The apostles experienced jail, beatings, and many were killed; some were well known, others not as much. Many Christians today, whose names are not known, labor daily to advance the kingdom under harsh circumstances. When we are obedient to God's plans, we are not promised notoriety, success, or even recognition as the world defines those things.

Father, remind me daily that although I work to advance my music ministry, I work in obedience to Your call and plan.

April 26

Excuses and Talents

"'Yes,' the king replied, 'and to those who use well what they are given, even more will be given. But from those who do nothing, even what little they have will be taken away.'"

Luke 19:26

The story of the ten talents—we know it and understand the concept. Yet, somehow there is a disconnect when we apply it to ourselves. Notice in the story that the king does not accept excuses or reasons why the servant did not make the most of what he had been given. But we often allow ourselves the luxury of excuses. "I just don't feel like doing that today" or "I don't know how" (with the implied, "I might be able to find out but I don't want to") are some common examples. But we also use God to spiritualize our lack of effort. How about, "It's just not my gifting" or "God has not provided a way for me to do that." Sometimes we even blame other people for not "receiving our ministry" when we have not made the effort to learn how to do booking correctly. We are talented but we have many excuses.

Why do we allow ourselves these excuses? We are not satisfied with the lack of results and we know they do not please God. Excuses do not get us what we want. The reasons we use excuses are varied, but they are almost all rooted in sin, which is why God does not accept excuses. Laziness, pride, unforgiveness, and fear are the most common reasons for excuses. Whatever the excuse, whatever the sin, God expects us to face it head on and work towards becoming victorious over it. We may not get it right all the time, but we have to start getting it right some of the time. We should certainly be consistently improving; the future of our ministry depends on it.

Father, thank You for the talents You have given me. Reveal to me the roots of my excuses for not making the most of my talents. Help me to be victorious over them.

April 27
Ordinary Men with Jesus

"The members of the council were amazed when they saw the boldness of Peter and John, for they could see that they were ordinary men with no special training in the Scriptures. They also recognized them as men who had been with Jesus."

Acts 4:13

How do you want to be recognized? If you were walking down the street and someone saw you and said, "Hey, there's that guy who _____." How would they fill in the blank? The guy who is in that band; the guy who looks like a rock star; the guy who just cut me off in traffic. How would you like them to fill in the blank? The guy who plays guitar for that famous Christian band; the guy who played with his band at our church last week; the guy whose band was on that magazine cover.

What about being known as the guy who knows Jesus? What would it take for us to be recognized as someone who knows Jesus, before we are recognized for being in a Christian band? How much effort do we spend promoting our band each day? How much effort do we spend getting to know Jesus?

Jesus has an overwhelming impact on our lives. The more we know Him, the closer we become to being like Him. We can never fully know all that there is to know about Jesus and we can never fully become like Him while we are on earth. But we can get closer each day through relationship with Him. It is not about us changing ourselves so that other people can recognize that we are Christians. It is about us knowing Christ. The change is the byproduct. Recognition of that change is the effect. Our western culture teaches us to affect change. But God's way is to know the one who never changes. Above all else, we must know Jesus, His character, His ways of thinking, and His ways of doing things.

Father, show me more about You. Give me something of Yourself today that I have never seen or experienced before.

April 28
But Afterward

"No discipline is enjoyable while it is happening—it's painful! But afterward there will be a peaceful harvest of right living for those who are trained in this way. So take a new grip with your tired hands and strengthen your weak knees. Mark out a straight path for your feet so that those who are weak and lame will not fall but become strong."

Hebrews 12:11-13

God does not want Christians to be weak and lame; of course, He does not want Christians to fall. In fact, one of the main reasons we are in the music ministry is to help keep people from doing just that. We hope to encourage and strengthen others as they walk through the difficult times of life. The challenge for us is to be able to do our ministry well while we are the ones being disciplined. Our hands get tired from the daily workload of our ministry. Our knees get weak as we walk on stage once again when we feel like we have nothing left to give. We become the weak and the lame. How can we continue to be faithful servants and ministers?

The key word in this verse is "afterward." We do not enjoy the pain of training and discipline. We do not like feeling tired and weak. But we can look past the current situation, to the afterward, even while circumstances have not yet changed. The ability to know that God is working in our lives, through the discomfort, and to trust Him to use the pain to bring about change in us will carry us through the now. We can envision ourselves becoming more like Jesus: more patient, kinder, less envious, having more hope, gaining endurance, having stronger faith, being persistent, forgiving, and less prideful. We can look to the afterward to see who we are in the process of becoming.

Father, reveal how You are changing me to become more like Jesus. Put a longing in me to do whatever it takes to change.

April 29

Lukewarm Routines

"And so the Lord says,
'These people say they are mine.
They honor me with their lips,
but their hearts are far from me.
And their worship of me
is nothing but man-made rules learned by rote.'"
Isaiah 29:13

Going through the motions, walking out the routine... we all live life this way from time to time. Often the routine is comforting and serves us well; but not so when it is applied to worship. Our Father desires our hearts, not our routines. We stress this concept to audiences as we attempt to keep their experiences with God new and fresh. Many lukewarm people attend worship services and Christian concerts. So, we are constantly looking for the latest tools and methods to try to help make Jesus more real to our fans. This search comes from a heart that genuinely desires to lead other people closer to Jesus.

While the desire to lead people into a more genuine experience with Jesus and the search for new methods to do so is good, the focus on other people can cause us to become lukewarm in our own experience with Jesus. Our rote man-made rules can be defined as helping other people to worship. Even though we are doing good works, we ourselves are lukewarm in relationship to God. Let this never be so! Let us pledge to never again let the ministry come before our personal relationship with God. We refuse to be lukewarm Christian music ministers. Our hearts will be on fire with His love and His presence. We will be known by God because we have spent time getting to know God.

Father, I want to be known by You; I want to know more of You. Interrupt my routines. Speak to me, change me, change my ministry. Cause my heart to long for You.

April 30
Persistent Endurance

"So do not throw away this confident trust in the Lord. Remember the great reward it brings you! Patient endurance is what you need now, so that you will continue to do God's will. Then you will receive all that he has promised."
Hebrews 10:35-36

Quitting is easy. Living a safe, comfortable life is easy. Doing God's will, becoming and doing all that He has for us is challenging. Christian music ministers do not have the luxury of living a safe, easy life. The very nature of what we do requires living and thinking differently than most people. Living our unconventional lives becomes more difficult as we watch people with safe lives prosper while we continue to struggle with the basics. But we must press on; continuing to do all the things God has called us to do, if we are to lead people closer to Jesus.

Endurance and persistence give us the ability to fall, get up, and try again as necessary. We do not need to be the first, or fastest, or strongest, or best, or perfect to be all that God wants us to be. We simply need to be consistently persistent and relentless in pursuing God first, and then what He has for us to do in our ministries. We can do that! We do not need to give up on our ministry goals and dreams; we need to get up and try again. We don't need to listen to opinions that infer we should grow up and conform. We need to persistently seek out what God has for our lives. We don't need to ask, "Why bother, what's the use?" We need to confidently trust in God's plan for us and our ministry. This confidence will give us the patient endurance and relentless persistence we need to succeed at being and doing everything God wants us to be and do.

Father, give me what I need to succeed. Teach me, train me, discipline me; I will not quit. I am Yours, committed to living the life and doing the ministry You have planned for me.

May 1
God's Power and Work

"And now I will send the Holy Spirit, just as my Father promised. But stay here in the city until the Holy Spirit comes and fills you with power from heaven."

Luke 24:49

At the time Jesus spoke these words the disciples were already the most highly trained Christian men and women on the earth. The disciples had learned from His teaching and His example, living life with Him daily. They knew how to do what needed to be done. But Jesus said, "Wait, for the Holy Spirit and His power." Once again, we see Jesus reinforcing the concept that it is not by our might or power, not all our training and talents, which gets the work of the kingdom accomplished. True kingdom change occurs by the power of the Holy Spirit and God's hand at work. Perhaps the disciples had to wait in Jerusalem until they were filled with power from heaven to ensure that they would be vessels of that love and power rather than calling attention to themselves. They were, after all, the closest friends of Jesus—the most spiritually qualified people on earth to lead the new church. But when they were overcome with the fullness of the Holy Spirit, they simply became His vessels.

After the music is done and band leaves the venue, what remains is the work that God has done. Of course, we want the fans to remember our band and our music. But the most important part of every show we play is the work that the Holy Spirit does through us and our music. This work is what we want fans to remember most: how God changed their lives and the lives of the people around them. We want them to be changed forever by the love and character of God as it works through us.

Father, help me to get out of the way of Your hand at work on and off stage. Show me how to call attention to Your love and character rather than myself, my band, and my music.

May 2
Powered By Prayer

"Keep watch and pray, so that you will not give in to temptation. For the spirit is willing, but the body is weak!"
Matthew 26:41

Prayer is the core, the foundation of every ministry that is successful in God's eyes. We must actually pray to please God. This does not mean studying about prayer, or teaching and attending seminars on prayer. Prayer is something we do that requires time, self-discipline, and focus. So, our flesh is not very eager to do it. We will be tempted to do anything and everything before prayer. Even good things, the works of the ministry, can become a temptation away from prayer.

We can learn all the mechanics of being excellent music ministers including songwriting, social media, marketing, business management, stage presence, etc. We can do all the tasks excellently and correctly. We can lull ourselves in to a sense of secure slumber after the tasks are accomplished. But without the power of God that comes through prayer, all our good deeds are not effective. If they were, people would be brought closer to Jesus just because they like us or our music.

Prayer is the power behind the ministry, and prayer is the one thing that cannot be bought. Each person must wrestle with their own prayer life. Each person must struggle through their own self-discipline, their own distractions and excuses, to come to a place of being alone with God. It is there that the true Christian faith begins to be worked out often through tears, fasting, weariness of soul, and finally surrender. No one can do this for another person. No ministry can please God without the people involved first meeting God alone, consistently in prayer.

Father, I want to become a person of prayer with a ministry that is powered by prayer. Help me to overcome the tendency to focus on ministry tasks more than relationship with You.

Hear From God

> *"Who is this that questions my wisdom*
> *with such ignorant words?*
> *Brace yourself like a man,*
> *because I have some questions for you,*
> *and you must answer them.*
> *Where were you when I laid the foundations of the earth?*
> *Tell me, if you know so much.*
> *Who determined its dimensions*
> *and stretched out the surveying line?*
> *What supports its foundations,*
> *and who laid its cornerstone*
> *as the morning stars sang together*
> *and all the angels shouted for joy?"*
>
> Job 38:2-7

Have you ever simply stood in front of God and said nothing? Perhaps we should all do this more often. We need to hear from God more than we need to be heard by God.

We say that our ministries are dependent upon God, but often our ideas of what we think God is like are skewed. In our limited understanding, we believe we know what God thinks about any number of topics, including what He wants for our ministry. But, as Job's friends discovered, even our best interpretations and most sincere efforts can be wrong. We simply are not God. We do not know the future and we do not have His understanding of the present. So today let us acknowledge His sovereignty, His magnificence, His omnipotence, and all the things that make Him God. Let us stand before Him in awesome wonder and silence simply to hear what He has to say to us.

Father, I stop my thoughts and shut my mouth before You. You choose the topic of conversation and say whatever You want to say. I will listen as I stand in awe of You.

May 4

Faith vs. Planning

"But Jesus said, 'You feed them.'
'With what?' they asked. 'We'd have to work for months to
earn enough money to buy food for all these people!'
'How much bread do you have?' he asked. 'Go and find out.'"
Mark 6:37-38

There are financial considerations in every ministry. It would be foolish to attempt any project without first asking, "How much will this cost?" There are many Bible verses that talk about wise financial planning. But then, there are verses like this one that seem to blow good financial stewardship out of the water. They ask us to ignore the money issue and have faith that God will take care of it. How can we reconcile these two seemingly opposing viewpoints or doctrines?

The answer to faith vs. planning is not an either or situation; both are true and right. Hearing from God, or discernment, is the key. Most of the time Jesus operated His ministry in what we would consider today to be a relatively "normal" way. Funding came primarily from donations and a treasurer kept track of the money. But every once in a while Jesus chose to go outside the norm and provide for the ministry with a miracle, such as this instance of feeding the crowd, and paying temple taxes with money from a fish.

It is our job as ministers to stay in tune with what God is doing and how He is doing it. Much of the time in our ministries He will want us to plan and budget, to be good financial stewards. But other times, He will want to do things in an unusual way and we must be prepared to believe Him for that as well. Our goal should be to hear God's plan and do it His way.

Father, I prefer to do things a certain way. But, help me to trust You to do my ministry in whatever way you choose. Give me discernment to know what You are doing so I may follow.

May 5
Backed By His Name

"I give you thanks, O LORD, with all my heart;
*   I will sing your praises before the gods.*
I bow before your holy Temple as I worship.
I praise your name for your unfailing love and faithfulness;
*   for your promises are backed*
*   by all the honor of your name.*
As soon as I pray, you answer me;
*   you encourage me by giving me strength."*

Psalm 138:1-3

There are times when our faith is not strong. There are times when our love is not all it should be. There are even times when we are more confident in ourselves than we are in God. Music ministers are not exempt from lows in our spiritual walk. Wouldn't it be great if once we took on the calling of working for Jesus our spiritual life leapt ahead to make us all we needed to be—strong, loving, and unwavering in our commitment? But, we are human so we know it does not work that way. From time to time we will not live up to what we want to be.

Thank God that our calling and spiritual lives are not solely dependent on us! God's promises are backed by the honor of His name. Our confidence is in Him, not in our best human efforts. There is no possible way that we can attain all that He wants for us and for our ministries by "getting it all right." If He does not complete the work, it will not get done! If we expect to complete the work by our own efforts, it will not get done.

Our ministries will only attain all that God has planned when He is actively involved. We are simply blessed enough to be chosen to work with Him in the endeavor!

Father, thank You for relieving me from the burden of expecting myself to be perfect as I work in Your ministry.

May 6
Relationship Harmonies

"So then, let us aim for harmony in the church and try to build each other up."

Romans 14:19

When a vocalist sings harmony, they are singing a different note than the lead. The notes complement each other and work together, but they are not the same. Yet, somehow we view harmony differently within our relationships, especially within the church and our ministries. We tend to think of living in harmony as everyone thinking alike and doing the same things.

In most music ministries, there is usually one strong leader with the rest of the members following. Certainly nothing is wrong with this model as long as the leader is striving for harmony rather than everyone "singing" lead. Just as there are a variety of instruments and vocal parts in most music, each band member has gifts and strengths that enhance the whole composition of the band. When we all play the same note as the leader, the ministry loses out on the depth and effectiveness that God desires. Instead of holding back our gifts or leading by creating an expectation that everyone will sing lead, we need to value our own gifts as well as each other's gifts. A tenor should not sing bass, but a tenor might have a great suggestion for how a bass part could be made stronger or more interesting. Our relationships can work the same way. As we learn to respect how each of us thinks and does things, we will begin to work together in harmony. We will build each other up by encouraging one another to contribute and express their opinions and gifts. We can follow the leader by playing the same song while each expressing our own parts to the music. In the same way, we can appreciate the fullness and beauty of the ministry as we work together to build up the entire body of Christ.

Father, help me to value my gifts as much as I value those of my band mates. Show me ways to build them up.

Because You Belong to Him

"Now I appeal to Euodia and Syntyche. Please, because you belong to the Lord, settle your disagreement."
                                              Philippians 4:2

Disagreements are bound to occur. Notice that this verse does not say, "Do not have disagreements." It does not in any way imply that we will always agree on any one thing, but it does infer that we should not let our disagreements affect our relationships. Somewhere along the line we will have to submit our will, our way of doing things to someone else just to keep peace and friendships. Submitting is not a bad thing. It teaches us humility, broadens our experience to new methods, and keeps our mind sharp as we learn new things. Settling our disagreements by submitting to one another in brotherly love is a Biblical mandate. In other words, we can expect to not always get our own way. Jesus certainly did not get His way when He was crucified, but He submitted to the Father's will.

Unfortunately, on the day of a show, submitting in love is one of the last things on our minds. We have a million things to do. We have to tear down equipment and then load it all up only to set it up and repeat the process after the show. How often have you gotten tense with a band mate during this process? Often, we have disagreements on business issues such as how many or which shows to accept, or how the band website should look. These kinds of disagreements can be the start of broken relationships if we do not settle them. One unsettled issue can pile on top of another and before we know it, it is too late. Because we belong to Christ, we are expected settle our issues before they cause problems in our relationships and ministries. Take time to take care of the issues and the relationships.

Father, help me to be more sensitive to my band mates. Teach me how to resolve disagreements by submitting.

Attractive Words

"Let your conversation be gracious and attractive so that you will have the right response for everyone."

Colossians 4:6

The Greek for the word "attractive" here is literally translated "seasoned with salt." We do not think much about salt because it is so common, so the word attractive is a more accurate translation of the meaning and intent of the word for today's readers. Imagine eating most of your food without salt. Worse yet, can you imagine living in a desert climate without salt? An invitation to dinner at the home of anyone who cooked with and served salt would definitely be accepted.

Many of our fans are in a similar situation; there is no nourishment, no nurturing conversation, no compliments, no verbal acceptance of any kind present in their lives. They are thirsty. One word, one encouragement from any member of a band they admire can change their perspective on their lives. In our rush to do all the tasks of our ministries, we often forget how empty and black the world can be. We live in a world full of salt, so we take it for granted. We have the camaraderie of our band mates and Christian friends. We have family and churches for support during difficult times. But many of our fans are struggling just to get through one more day. Some of them have become numb to the struggle and simply try to exist. One kind word, one compliment, or one word of encouragement form you may be all they receive and may be just enough to bring life to them. Speaking one-on-one to fans before and after a show can affect their lives forever. Do not underestimate the power of influence you have with your fans. Make time for this most important ministry. Attract them to Jesus with gracious words.

Father, help me to be salt to my fans. Give me gracious words to say to each one of them to attract them to You.

Success as a Result

"In all that he did in the service of the Temple of God and in his efforts to follow God's laws and commands, Hezekiah sought his God wholeheartedly. As a result, he was very successful."

2 Chronicles 31:21

Bookstores are filled with the latest books about how to become successful. The authors probably increase their income with the well-meant advice, but the majority of readers do not become successful. It really is too bad that most people do not understand that success can be a result of seeking God wholeheartedly and then following His commands.

Of course, not everyone who enjoys a measure of success finds it this way. There are always harder ways to do things. People will try anything to become successful. Some do it honestly by working long hours and often sacrificing their family life. Others try to manipulate the system, and still others lie and cheat in order to have a shot at becoming successful. Like them, we can strive to be successful Christian musicians, working hard to devote every minute of every day to our craft. We may even attain success in the world's eyes without sacrificing too much of our integrity. We might play all the big shows, be on the cover of magazines, and sell much music. Those may all be good things, but are they what makes a Christian music minister a success?

Success is a result, almost a byproduct, of seeking God wholeheartedly. We do not need to strive for success; we need to strive to have deeper, closer relationship with God. This deeper relationship will cause us to apply His word to our lives and obey His commands. Then, success will follow. Obviously, we need to be excellent at doing the tasks involved with being a music minister. But, do we work harder at seeking God wholeheartedly?

Father, above all else, I want o be successful at having the deepest possible relationship with You. Change my heart.

May 10
Standing Still

"But Moses told the people, 'Don't be afraid. Just stand still and watch the LORD rescue you today. The Egyptians you see today will never be seen again.'"

Exodus 14:13

There are times in every ministry that we must move quickly and work hard. We love those periods of heightened activity because we feel like we are accomplishing something and getting somewhere. At other times we can do nothing because we are completely boxed in, without options. We cannot, by our own efforts, move forward or retreat, and even our efforts at lateral moves to the right or left are thwarted. These times can cause us to become agitated and despondent. Nothing changes, no improvements are being made, and our ministries are not progressing. We have no choice but to stand still.

How we choose to stand still can make the time easy or extremely difficult. Do we stand trembling in fear, listening to the voices that talk about our forthcoming destruction? Or do we choose to stand still while trusting God? It is easy to trust when we can see what is happening and predict what the future will most likely be as a result. Trust is much more difficult when there seems to be no way out, no possible good future. So, from time to time, God places us in situations where we must stand still much longer than we would like. When we then see His hand work on our behalf, our faith is increased and we build our trust in Him. God is working in our lives, even during times of standing still. So the only question is, "How will you stand?" We choose to stand in faith and trust, worshipping our Lord without fear, resting in Him until He rescues us. We choose to stand still trusting in the love of God for us.

Father, increase my faith in Your love for me. Teach me how to stand without wavering in fear, in a way that honors You.

Powerless Foolish Things

"Remember, dear brothers and sisters, that few of you were wise in the world's eyes or powerful or wealthy when God called you. Instead, God chose things the world considers foolish in order to shame those who think they are wise. And he chose things that are powerless to shame those who are powerful."

1 Corinthians 1:26-27

It has often been said that the music industry is more about whom you know than how talented you are. There have always been and probably always will be door openers and gatekeepers in the industry. But God does not need them for successful music ministry. Instead, He chooses us, whom this verse describes as powerless foolish things, to do the work of ministry. Being considered as not wise, not powerful, and not wealthy is not a compliment. The description may be true but it is not something we are proud of. It is definitely not a recipe for success. So, why did God choose us to be music ministers rather than those who are already well connected in the industry and more talented than us? To show His power. We are proof that His hand is working on earth because we could not do our ministries with the little bit of talent and lack of connections we have.

God using our lack to demonstrate His power through our ministries should give us great comfort. We do not have to do it all perfectly. Given the limited talent, money, and connections we have we cannot make our ministries successful. That is the whole point. We must have God actively working in our ministries to make up for all that we do not have. We must continue to work hard at our ministries, but we can relax a little knowing that our success lies not in our efforts and abilities, but in God's choosing to use us. It's not about us; it's about Him.

Father, thank You for choosing to use me. Help me to rejoice in my lack because it demonstrates Your power.

Hungry Lions

"Stay alert! Watch out for your great enemy, the devil. He prowls around like a roaring lion, looking for someone to devour. Stand firm against him, and be strong in your faith. Remember that your Christian brothers and sisters all over the world are going through the same kind of suffering you are."

1 Peter 5:8-9

A lion that has just eaten and has a full stomach is far less dangerous than a hungry lion. Full lions will protect their domain but they are prone to take naps, choosing only the easiest and tastiest prey to attack. Hungry lions will strike at any prey they can find regardless of the personal risk or quality of the meat. Hungry lions will roam out of their territory to find prey.

Our enemy is compared to a lion. So, we should not be surprised when we think we are on the right track with our ministries and we get attacked. The lions are hungrier when we are doing well. They get downright nasty when we threaten their territory. Being blindsided by an unexpected circumstance or friction in relationships is not always an indicator that something is spiritually wrong with our ministries. Most often, it simply means the enemy is attacking. We have been trained to repel his attacks. We know what to do. We know how to be victorious. The enemy knows that we know, so with each attack he must get craftier, sneakier, and subtler. His only hope is the element of surprise, which is why these verses remind us to stay alert. Remembering that other ministries are also enduring these same types of attacks reminds us that we are not necessarily doing anything wrong. In fact, we might be doing most things so right that the enemy is compelled to attack. We must learn not to judge our own or other ministries by the ferocity of attacks.

Father, open my eyes to areas of attack by the enemy. Give me extra alertness and strength to repel his attacks.

Forgive the Church

> *"And forgive us our sins,*
> *as we have forgiven those who sin against us."*
> *Matthew 6:12*

Forgive: a familiar yet unpleasant word. We've heard this verse and the teachings that go along with it, and we know what to do. Most of the time we are successful at doing it with the people that hurt us. After all, we must live up to higher standard because we are Christian music ministers. But why are we so often depressed, frustrated, and angry? Why don't we feel love? Could it be that we still have more forgiving to do?

"Those who sin against us" are not always individual people. How do you feel towards a church that does not understand or support your ministry? What emotions come up when thousands are spent on church building improvements while your ministry is being limited due to lack of finances? How do we respond when it is implied that we should grow up and get a "real" job so we would have money to give to the church? What do we do with a church structure that pays those with the gifts of teaching and administration but not artists? How do you feel when yet another church asks you to donate a show? Musicians are not paid what they are worth. Very few of us will make it to superstar status and be able to earn a living from our music. So yes, choosing to use our creative gifts will most likely impact our finances negatively for the rest of our lives. But the church still needs musicians for services and special events. Many churches will continue to use us but not understand or respect us. They will pat us on the back and tell us we are doing good, all the while treating us as commodities. Can you forgive them for it? Do you love the Church as Christ loved the Church?

Father, forgive my anger and bitterness toward Your Church just as I have forgiven them.

May 14
Times of Famine

"One day Ruth the Moabite said to Naomi, 'Let me go out into the harvest fields to pick up the stalks of grain left behind by anyone who is kind enough to let me do it.'
Naomi replied, 'All right, my daughter, go ahead.'"

Ruth 2:2

Like Ruth, we sometimes experience famine in our ministries due to circumstances beyond our control. Venues and festivals have closed at an alarming rate; often, there simply seems to be no places to play. The money needed to get to gigs frequently is not in the bank account when we need it. Equipment breaks down at the most inopportune times. We can experience times of famine when we have done nothing wrong.

So what do we do when famine strikes? Like Ruth, we need to continue to do what is right. Famine is not the time to cut and run or to make drastic changes in our ministries. Most often, it is small changes that will release us from famine. We must continue to do what we know is right, and then do all that we can. In Ruth's case, this meant gleaning in the fields. It was not a glamorous task. Only the poor gleaned the scraps leftover from the harvest. But it was legal and set aside in Scripture specifically for people in this circumstance. For Christian musicians, this may mean playing less than great events, or holding a fundraiser for our own ministry. There is always something we can do. The small things we can do feel insignificant because they may not make enough difference to solve the entire problem. But those small steps often lead to our rescue from famine. The key is to trust God to take care of us and our ministries during the famine. We must cling to what is right, do all that we can, and then trust God for the rest.

Father, help me to work diligently and grow in trust of You during famine. Thank You for being in control of my ministry.

It's Not Only About Us

> *"A person without self-control*
> *is like a city with broken-down walls."*
> **Proverbs 25:28**

The walls of cities were the main defensive weapon for the people inside. So, walls were constantly being maintained, repaired, and guarded. Being a guard of the walls or the stonemason who repaired the walls were not glamorous careers. Neither the guards nor the stone masons were typically brought before the king and awarded medals. Those kinds of public acknowledgements were reserved for the heroic deeds of knights or the especially talented craftsmen of weapons. But the entire city could fall because of one breach in the wall. One stone mason who did his job poorly or one guard who was not diligent on his watch could affect the entire population of the city.

Have you considered the effect of our self-control on the lives of the people around us? When we lose self-control in any area, our families, friends, band mates, fans, and the ministries we work with all pay a price. Conversely, when we are diligent at applying self-control, all those people reap the benefits of our stability and safety. Exercising self-control is not glamorous. It is not something most people will notice as long as we are doing it well. But the moment we lose self-control people around us definitely notice that they are wounded. Unfortunately, exercising self-control is a matter of consistent maintenance. We cannot simply decide once and for all that we will have self-discipline in any area. Instead we must treat self-discipline like the city walls. We must be constantly on our guard, looking for places that need to be repaired and maintained.

Father, when it is time to make a decision about exercising self-control, remind me about everyone that decision affects. Give me the strength to exercise self-control.

May 16
Lend Generously

"Give to those who ask, and don't turn away from those who want to borrow."

Matthew 5:42

Every band does not take care of their equipment well. We have all run across the band who has forgotten or worse yet, broken a piece of equipment for the gig. Many musicians are hesitant to lend out their equipment because it may be damaged or misused. We tell ourselves that our equipment belongs to God and is used in His work, so we must take care of and protect it. Somehow we find it a little easier to lend equipment to another Christian band. But what do we do about the secular band that needs to borrow some of your gear? Clearly, this verse commands us to share with anyone in any circumstance. From God's point of view, people are more valuable than any piece of equipment, no matter how expensive it may be. It is our job to protect God's assets. Unfortunately, being human, we tend to value the tangible assets on earth more than the assets that God values most: people. He wants their hearts and He has already proven by the sacrifice of Jesus that He will pay any price to get them. Is any piece of gear worth more than Jesus? Is any equipment more valuable than a human soul? No. Surely, we cannot expect the instant results of a changed life when we share gear. But our generosity can be one more example of the love of Christ to a fellow musician. Eventually, that love demonstrated may become so overwhelming as to cause the musician to accept Jesus.

Beyond sharing with those who may need to borrow gear, what would happen if we planned ahead of time to meet some of their needs? What would happen if we carried extra supplies like batteries, sharpies, and duct tape specifically to give away to other bands? Small acts of generosity can change a heart.

Father, teach me value people more than equipment. Show me ways to give to musicians to bring them closer to You.

Imperfect Leaders

"We now have this light shining in our hearts, but we ourselves are like fragile clay jars containing this great treasure. This makes it clear that our great power is from God, not from ourselves."

2 Corinthians 4:7

Christian leaders are held to a high standard. Imperfections in people that would otherwise be overlooked are not given the same grace in our leaders. We expect our leaders to be perfect, and as leaders we often expect similar perfection from ourselves. But in God's eyes we are all just clay jars. Pastors are not more perfect than their congregation and music ministers are not just slightly less perfect than pastors but more perfect than their fans. We are each working through the process of becoming more Christ-like. Thank God that He uses us wherever we are in that process, in our imperfection.

It is easy to look at Christian leaders and believe that they have somehow arrived at a certain level of spirituality because they have arrived a certain level of notoriety in their career. We often equate working full time in ministry as a stamp of approval or reward for attaining a higher level of perfection. It simply may mean that God has chosen to use this particular clay pot in this particular way at this time. Certainly we must all be working toward greater Christ-likeness and progressing toward perfection. Just as certainly, we must be working toward doing greater works to advance the kingdom of God. But we must not automatically equate more public or famous workers with greater perfection. We also must not assume that we are more or less spiritually mature based on the popularity of our own music ministry. Our goal is to seek to become more Christ-like daily and to allow Him to use us, in our imperfections, however He sees fit.

Father, use me in ways that benefit Your kingdom the most. I do not need to be famous. I need to be more like You.

May 18
You Know You're Doing Something Right When...

"Tax collectors and other notorious sinners often came to listen to Jesus teach. This made the Pharisees and teachers of religious law complain that he was associating with such sinful people—even eating with them!"

Luke 15:1-2

People complain about other people. It is human nature to compare ourselves to each other and voice what we would do differently. We especially complain about those who work in our field but do not do their jobs well; "well" being defined as "the same way we would." So, it is typical (although not necessarily right) that pastors complain about other churches and pastors and music ministers complain about music ministries.

When we are the target of such complaining, we must consider the source before we consider the validity of the complaint. Is their viewpoint about ministry the same or similar to ours? If not, the complaint may actually be a compliment, such as in the case of the Pharisees complaint about Jesus. Certainly, they did not mean their comments to be taken as a compliment; the tone was condescending and arrogant. Jesus could have wallowed in hurt feelings. But He knew He was doing exactly what His Father wanted Him to do. He could have changed His ministry based on their complaints. Instead Jesus explained His ministry using the parable of the lost sheep.

Like Jesus, we can do our ministry with confidence when we know we are doing what God has called us to do, even in the face of complaints. Considering the source of the complaint may even turn it into a compliment.

Father, teach me to handle complaints appropriately, with no more or less weight than they deserve.

Love & Obey

"We know we love God's children if we love God and obey his commandments. Loving God means keeping his commandments, and his commandments are not burdensome."

1 John 5:2-3

What would happen if we changed our definition of love from "being nice" to "obeying God's commandments"? How would our relationships change? There are many scriptures that tell us how to handle specific situations in relationships such as go to your brother first and alone if he offends you, or if your brother does not have a coat give him yours, or do not gossip. Our lives, the lives of everyone around us, and our ministries would be dramatically affected if we put the highest priority on obeying God in our relationships rather than seeking to be liked by being nice. How would our ministries be changed if we placed a higher priority on obeying God than on being nice to people that might be in a position to help advance our careers?

Loving one another and ministering to each other by obeying God's commands causes us to remember that we are all children. Some of us may be a little farther down the road in our spiritual walk than others, but we all exist because of the love of God. We all fail, hurt, and struggle with things in our lives which we choose to keep hidden from most people. Booking agents, reporters, managers, pastors, club owners, famous musicians, and talent scouts are no different. We are all people who need to be loved by God and experience that love through His people. But how often do we miss opportunities to minister to someone in an attempt to advance our ministries? The best way to succeed in ministry is to love God and then love people by obeying God. If we focus on taking care of His people, He will provide for us.

Father, cause me to be more sensitive to people who are in need of a demonstration of Your love today.

Strong, Courageous & Obedient

"Be strong and very courageous. Be careful to obey all the instructions Moses gave you. Do not deviate from them, turning either to the right or to the left. Then you will be successful in everything you do."

Joshua 1:7

Everyone wants to be successful in what we do. If we could wish it to happen, we would all be successful. If we could be successful by creating our vision and mission and then doing a little goal setting, many of us would be successful. But it takes more than wishing plus a small amount of effort to be successful, and not everyone is willing to do what it takes. Strength, courage, and obedience are difficult character qualities to develop, yet they are what God says is necessary for success. Developing one or two is not enough; we must have all three.

Strength is defined as "the power to resist force or attack" and "the ability to deal with problems with determination and effectiveness." Courage is "the ability to do something dangerous or difficult." Obedience is "doing what an authority tells you to do." In other words, to be successful we must do what God tells us to do (follow His commands when, where, and how He tells us to do it) without wavering. We cannot be moved by force, problems, or difficulties because we are absolutely determined to accomplish God's will.

Are we willing to do that in our ministry? Are we willing to set aside what we want, or what we think is best to focus solely on what God commands? Are we so determined to live out His commands that we cannot be moved? If so, He promises that we will be successful.

Father, give me strength, courage, and the willingness to be obedient. I will do whatever it takes to get Your success.

May 21
Looking Away in Fear

> *"The LORD is my light and my salvation—*
> *so why should I be afraid?*
> *The LORD is my fortress, protecting me from danger,*
> *so why should I tremble?"*
>
> Psalm 27:1

Fear can make us run the other way. Fear can paralyze us. But most often, fear does a little of both. It makes us look the other way so that we are able to live with ourselves while we do nothing. After all, if we do not see a need or a problem, we are not responsible to deal with it, right? Too many of us have been raised with this mindset as the Christian way of life. We are afraid of people and their problems because they are messy. If we get involved we will get dirty, our reputation might be tarnished, and we will certainly be inconvenienced. Most likely we will be hurt because hurt people tend to hurt people. So, with fear as a root we avoid the whole issue by looking the other way.

For example: It is so easy to talk to the fans that want our autographs. It is much more difficult to start a conversation with the person who stands at the back of the room. Since we have the work of the ministry to do, we can easily look the other way by staying busy loading and unloading gear. But why should we be afraid to go out of our way to see a hurting person? We have the answer they need. The Lord IS our light and salvation. He does not merely give us light and salvation as gifts from time to time. He has already completely given us Himself; parts of His character are light and salvation. Because of this we never run out and we do not need to be re-gifted because there is always a steady supply. We are equipped to fearlessly see people's needs.

Father, destroy the root of fear in me. Cause me to be so aware of Your light and salvation that I cannot look away from hurting people without doing something to help.

May 22
Apply What You Know

"Anyone who listens to my teaching and follows it is wise, like a person who builds a house on solid rock. Though the rain comes in torrents and the floodwaters rise and the winds beat against that house, it won't collapse because it is built on bedrock. But anyone who hears my teaching and doesn't obey it is foolish, like a person who builds a house on sand. When the rains and floods come and the winds beat against that house, it will collapse with a mighty crash."

Matthew 7:24-27

The heart of this teaching is that it does not matter how much you know as much as it matters what you do. You can know how to be a great musician with excellent instrument skills, amazing marketing and business abilities, and even own the best equipment. But if you do not actually use and do any of it, no one will ever hear your music. You will fail as a musician.

The same principle applies to our relationship with God and our ministry. We could have graduated from the best seminary in the world, but that does not mean we have applied any of our knowledge. The solid foundation is built not by hearing only, but by doing. What would our relationship with God and our ministries look like if we started by simply applying the absolute basics of what we know: love God first, and then love people? If we started today, how would today be different than yesterday?

Relationships and ministries are built over time. Both are built on one small choice after another. Often it is the small choices that keep us from applying what we know because they seem insignificant. But if we apply what we already know of the teachings of Jesus to the small daily choices we will have a solid foundation to hold us up when the storms try to knock us down.

Father, cause me to see the impact of my small daily choices. Show me better ways to apply Your teachings to my life.

May 23

Very Precious to God

"And the man said to me, 'Daniel, you are very precious to God, so listen carefully to what I have to say to you. Stand up, for I have been sent to you.' When he said this to me, I stood up, still trembling."

Daniel 10:11

Every once in a while we need to be reminded that we are very precious to God. We get distracted with all we need to accomplish each day and we focus on the areas of ourselves that need to improve. There is always so much to do. As we progress in ministry, there are usually more tasks to do, not less. So, a reminder and a moment's pause to reflect on how much God loves us is in order. Remember all that Jesus endured on the cross, and then remember His resurrection. Picture heaven in your mind as our promise and future reward. Feel the love of God pouring out to us right now, in this very moment.

Only after knowing that we are very precious to God can we listen carefully and then stand up to do His will. When we try to hear and do God's will before experiencing His love, we work in our own strength. Eventually we will fail. This is not new information to us. But somehow in our humanness we still feel the need to rush ahead each day with our "to do" list. Today is the day to return to basics: experiencing the love of God and then using the strength from that love to listen to and do God's will for the day. Our ministry is the overflow of God's love from our own life. So, we must start with an overflow before we can effectively minister. Take time to remember just how very precious we are to God first. Allow Him to fill us up and then overflow to everyone around us.

Father, forgive my busyness. Thank You for reminding me that my strength comes from Your love, my ministry comes from Your love, and all that I am is very precious to You. I cannot express how much it means to me that You love me.

May 24

~~Random~~ Acts of Kindness

"Your love has given me much joy and comfort, my brother, for your kindness has often refreshed the hearts of God's people."

Philemon 1:7

Random acts of kindness can change a person's day. What was a long, boring, or difficult day becomes a source of encouragement and sparks a belief in what is good. Both the recipient's and the giver's hearts are refreshed by a simple act. But in the end, the effects of these acts are limited because they are random, done and received sporadically by a few people.

Although our schedules can be erratic, Christian music ministers do not live randomly. We are not hot one minute and cold the next simply because we do not keep regular office hours or punch a time clock for each shift. In fact, our irregular schedule allows us to live intentionally and purposefully. Like Philemon, we have the ability to live out the love of Christ with regular, consistent, daily acts of kindness. Our "normal" routine of playing gigs is already special because it is an interruption to the "normal" routine of everyone we meet in the process, from the gas station attendant to the toll booth worker and waitress, as well as our fans. Our lifestyle and creativity are interesting to them, and so their curiosity opens a door for regular, purposeful, and intentional acts of kindness. These kindnesses do not always have to cost money; they can be as simple as helping a stranger lift heavy purchases into their car or holding the door open for a mom with children in tow. Consistent kindness refreshes the hearts of people because the act says that we notice them. When we are known for consistent kindness, people look forward to being around us because of the joy and comfort we bring.

Father, open my eyes to ways that I can demonstrate Your love by living out consistent kindness. Show me how to impact people I usually overlook with Your loving kindness.

May 25
The Trouble We Are In

"But now I said to them, 'You know very well what trouble we are in. Jerusalem lies in ruins, and its gates have been destroyed by fire. Let us rebuild the wall of Jerusalem and end this disgrace!'"

Nehemiah 2:17

The people of Jerusalem LIVED the trouble. They were present when the city's gates were burned and the city was ruined. They survived the ordeal and its aftermath. The threat of destruction had come to pass and then they continued on with life. Did survival mode continue on so long that their mindset changed? Did they get used to the burned gates and the threats from their enemies? Living in a ruined city became normal as they survived and slowly adjusted to their circumstances. So even though the people knew the gates were burned and the city was in ruin, Nehemiah had to get them to really see their predicament before they could take action to rebuild.

We are often like the people of Jerusalem, not taking action against the true danger of our situation because we have adjusted down to the circumstances of life. Often the works we need to do to stay strong spiritually are outweighed by the daily tasks of life and ministry. We need outside help, people who can show us what we need to see, so we can fortify weak areas in our life and ministry. How much farther could we go, how much more ministry could we do, how much closer could we be to God if only we could see and avoid dangerous situations? Much of the trouble our ministries and we are in, or will be in, is a result of allowing our circumstances to dull our spiritual life. We, like the people of Jerusalem, do not always see the full value of maintaining our protective walls until someone opens our eyes.

Father, give me wisdom to know who to listen to. Send me people like Nehemiah who will open my eyes to areas in my life and ministry that need to be repaired.

May 26
Getting What We Want

"I gave you your master's house and his wives and the kingdoms of Israel and Judah. And if that had not been enough, I would have given you much, much more. Why, then, have you despised the word of the LORD and done this horrible deed? For you have murdered Uriah the Hittite with the sword of the Ammonites and stolen his wife."

2 Samuel 12:8-9

In ancient times, kings were entitled to any woman they wanted, except those who were already married. As with most humans, kings often found what they could not have to be far more desirable than what they could have. So, the custom was to kill the desired woman's husband, thereby making her available. David was abiding by the accepted customs of kings when he murdered Uriah. By the time David first saw Bathsheba he had already endured the hardships of becoming king: living in caves, running from Saul, and forming an army from malcontents. He knew what was right in God's eyes and had years of experience walking out his faith. But David found what he could not have to be so desirable that he was willing to do things according to the customs of the world rather than God's way.

We can judge David because he had so much and committed such a heinous sin, or we can realize just how much like him we are. Are we willing to compromise on how God would have our ministry operating in order to get ahead in the music industry? What about talking negatively about another band in order to get a really amazing gig? Do we exaggerate our fan base or what God has done through us to make our ministry seem more important? Have we ever hurt another person, through disrespect or neglect, to get ahead? If so, we are just like David.

Father, keep me from being overcome with the desire to have anything other than what You are willing to give.

May 27
Who is Doing the Fighting?

"'Do you intend to stay here while your brothers go across and do all the fighting?' Moses asked the men of Gad and Reuben."

Numbers 32:6

Some gigs are more fun and prestigious than others. In fact, when there are larger crowds who respond well to us and we get paid more than enough to cover our expenses, gigs do not feel like work at all. So, we seek out and prioritize those shows during the booking process. There are many other gigs that most people do not want to play because they are difficult. Nursing homes, jails and prisons, tiny youth groups and prayer meetings, and homeless shelters are all venues we generally try to avoid. Those are typically the places that the warfare is heavy. When we play difficult venues, we often spend more than we make, we do not significantly enlarge our fan base, the audience response is minimal because the audience is so small, and we tend to get discouraged because we do not see the effects of our ministry in either advancing our careers or the kingdom.

But is avoiding difficult shows the appropriate response? If so, in the end a few musicians must try to meet the needs of all the difficult venues or the needs simply go unmet. If we avoid difficult shows, how will we ever grow stronger as music ministers? A better response would be to join our brothers in ministry by playing as many difficult venues as our schedules and finances will allow. We do not have to play every free or smaller show we are asked to play, but we do need to consider doing our share. Playing some free and smaller shows will keep us strong and focused on ministry, meet the needs of all the venues, and help our fellow music ministers to fight the good fight.

Father, the music industry tells us to only seek out the most prestigious places to play. Help me to seek ministry above prestige. Show me where to play to accomplish Your ministry.

May 28

Living Outside the Norm

"But Peter and the apostles replied, 'We must obey God rather than any human authority.'"

Acts 5:29

Most preachers use this verse to support civil disobedience if a government's laws contradict God. But there are other authorities that affect our lives. People who try to force cultural norms upon our lives can be a source of heartaches and headaches for many music ministers. Most western cultures are made up of people that work jobs that they do not enjoy with regular hours. They exist financially paycheck to paycheck, using steady paychecks as their primary source of income and security. But music ministers often live outside that norm, with irregular income from multiple sources and God as their security. People with regular jobs tend to say things like, "Grow up and get a job" or "If you don't work, you don't eat" to musicians. In reality they are attempting to force cultural norms on those people who may be called to live differently in obedience to God.

Cultural norms and even our western way of doing church are not always God's plan for everyone. If God calls us to live outside the norm, we are in sin if we conform to whatever makes the people around us comfortable with our life. We may desire to live the way someone else lives and have what they have; but if we do, we will not attain all that God has for us. Living outside the norm causes us to put our security and trust in God's love for us. We are forced to grow in our trust of God. As we continue to do what is right and sacrifice even our lifestyle, God takes an active role in our lives to bless those sacrifices. A normal lifestyle may produce plans that are successful now, but an obedient lifestyle is blessed and multiplied by God forever.

Father, give me the courage to live obediently, whether that follows the norms or not. Bless my obedience and sacrifices.

Next Door Neighbors

"For you have been called to live in freedom, my brothers and sisters. But don't use your freedom to satisfy your sinful nature. Instead, use your freedom to serve one another in love. For the whole law can be summed up in this one command: 'Love your neighbor as yourself.'"

Galatians 5:13-14

All too often we think of our neighbors only as the fans we meet at shows or the people we encounter in our travels. We tend to forget about the people who live right next door, those who are literally our neighbors. If we could get an honest answer from them, what would our next door neighbors say about us, our band, and our ministry?

Christian music ministers tend to expect a certain amount of grace and patience to be given by the people around us because we assume they understand and support what we do. But we have habits that annoy people, especially people who live on a more normal schedule. We come home in the middle of the night and unload gear; sometimes we are not as quiet as we could be. We practice and practice and practice, the same songs over and over again. Everyone who can hear us has the song memorized but not necessarily because they love it. We get upset when people call or text us too early in the morning but sometimes forget what time it is and call or text people later at night. We are free to live on an unusual schedule but that can be annoying to our neighbors. What are we doing to thank our neighbors for putting up with us? How are we demonstrating love to them? When was the last time we went out of our way to serve our next door neighbor?

Father, open my eyes to the needs of my next door neighbors. Cause me to be more sensitive to things that I do to annoy them. Show me ways I can demonstrate Your love to them.

Plan + Work = Prosperity

"Good planning and hard work lead to prosperity,
but hasty shortcuts lead to poverty."

Proverbs 21:5

We have all heard the stories of the construction worker that becomes an overnight star by "being discovered" while remodeling an office. We tend to focus on the being discovered part but not all the hard work and career management that went into the "overnight" success. This same principle is why lotteries are so successful—spend a dollar, win enough money to last a lifetime—instant fortune. But most lottery winners are bankrupt shortly after receiving their money. Why? No plan, no hard work. Hasty shortcuts lead to poverty. When we take shortcuts, we do not value what we receive because we have not had to work hard or fight for it. We do not make plans to maintain or improve what we have. We treat it lightly and eventually lose it.

The best plan for our ministry comes from God. We can seek out this plan through prayer, counsel from other people, and gaining knowledge about the topic. Creating a plan for ministry is critical to the success of the ministry. But a plan is useless without the hard work of implementing the plan. There are days that the work is overwhelming and exhausting. Seasons will come when we just need to buckle down and work hard, really hard. There are times when, after all the hard work, the plans just don't seem to work out. We have to go back and reevaluate and adjust the plan. Why do we go through all this? God values ministry because He loves people. He asks us to plan and work hard so that we will value the ministry and the people we serve as much as He does. He wants us to succeed at bringing people closer to Him—they are the true heavenly wealth.

Father, I love Your people. Give me Your plan for them and the strength to accomplish it. I want kingdom prosperity.

Ignorance & Repentance

"God overlooked people's ignorance about these things in earlier times, but now he commands everyone everywhere to repent of their sins and turn to him."

Acts 17:30

God's expectation of us changes over time. This verse states that in the past He overlooked the ignorance of these people worshipping wooden idols but then He expected people to repent. What made God change His expectations? The disciples brought the knowledge of the good news. Once the people received knowledge, God expected them to apply it and grow closer to Him because of it. Ignorance is not overlooked forever. It is only overlooked until knowledge of the truth is received. After that, it's up to us to apply the knowledge and change. Willful ignorance, choosing to remain ignorant so we do not have to change, is not overlooked. We are expected to grow beyond what we know today. Choosing to remain ignorant when knowledge is available is sin and requires repentance.

Everyone has areas we love to work on and are good at. Everyone also has areas that we prefer to ignore or put off working on because we are not so good at them. What areas have not grown in our lives and ministry? Relationships, finances, self-discipline? Where do we seem to be perpetually stuck? Job, health, avenues for ministry? Could willful ignorance and the unwillingness to change be the cause of some of our stagnation? We need to seek out God's knowledge, both through His Word and through carefully chosen people who will hold us accountable to apply what we have learned.

Father, I repent today of all the areas I am stuck in because I choose not to seek out Your knowledge and change. I have simply accepted many of these areas, so bring them to my attention once again. Show me where and how to change.

June 1

Fortuitous Happenstance

"So Ruth went out to gather grain behind the harvesters. And as it happened, she found herself working in a field that belonged to Boaz, the relative of her father-in-law, Elimelech."

Ruth 2:3

Isn't it amazing how things "just happened" to work out so well for Ruth? Sometimes it seems like things work that way for other Christians and their ministries; they prosper in spite of difficult circumstances, while we struggle along trying to get by. But before we get too carried away comparing ourselves to other people, let's look at Ruth's submission and obedience. First, she was committed to God. She was not born a Jew but chose to become one. Ruth was submitted to Jewish law; she followed the commands of God. When things got tough, she did not go back to her old ways; instead she upped her commitment level, staying with Naomi even when the future looked like it would hold poverty. Ruth was also committed and submitted to the authority God placed over her—her mother-in-law. She went where Naomi told her to go and did what Naomi told her to do, even though the work was humble and tiring. Eventually Ruth found a husband and became co-owner of the fields she had gleaned. It was not fortuitous happenstance; it was God setting the whole plan up. But Ruth had to consistently do her part.

It is easy to look at ministries that have achieved a level of success and wish that like them, we could have been in the right place at the right time or that we knew the right people. But first we should check our own commitment, obedience, and submission. What has our track record been over the long haul? God plans fortuitous happenstance. He does not withhold good from us, but we must consistently do our part to follow His plan.

Father, show me where I am falling short in obedience to You. Strengthen me to serve You well over the long haul.

June 2
What's Important

"It's not important who does the planting, or who does the watering. What's important is that God makes the seed grow. The one who plants and the one who waters work together with the same purpose. And both will be rewarded for their own hard work."

1 Corinthians 3:7-8

Some music ministries are more famous than others. Some have more fans, more equipment, play more shows, and sell more music. We tend to be jealous of them, to want what they have. Generally, we do not like to admit our jealousy but it shows up from time to time in our comments, especially when we have to work with them. As always, our mouths speak from the abundance of our hearts. What our hearts do not seem to understand is that all ministry belongs to God. He is the power behind every ministry. So, if one band has a different ministry than another, praise God! He is working through each of them to accomplish His goals. Why should we be jealous of another band when everything they have is kingdom property and power?

We will all be rewarded for our hard work regardless of what our work was or how it was received on earth. God rewards obedience, not fame. If we can let this principle sink deep into our hearts, we will be free from the concern of who does what and who has what on earth. We can then focus on doing whatever God has for us to do. When it comes time to work with another band or ministry, we can truly work towards the same purpose without competition or comparisons. We may even get to the place of understanding the importance of doing everything we can do to help them succeed in their ministry! Is their ministry advancing the kingdom of God? Rejoice and help them, they are your allies not your competition.

Father, help me to value other Christian bands as co-workers and allies, all on Your side of this battle.

June 3
Rest & Refreshing

"You have six days each week for your ordinary work, but on the seventh day you must stop working. This gives your ox and your donkey a chance to rest. It also allows your slaves and the foreigners living among you to be refreshed."
Exodus 23:12

Music ministers are notorious for working way too much. We love doing what we do, so we do it to the extreme. We are obsessed with music, songwriting, performing, and holding endless discussions on instruments and gear as well as the latest technology for our websites and social media. Most of the time, this does not feel like work to us so we do not realize how wearing we can be on the people around us. A Sabbath day's rest is not only for us, but for everyone associated with us. Would your family be astounded if you went an entire day without working on music? Would they be shocked if you spent a whole day with them, talking about them and not your music? If so, you and they need a Sabbath day's rest.

Originally, all the Jews rested on the same day of the week, the Sabbath. Most musicians cannot adhere to this schedule, which technically would be from Saturday at sundown to Sunday at sundown. Our current culture simply does not choose to shut down on any given day. But we can adhere to the principle of one day of not working for every six of working, even if that day is a Monday or Wednesday. Most of us probably cannot keep the same day each week for rest. But we should not use our erratic schedule as an excuse not to rest. Every minister needs a break from ministry. We need to be refreshed, and those around us need to be refreshed. We must have time set aside for our relationships with God and our families to be effective ministers.

Father, show me how to truly rest. Teach me how to be refreshed and to be part of refreshing my friends and family.

June 4

Giving Up Your Life

"If you try to hang on to your life, you will lose it. But if you give up your life for my sake, you will save it."

Luke 9:24

People think that "giving up your life" means to die as a martyr. While that is true, this verse has more to say about our daily experience in dying to our own will. We have ideas about the kind of life we want to live and the kind of lifestyle we want. For some of us, that means owning certain possessions; for others it means living a life of purpose and significance. Still others of us simply want to live to live life on our own terms, doing exactly what we want to do in any given moment. Most of us say that we would give any or all of these things up "if"... "if" we knew we were going to change the world for God, "if" we were part of a national band, or "if" we could somehow see the results of our sacrificial living. But what if the results are not seen?

When we give up our lives by daily dying to our own wants and desires we are not given the promise of seeing changes in other people's lives. Laying down our lives cannot be based on seeing the results of our sacrifices. If it is, we will change course whenever we do not see results and our ministries will flounder for lack of consistent direction. While the method of changing the plan when the desired outcome does not happen is commonly used in business models, it is not appropriate for ministries that claim to be following the direction of God. We must make changes under the direction of God, not under the pressure of perceived results. We must stick to God's plan, no matter what we see or do not see, because it is He who will save us when we give our lives to Him. Giving up our lives must simply be based on obedience as a demonstration of our love for Christ.

Father, deepen my love for You and my obedience to You. I desire to serve You out of love, not because I see results.

June 5
It's OK to be Weak

"That's why I take pleasure in my weaknesses, and in the insults, hardships, persecutions, and troubles that I suffer for Christ. For when I am weak, then I am strong."
2 Corinthians 12:10

No one knows how to do everything that needs to be done to succeed in music ministry. In fact, none of us can perfectly live up to the Biblical standards of being a leader, elder, or teacher. Most of us do not even live up to the lifestyle expectations we have for ourselves. None of us gets it right all the time. We all have a variety of weaknesses in ourselves. These weaknesses range from areas where we are especially vulnerable toward sin to areas where we simply do not have the knowledge to accomplish our tasks. When we add in the extra spiritual warfare targeted towards us by our enemy because we are leaders, we cannot logically expect to succeed by ourselves. Yet, we often fall into the trap of trying to rely on our own strength, knowledge, expertise, and wisdom. We want to be right, we want to be strong, and most of all we want to be perceived as a person who is successful at being Christ-like.

The problem is that the world's definition of Christ-like is to be their version of "perfect." So, we consistently hear Christians being called hypocrites and being judged by standards that change with culture and time. Sometimes those judgments against our actions are correct and sometimes they are not. What is important is not how close we come to the world's version of perfection, but how much we rely on Christ's strength in our weakness. The gospel message is not that God instantly changes us to be perfect, but that God loves us in our weakness.

Father, I want to strive to be more like Christ each day. But release me from the chains of perfectionism. Show me how to rejoice and rely on Your strength in my weakness.

June 6

Private Examination

"But if we would examine ourselves, we would not be judged by God in this way. Yet when we are judged by the Lord, we are being disciplined so that we will not be condemned along with the world."

1 Corinthians 11:31-32

Private examination of ourselves keeps us from public condemnation. We can deal with problems when they are small privately, or we can face God's judgment and discipline. After that, if we do not repent, God will even allow public humiliation because He does not want us to be condemned with the world. Satan loves to see Christians humiliated publically, especially if the embarrassment affects many people. Attacks against Christian leaders are far more intense than for the average person because leaders have a greater sphere of influence. If our enemy can get a leader to fail publically he can use the failure to undermine the faith walk of many other people. Unfortunately, this means Christian music ministers are targeted for greater attacks because we work hard to develop our fan base; and since we are human, we know that we will fail from time to time.

But God has provided a way for us to escape public humiliation: deal with Him privately. If we had no other reason for spending time in one-on-one relationship with God, private examination and repentance would be enough. The Holy Spirit can show us problems before they become issues that cannot be dealt with privately. But, we must take the time to ask, to listen, and then to repent. We are aware of this principle, but we fall prey to attacks of busyness and over-confidence in our own ability to avoid sin. Our enemy loves it when we are too busy doing ministry to allow the Spirit to reveal our failures. If we are to succeed publically, we must make private, regular, consistent time to examine ourselves before God.

Father, I am here now to listen for changes I need to make.

June 7

Look Back for Courage

"But David persisted. 'I have been taking care of my father's sheep and goats,' he said. 'When a lion or a bear comes to steal a lamb from the flock, I go after it with a club and rescue the lamb from its mouth. If the animal turns on me, I catch it by the jaw and club it to death. I have done this to both lions and bears, and I'll do it to this pagan Philistine, too, for he has defied the armies of the living God! The LORD who rescued me from the claws of the lion and the bear will rescue me from this Philistine!'"

1 Samuel 17:34-37a

Is the challenge set before us huge? Absolutely! Christian music ministers want to draw people closer to Jesus. But we face temptations within our own attitudes, judgment from other Christians, condemnation from unbelievers and the daunting task of learning all the skills we need to accomplish our mission. The old ways of the music industry no longer work and the new ways have not been completely defined, which makes our mission easier and more difficult at the same time. It would be easy for us to give up, give in, and walk away in defeat on any given day. But no, we are God's champions!

When we need courage to face the day, the tasks, and the ministry that must be completed, we simply need to look back and see what God has already done for us in the past. We have already overcome so many things! We have learned new skills, influenced people, and lived a life that demonstrates the love of Jesus during difficult times. God has given us grace to get through the tough times, resources to meet our physical needs, and brothers to walk alongside us. The God who has always been with us in the past will always be with us in the future.

Father, give me courage for today. I remember all that You have done in my past and I look forward to our future.

June 8
Forgetting the Past

"I don't mean to say that I have already achieved these things or that I have already reached perfection. But I press on to possess that perfection for which Christ Jesus first possessed me. No, dear brothers and sisters, I have not achieved it, but I focus on this one thing: Forgetting the past and looking forward to what lies ahead, I press on to reach the end of the race and receive the heavenly prize for which God, through Christ Jesus, is calling us."

Philippians 3:12-14

Let's face it: simply because we are Christian music ministers, we are demonstrating that we already have a certain amount of spiritual maturity. We have been around the block a few times and attained some experience and wisdom. In many areas, we know what we are doing. People should be coming to us for advice and giving us some respect. Unfortunately, at this point in our walk, we tend to allow self-righteousness to sneak in. We mentally use their respect as evidence that we are who we should be in Christ. If they do not respect us, we judge people by what we have attained. In either case, feeling that we have become who we should be allows us to stay the way we are.

When we hear that it is our past that often holds us back, we tend to think of past sin, trauma, and experiences we struggled to overcome. But even more often, the past that holds us back is our successes, attainment of spiritual maturity, and the popularity of our ministry. Certainly at the time he wrote these verses, Paul's ministry was growing, he was famous, and he had a deep level of spiritual maturity. It was at this time in his career that he talked about forgetting what was behind and pressing forward to become more and more Christ-like.

Father, show me my self-righteousness. Grant me the courage to put my past behind and press forward to the end.

June 9
What's Stealing Your Peace?

"I am leaving you with a gift—peace of mind and heart. And the peace I give is a gift the world cannot give. So don't be troubled or afraid."

John 14:27

The gift we have been given is not freedom from trouble or reasons to fear. What we have been given is the ability to have peace of mind and heart in the midst of troubles that we are currently experiencing, as well as trouble we fear may come in the future. We are not told that we will not experience feeing troubled or afraid. But, we are told not to continue to be troubled or afraid because we have this gift. We must discipline ourselves to use the gift of peace of mind and heart during trouble; it is up to us to apply the gift in the situation.

Christian music ministers are not exempt from trouble. In fact, because we are in leadership positions, we are attacked by our enemy more harshly and frequently. We are away from home more than most people, which causes us to be concerned for our families in addition to the problems of running a ministry. It is no wonder we feel anxious and fearful from time to time. But are all the trials and circumstances really what steals our peace? We know trouble will come; we know that when we make it through the current trouble, a new one will eventually follow. It is a never-ending cycle, as we are not destined to live a trouble free life. Since we know this, we must consider the possibility that what steals our peace is not any particular trouble itself but our inability to apply the gift we have already been given in the situation. The next time trouble comes, and we know it will come, let us not be surprised and become anxious and fearful. Instead, we will remember that we have been given the gift of peace of mind and heart and apply it in the moment of trouble.

Father, show me how to use the gift of peace of mind and heart so I can be unwavering in the face of difficult times.

Don't Water the Bitter Roots

"Look after each other so that none of you fails to receive the grace of God. Watch out that no poisonous root of bitterness grows up to trouble you, corrupting many."
Hebrews 12:15

Have you ever watched a plant cutting grow roots? The cutting goes into water and at first nothing happens; and then, almost imperceptivity, a small white nub forms. That little nub grows longer daily until it eventually spreads and combines with other little nubs to form an entire root system for a new plant. As the root system expands the plant grows and forms new shoots and leaves. This is great when it is a good plant. But the best way to stop unwanted plants from spreading is not to water the roots.

Have you noticed that most of us feel a need to join in when someone else complains? We may not have paid attention to the complaint until someone else brought it up. But after it has been spoken, it becomes a part of us. When someone else's complaint turns to bitterness and they give voice to their bitterness, we tend to empathize and see their point of view. This is how bitterness affects many and why we must watch for it in each other as well as ourselves. Bitterness changes our perspective. For example, how many musicians do you know who are bitter that the music industry has changed? They say no one can make a living at it now. Is that true, or is that their bitterness talking? Obviously, there are many people making a living with music, they are simply doing it differently than in the past (and many of them love the change). But, how many people has that one bitter concept affected? Like plants, the best way to stop bitterness from changing our perspective is to stop watering the roots with our words.

Father, cause me to be aware of roots of bitterness. Change my perspective and my words to match Yours.

June 11
Blaming God

"In all of this, Job did not sin by blaming God."
Job 1:22

It is very easy to look at successful people and assume they are blessed by God. It is even easier to assume that popular ministries are blessed by God. We also tend to assume the opposite, that God approves less of the less successful people and ministries. When bad things happen, our first reaction is often to ask God what that person or ministry did wrong. But when our equipment is stolen or our trailer catches on fire, our first reaction is often to blame God. After all, we are working in His ministry so we deserve His protection, right?

Job proves that our current circumstances are not always related to God's approval or blessing on our lives and ministry. Still, we persist in asking, "Why?" especially when our ministry takes a hit. There are many possible reasons; we may have done something wrong, we live in a fallen world so bad things simply happen, God may be implementing a bigger plan we don't see yet, or we may be experiencing an attack by our enemy, etc. But in that catastrophic moment we are probably not going to have a high enough level of discernment to find out the answer to "Why?" In that first moment we really do not need to know. We can search out the answer to "Why?" later. What we do need to do is to trust God rather than blame Him. It is pretty tough not to blame God if we still believe that our circumstances are tied to His approval. When a difficult, unexpected situation occurs, is our first reaction to curse or pray? When we trust in God's love for us in the midst of every circumstance, even the worst problems our ministry encounters, we demonstrate the maturity of our love for Him. His love for us will carry us through anything.

Father, give me wisdom and discernment to see problems and failures through Your eyes. Give me courage to trust You.

June 12
Ask God for It

"You want what you don't have, so you scheme and kill to get it. You are jealous of what others have, but you can't get it, so you fight and wage war to take it away from them. Yet you don't have what you want because you don't ask God for it."

James 4:2

What kind of ministry do you want? Do you have a clear vision of that ministry in your mind? Does your vision line up with God's vision for your ministry? If so, what is keeping you from attaining it? Most likely the hindrance is not that the music market is saturated. We tend to think that only a certain few can really make it in music ministry, but the world has a wide variety of needs. So, certainly there is enough ministry opportunity to go around. Do we need to be competing with other music ministers? Do we need to be scheming to get ahead in the music ministry? NO. We need to be asking God to show us what to do next to get to where He needs us to be in ministry.

God has a plan for each of our music ministries. We need to seek out what that plan is and do it. In God's plan, one of us does not have to fail in order that another of us succeeds. It is not a competition where only one or two can win the prize. The ministry opportunities are limitless because the need is so great. By recognizing that God has everyone's music ministries orchestrated to fit into His overall plan, we can eliminate competition and jealousy. We do not have to strive and scheme to get ahead at another's expense but can support each other in our ministries. We can have the kind of exciting, effective ministry we dream of if we ask God. Ask God for the dream and then ask God daily for the steps to take to attain the dream. We must never give up asking and doing whatever He leads us to do.

Father, show me ways to help other ministries attain their dreams while we all work together to advance Your kingdom.

Human Thinking

"Don't let anyone capture you with empty philosophies and high-sounding nonsense that come from human thinking and from the spiritual powers of this world, rather than from Christ."

Colossians 2:8

We are not stupid; we are trained Christian music ministers. So, we are not going to fall for the deceptions of other religions. But we easily fall prey to human thinking. The problem with human thinking is that it removes the sovereignty of God from our lives. We solve problems using the common sense logic of the world's ways. These methods do not take into account God helping us or intervening in our lives and ministries.

One great example of using the "logical" world's methods is going into debt to record a CD in an attempt to be signed to a label. There is nothing wrong with recording a CD or with being signed to a label, if that is what God has planned for your ministry. But the Bible has quite a bit to say about when debt is and is not appropriate. Still, many of us took the process into our own hands because for years we were told that this is the way things are done. We went into debt to record a CD that had a small chance of getting heard by a record executive in the even smaller hope of being offered a recording contract that may or may not ever repay the initial debt (not to mention all the other debt incurred along the way). We told ourselves that we were acting faith to believe God for successful ministry. But in effect we believed men rather than God's Word and removed the sovereignty of God from our ministry.

Human thinking is normal to us because we are human, so we do not easily recognize it. But God's way of thinking is always better. What other things have we so easily believed?

Father, reveal all the areas that I am following human thinking instead of Your ways. Show me Your best way to go.

June 14
Shining on Everyone

"In the same way, let your good deeds shine out for all to see, so that everyone will praise your heavenly Father."
Matthew 5:16

In his book Forgotten God, Francis Chan says, "Being a Christian is not about knowing a set of propositions—it's about knowing Christ and acting on His behalf in the world". Christians often get caught up in our own world: the people who attend our church. Our good deeds shine brightly to those around us, so Christians end up shining light in each other's faces while the world is in darkness. We do not intentionally do this; it is simply easier to be with people most like us. We act on Christ's behalf in the church because the church has become our world.

Music has the ability to touch everyone, both Christian and non Christian alike. While most of the church understands that Christianity is not a set of rules, most of the world does not. They expect Christians to live like hypocrites under the law. Music ministers can change their perspective of Christians using our gift of music. But that gift is not only used while we are on stage performing at gigs. A musician's life and lifestyle is intriguing to many people. We tend to forget how unusual our creativity is to people we interact with daily, like bank tellers, grocery store cashiers, doctors, and even our next door neighbors. As we talk about what we do and more importantly why we do it, people will begin to see that something is different about us. We will not live up to their expectations of a Christian, but we may open their eyes to real Christianity. When we expand our world to include everyone around us, we can then share our good deeds using our creativity with the world. Then, everyone has the opportunity to praise our Father.

Father, open my eyes to all the people around me. Show me ways to share my creative life and represent You to them.

June 15

Secret Deeds

"In the same way, the good deeds of some people are obvious. And the good deeds done in secret will someday come to light."

1 Timothy 5:25

Good deeds in the limelight come with a certain amount of reward. Donating our time to play free shows for a charity is one of the best ways Christian bands have to support other ministries and help people. Those good deeds please God. But, we reap a certain amount of harvest from them right away, for example in respect from people, exposure, and merchandise sales. We feel satisfied when people acknowledge that we have done something to make the world better.

Good deeds when no one knows are often smaller and seemingly less important. Carrying an older person's groceries to their car, giving a card of encouragement or anonymous gifts, intercessory prayer, and visiting shut-ins are all examples of good deeds done in secret. These deeds also please God. God sees them and He remembers us for doing them. But deeds done in secret come with little earthly rewards, and so it falls on God to reward us. The Bible repeatedly encourages us to do things like entertaining strangers and helping the poor, who cannot pay us back. Why? Because God Himself wants to reward us. This is part of the principle "the last shall be first." Those who serve without earthly reward store up treasures in heaven; they receive heavenly rewards.

Pastors, prominent Christian authors, and even Christian musicians reap a measure of their rewards here on earth in the form of respect, wages, and recognition. It is not enough to simply do ministry jobs well. We must go deeper into ministry, serving and doing good deeds in secret. When we live that way, God alone sees, remembers and becomes our reward.

Father, show me opportunities to do good deeds in secret.

June 16
Blessed to Work Hard

"You know that these hands of mine have worked to supply my own needs and even the needs of those who were with me. And I have been a constant example of how you can help those in need by working hard. You should remember the words of the Lord Jesus: 'It is more blessed to give than to receive.'"

Acts 20:34-35

Many music ministers believe that they are not truly ministers until they are working full time in their ministry. Musicians who have a day job are often viewed as less spiritual and professional than full time musicians. But these verses and Paul's life proves those beliefs to be untrue. Working hard as a tentmaker did not diminish Paul's ministry, but enhanced it. Paul demonstrated that making money is a holy activity when the money is used to support ministries that help people.

So, why do people tend to esteem full time music ministers more than those who have day jobs? Perhaps this is another pattern the Christian music ministry has adopted from the secular music industry. In the secular industry, the goal is to become famous. Fame brings money but it also requires attention to be drawn to the artist as a cultural icon. In the Christian music ministry, the goal is to bring people closer to Jesus. The artists' goal is not to bring fame to themselves but to call attention to Jesus. Fame may come through excellent music and marketing, but ultimately the fame, music, and marketing are all simply tools we use to advance God's kingdom, not our kingdom. We need to start thinking like God rather than patterning our ministries after the world. Before we implement the strategies of another ministry, we should ask how effective they are at bringing people closer to Jesus and then continue accordingly.

Father, constantly remind me that my goal is to bring people closer to You and to be willing to do whatever that takes.

June 17

Crop of Love

"I said, 'Plant the good seeds of righteousness,
and you will harvest a crop of love.
Plow up the hard ground of your hearts,
for now is the time to seek the LORD,
that he may come and shower righteousness upon you.'"
Hosea 10:12

When we plant bean seeds we get beans. When we plant carrot seeds we get carrots. So, how do we get a harvest of love from seeds of righteousness? God cannot help but love us because He created us to love and to have relationship with Him. Righteousness allows us to stand in His presence and enables us to have that relationship. When we are in His presence, His love overflows to us and then through us. His overwhelming love becomes our harvest to share because we cannot possibly contain all that He gives us. How do we get seeds of righteousness? By plowing up the hard ground of our hearts and seeking God. We cannot attain righteousness on our own, but God showers it on us when we seek Him wholeheartedly. So, here is the progression: we plow up the hard ground of our hearts, and then seek God wholeheartedly. After that, God covers us with His righteousness so He can overflow His love onto us. We accept His righteousness and love, and we overflow it on to other people.

Too many times we try to overflow love onto the people without taking the first step of plowing up the hard ground of our own hearts. We try to love in our own strength with our own love. Eventually we use up our strength and become exhausted. When we feel our love is exhausted, we have only to look at the hardness of our own hearts and our search to be closer to God. The people we are ministering to cannot exhaust God's love.

Father, reveal the hardness of my heart. Give me the desire to seek after You so that You may love through me.

June 18
God's Presence

"How will anyone know that you look favorably on me—on me and on your people—if you don't go with us? For your presence among us sets your people and me apart from all other people on the earth."

Exodus 33:16

What makes us different from other bands and musicians in the world? God's presence. We can sing about God, we can write Christian songs, we can even quote Scripture from the stage. But to the world we become just another band promoting their cause if we do not have God actively working through all that we do. We cannot change the world by promoting a cause; only the presence of God's Spirit moving through us will change the hearts of people. We acknowledge this to be true. We may even say it to fans when they compliment or thanks us. But if we really do believe it to be true, what are we doing daily to cultivate God's presence in our lives and ministry? Is the highest priority in the 24 hours we are given each day to be close to God? We can read the Bible through in a year, checking off the boxes for the Scripture we have read each day. We can have a daily devotional time, sing worship songs, and give of our time and money to help others. We can do all the right works and tasks in our ministry and still not experience God or His presence.

Have you ever been on a date with someone who is present but obviously thinking about something else? We say "they aren't there," even though they are physically present in the room. We are not very motivated to set up another date with that person. How often have we done this to God? How often are we thinking about our ministry when we should be first simply spending time with God? God's hand in our ministry comes from knowing God personally, not from knowing about God.

Father, forgive me for placing a higher priority on working for You than knowing You. Show me how to change.

June 19

Being Exalted

"'Everything they do is for show. On their arms they wear extra wide prayer boxes with Scripture verses inside, and they wear robes with extra long tassels. And they love to sit at the head table at banquets and in the seats of honor in the synagogues. They love to receive respectful greetings as they walk in the marketplaces, and to be called 'Rabbi.' Don't let anyone call you 'Rabbi,' for you have only one teacher, and all of you are equal as brothers and sisters.'"

Matthew 23:5-8

The Pharisees were masters at putting on a spiritual show, but they were not so good at bring people closer to God. Learning how to lead an audience in a meaningful concert experience, which brings them closer to Jesus rather than only putting on an awesome show, is a sign of great spiritual maturity. It requires us to lay down our position as divas and rock stars to walk in the humility of God's grace. Walking in God's grace acknowledges that we all sin, requiring God to act on our behalf to make us worthy to even be invited to the Lamb's wedding feast. When we are walking in the knowledge of our need for God's grace, it is easy to set aside diva and rock star attitudes. We see everyone as equals to us in needing His grace. So, it becomes natural to reach out in love rather than to expect people to extend honor and respect to us. This kind of honest humility in acknowledging our faults and genuineness in our love for Christ is what people want to see demonstrated rather than only taught.

When we connect our fans with the love of God, a concert becomes more than the music and we become true music ministers. Leading people closer to Jesus is the most exalted position any human can have.

Father, teach me to walk in humility so I may bring people closer to You. Show me ways to reach out with Your love.

June 20
New Songs

"I will sing a new song to you, O God!
I will sing your praises with a ten-stringed harp."
                                                    Psalm 144:9

Why do we need new songs? In Revelation we read that the elders and heavenly beings sang the same words over and over again. Surely God does not need to keep up with the latest cultural trends or be worshipped with new words and melodies. Perhaps it is us humans who want new songs. But if that is true, why do we resist change? Change from our hymns to choruses, change from piano and organ to electric guitars and drums—none of this was done without struggle. We even love the same Christmas carols year after year. Most people tend to like the familiarity of sameness and tradition.

So, if God does not need it and most of us do not want it, why does David present new songs in this verse as a good and desirable thing? New songs are written and sung in collaboration and in relationship. New songs come from our experiences in life. They are an expression of our hearts during those experiences, and as Christians we have all those experiences with God. When we write new songs we are not only writing about an experience we shared with God, we are collaborating in the creative process with Him. Then we share our creation with people around us. Hopefully, our new song inspires an experience between God and the people hearing or singing it and they are brought closer in relationship to Him.

Neither we nor God needs new songs if they are simply new songs. What we do need is creative heart expressions and experiences in relationship with each other.

Father, I do not want to create new songs in Your name. I want to experience creating new songs in collaboration with You as an expression of our relationship.

One Step at a Time

"I know, LORD, that our lives are not our own.
We are not able to plan our own course."
Jeremiah 10:23

God often gives us the overall vision for our ministry. We generally know the direction we are headed, though many times we do not know how or when. The details get fuzzy and figuring out how to pay for it all can be a nightmare. We can easily be overwhelmed with all the available career and ministry advice using what has worked for other people in the past. The steps we think we should take do not always line up with the steps we have the means and ability to take. Choices can be confusing.

But God is a God of order. He has already made a way to get us exactly where we need to be. The confusion comes in when we try to figure out more of God's plan than He wants to show us right now. We think we have our ministry all mapped out and then out of the blue something entirely different happens. God's plan collides with our plan. While it is absolutely essential to continually seek out God's plan for our ministry, there will be limits to how much He will show us at any given moment. His goal is not to keep secrets from us, but to build our trust in His love. We would not have to trust Him if He laid out the next five years completely for us. We would not grow in our faith and trust if we could do exactly the same things as another successful band and get the same ministry results. Instead, He most often tells us the general direction we are headed and then expects us to come back each day for more specific directions. So, we build our ministry one step, one day at a time. We do not have to know it all, nor do we have to do it all in one day. We simply have to be consistently seeking direction and applying what we know to do.

Father, thank You for working on building my trust in Your love. Show me how to walk one step at a time in ministry.

June 22
God Still Works

"But Jesus replied, 'My Father is always working, and so am I.'"

John 5:17

People who say that God doesn't do anything nowadays are wrong. God the Father did not stop working after He created the earth; He only took a Sabbath's rest. God the Father, Jesus, and the Holy Spirit are all at work yesterday, today, and forever. This is exciting news when we stop to think about what they are doing on the earth we now live in. God Himself, the creator of the universe, is still actively working within that creation!

God still working changes everything—we do not have to do things for God or in His name, as if we are standing in for Him while He is busy elsewhere. Instead, we can do things in collaboration with God! Working with God instead of working for God changes how we approach life and ministry. When we work with God, we simply have to find out what He is doing right now and do that too. God is excited to work with us because the work becomes part of our relationship. This is why He did not create the world and then step away to see what we would do. He does not want to observe our actions; He wants to participate in our lives, in relationship with us. As we are working on a project together, God guides us and pushes us to grow. We make Him happy when we experience His participation in our lives and press in to become more and more like Him.

Working in collaboration with God—what a privilege and honor! Our songs, our music, our ministry does not have to be our own, born of our own ideas or performed in our own strength. We do all this with God, with His input, His strength, and His power. To work in collaboration with God we must simply find out what He is doing, and then take the time to do that work with Him.

Father, I do not want to be independent—to do it all myself. Show me how to collaborate in the work You are doing.

June 23

Seasons of an Olive Tree

"But I am like an olive tree, thriving in the house of God.
I will always trust in God's unfailing love.
I will praise you forever, O God,
  for what you have done.
I will trust in your good name
  in the presence of your faithful people."
Psalm 52:8-9

When we picture an olive tree thriving in the house of God, we tend to see a huge mature tree with beautiful silvery green leaves, small white flowers and a huge harvest of olives hanging off the branches at all times. While this is certainly picturesque, it is not a snapshot of a healthy olive tree. Olive trees, like most trees, need to experience seasons in weather to produce fruit. The trees must have times without flower or fruit to rest and rejuvenate. A thriving olive tree has a very long lifespan but it must endure pruning annually. Olives are ready to harvest only towards the end of the year, in fall and winter. Most trees have a small harvest each year but do not typically produce a large harvest two years in a row. The most mature olive trees produce an enormous harvest only once every six or seven years. So, we can see from this information that a healthy, thriving olive tree does not always look as pretty as we pictured.

Like olive trees, we must experience different seasons to remain healthy. It is not God's plan that our ministries will always be in a state of harvest. In fact, it is much more common to experience just as many seasons of pruning and rest as harvest. It is during the non-harvest seasons that we sink our roots deep and grow in our trust of God and His love for us.

Father, teach me to see the value in and welcome seasons of rest and pruning. Budding and harvesting are much more exciting but I want to be rooted deeply in You.

June 24
Hiking in the Dark

"Your word is a lamp to guide my feet
and a light for my path."

Psalm 119:105

Hiking in the dark is not a recommended activity. Most of us do not enjoy trying to find a path from one place to another without a flashlight. If we try, we will probably stumble and fall over branches and into holes repeatedly. Attempting to find our way in this world without God's Word is like hiking in the dark.

But, is the Bible going to tell us each step to take to build our ministry and to rebuild the Christian music industry? Obviously there are no Scriptures to direct us to the best platform to sell our music, the next great app we need to use, who to call to get booked for the next show, or social media to reach our fans. What it does is to teach us principles and give us examples from other people's lives. It illuminates the way by showing us where the path is clear and where the potholes and branches that will trip us up are located. Unfortunately, because the Bible speaks in generalities, principles, and examples, we tend to set it aside when something more "logical" or culturally acceptable presents itself. We often make these choices without even noticing that we are violating God's principles because they are normal in today's society. The results are much easier to see in hindsight. For example, many people believe the Christian music industry is failing because it was built by copying the secular music industry rather than God's principles. This is very easy to see in hindsight, not easy during its inception. Now that we are essentially rebuilding the way music is marketed and sold, are we doing any better? We need to carefully examine every aspect of our ministry in light of God's Word and principles.

Father, bring light to dark places in my ministry. Show me how to line up to Your Word rather than cultural norms.

June 25

Rest in the Storm

"But soon a fierce storm came up. High waves were breaking into the boat, and it began to fill with water. Jesus was sleeping at the back of the boat with his head on a cushion. The disciples woke him up, shouting, 'Teacher, don't you care that we're going to drown?'"

Mark 4:37-38

Jesus was with the disciples and they were doing what He asked. There was no disobedience or loss of fellowship. But Jesus was asleep and the disciples were afraid and miserable. The water was everywhere, they were wet and the storm was getting worse; the boat could sink if this continued. These disciples were professional fishermen; they were not afraid without good reason. They had seen this kind of storm before and they knew what was at stake. Why didn't Jesus stop this? Didn't He care? Surely His sleep was not more important than the boat sinking.

Notice that there was not a lack of faith in Jesus' ability to calm the storm. There was a concern that Jesus would not notice this storm. In our lives and our ministry, this is often where we live. We know He can do it ("it" being whatever is needed at the time to calm the storm); we just are not so sure He will. This uncertainty is one of the main reasons God allows storms into our lives and ministries. He uses it to demonstrate His continuing love for us and to grow our faith in that love. As children we expect that Jesus' presence equals our comfort, often judging other people who are experiencing storms. In our spiritual adolescence we hope that He will work things out as we seek to understand the why's of it all. But as fully mature adults in our faith we can mimic Jesus, resting in the love of the Father. From this place of rest we can work to calm the storms of life.

Father, teach me to encourage others through the storms of their lives. Show me how to rest in the storm.

June 26

Submission vs. Sacrifice

"But Samuel replied,
'What is more pleasing to the LORD:
your burnt offerings and sacrifices
or your obedience to his voice?
Listen! Obedience is better than sacrifice,
and submission is better than offering the fat of rams.'"
1 Samuel 15:22

Humans do not like doing what they are told. In fact, many of us will go out of way to do anything other than what we are told. We justify ourselves by doing things that are more sacrificial than what we were originally told to do. Then, in our hearts we say, "Isn't this so much better than if I had done what I was told?" Musicians do this frequently when we do not follow the little prompts we get from God such as "Go, talk to that person" or "Help that band unload their equipment." We usually choose an activity that seems much grander like chatting up the promoter or updating our social media. But those little prompts can result in big ministry; not following them is disobedience.

God is not pleased when we put in a twelve hour day doing a free show but do not follow His prompting while we are there. In our hearts we commend ourselves for the long hours doing ministry. Sometimes we get so frustrated with the lack of fruit from our efforts that we discuss when we are going to play a "good show" with the band. But God's heart says something like, "I sent you there to talk to them. Your long hours of work were wasted because you were not obedient." Music ministers make many sacrifices of long days with little or no pay. God does not ask us to make sacrifices without a purpose. We must learn to focus on being obedient to His plan by obeying His promptings.

Father, teach me to be a better listener to Your promptings.
Show me ministry opportunities and how I can meet them.

June 27
Communication Builds Trust

"You will keep in perfect peace
all who trust in you,
all whose thoughts are fixed on you!"
Isaiah 26:3

This verse is often quoted as a means of encouragement to stay focused on God during times of catastrophe. When those big life-changing moments come upon us we are often surprised, but we somehow manage to cope and come out the other side of the event stronger. Although there are always long term repercussions, we find comfort in the knowledge that most catastrophic events are only temporary. So, once the initial shock is over, we are usually able to walk through the situation with some measure of peace.

When do we lose our peace almost completely? During the hustle and bustle of everyday life. There are too many tasks to do and not enough time to do them, too little money and too many bills, not enough time to meditate and pray as life steadily spins out of control. We do not usually lose our peace in one fell swoop; most often it slips away incrementally. When we finally stop to examine our lives we are appalled at the unintentional mess. Music ministers are especially adept at becoming distracted with all the tasks of ministry—working for God rather than working with God. One of the first signs of the loss of peace is irritability. When we catch ourselves responding in irritation we need to pause immediately and check our inner peace. Most likely we are irritated because we are not focused on relationship with our Father, but on the tasks we need to accomplish for Him. Relationship involves communication and communication leads to trust. Trust allows us to walk in peace regardless of the situation.

Father, keep me from the trap of working for You rather than working with You. Give me ears to better hear Your voice.

June 28

Name Recognition?

"You see, we don't go around preaching about ourselves. We preach that Jesus Christ is Lord, and we ourselves are your servants for Jesus' sake."

2 Corinthians 4:5

Much of the music industry is built around expanding our fan base in an attempt to sell more music. To build name recognition, we create an image and a brand for ourselves, our music, and our ministry. One of our primary marketing goals is to have our ministry's name come to mind whenever a fan sees our logo. Hopefully that fan will talk about us to their friends and we will gain new fans. While marketing is not evil or wrong, it must not be the primary focus of Christian music ministers. Our goal is to bring people closer to Jesus. We lay down our lives, our finances, and potential success in the music industry to do so.

The apostle Paul could have been a famous Jew. He had the family background and education to make a good name for himself. But he chose to follow Jesus and become a servant to all. He could have been the most famous Christian of his time. Instead he openly rebuked Christians for causing division by promoting whichever apostle they followed. His goal was to see Jesus preached by whatever means possible.

So, we must continually ask ourselves, "At the end of each show whose name is the audience most likely to remember? Ours or Jesus'? Have we been building our own music kingdom or have we been using our music to advance His kingdom?" The lines are often very blurry in our marketing. We will not always make the best ministry and marketing decisions. But we cannot afford to blur the lines in our hearts. Our motivation for Christian music ministry must be extremely clear every day: we want to bring people closer to Jesus using music as a tool.

Father, help me to avoid the trap of seeking my own fame and recognition. Show me how to bring people closer to You.

June 29

Unsuccessful Ministry

"What shall we say about such wonderful things as these? If God is for us, who can ever be against us?"

Romans 8:31

We usually interpret this verse to mean that since God is on my side, I am going to win. But that simply is not what we experience. We do not always win. Does that mean that God is not always on our side? Was He on our side when we won and not on our side when we lost? Do we always win when we do everything right and lose when we do anything wrong? Of course not. So, we must not look at every unsuccessful ministry, bands that break up, labels that fail, or venues that close as God abandoning the ministry because the people involved fell short.

This verse shifts our focus from us and our side to God and His ministry. When we are aligned with what God is doing, when we do not have our own side, no one can be against us. They attempt to stand against God. But God will always win. In other words, people are used by God when cooperating with His will, or used by God unwillingly to accomplish His will. Either way, His ministry is going to be done. So perhaps when a ministry appears to be unsuccessful it would be more appropriate to ask, "What is God doing?" than to start by judging the people.

We strive to do effective ministry throughout our life, but being part of a ministry is not the most important thing. What is important, what cannot be changed by outside influences, is that we cannot be separated from the love of God. It's not all about winning or losing at ministry, or how we do ministry, or even which ministry we are currently doing. It is all about who we are in ministry with—God. God does not remove the challenges and battles of ministry from us. But, our success, our victory is this: we are loved by God through it all.

Father, give me discernment to know what You are doing.

June 30
The Next Generation

"Know the state of your flocks,
  and put your heart into caring for your herds,
  for riches don't last forever,
  and the crown might not be passed to the next generation."
                                              Proverbs 27:23-24

In Old Testament times, the wealth of a family was determined by the state of their flocks and herds. Obviously, most of us no longer have herds or flocks. Our wealth is determined by other assets such as bank accounts, investments, real estate, and intellectual property. But the principle remains: know the state of your assets and put your heart into caring for them. The principle comes with a warning: wealth does not automatically get passed down to the next generation. Most creative people really do not like to do financial planning and management. In our hearts we tend villanize the financial industry and would much prefer to do the more spiritual tasks of ministry. Yet, here it is, another verse in the Bible telling us to take care of our wealth. Why is a God who is so concerned about people so interested in how we take care of our assets?

Managing wealth for wealth's sake is just as pointless as being rich and spending everything on you. But this verse connects managing wealth with taking care of the next generation. We might not be able to motivate ourselves into taking care of our assets to benefit ourselves, but we can certainly find motivation in caring for the next generation. We use our assets to take care of people, and that is what makes money management a spiritual task. The task may be just a little more pleasant when we stop to consider how it will affect those around us. Do not procrastinate any longer; let us demonstrate our love by putting our finances in order.

Father, give me the help I need to overcome in this area.

July 1

Growing Through Hardship

> *"If we endure hardship,*
> *we will reign with him.*
> *If we deny him,*
> *he will deny us."*
>
> *2 Timothy 2:12*

Christian testimonies are full of sensational stories of deliverance and rescue. We love to hear about dramatic changes in difficult circumstances because that is what we hope will happen to us too. But experience has taught us that most often God asks us to endure through rather than be delivered from trying hardships. Could it be that He cares more about growth in our faith walk than our comfort or a sensational testimony?

There is really only one way to grow in endurance: to go farther than you did last time. We cannot grow by researching it, watching other people's examples or even writing a great sermon about endurance. We simply have to experience more endurance. In ministry, unlike training as an athlete, we do not have control over when we will work on our endurance. Hardship will come at any given moment and then we simply must endure. Of course, hardship usually comes at the most irritating and inconvenient times, often in front of people we would prefer not to see us struggle. Our only option is how we respond. Our response is exactly what God is interested in because He is training us to reign with Him. Does it seem that you are asked to endure longer and more difficult hardships than the people around you? Is your ministry difficult to understand right now? Praise God, you are being trained for greater things. Do not give up; do not decide to stop where you are. In doing so, we deny the Lordship and character of God. Press on in endurance knowing that you are growing closer to all that God has planned for you.

Father, I need Your strength and courage to go on. Help me to train and grow in endurance.

July 2

Love Covers Sin

"One day he drank some wine he had made, and he became drunk and lay naked inside his tent. Ham, the father of Canaan, saw that his father was naked and went outside and told his brothers. Then Shem and Japheth took a robe, held it over their shoulders, and backed into the tent to cover their father. As they did this, they looked the other way so they would not see him naked."

Genesis 9:21-23

Noah was drunk and exposed himself shamefully. He knew better, it was stupid, it was wrong, but it happened. While we may not have done exactly the same thing, we have all done something similar. We will probably do something similar again because we are human and we tend to fail from time to time. We do not want to and we do not plan to fail, but we do. The issue in this passage was not so much Noah's actions as the actions of his sons. Ham could have covered his father and had a private conversation with him later about what had happened. But, he had to broadcast the problem. Why did Ham act this way? We are not told, but it certainly was not out of love and respect for his father. Would Ham have been upset if the shoe was on the other foot and his father broadcasted his problem? Absolutely. When our brothers or sisters fail how do we act? Love covers sin. It does not hide or ignore sin but it also does not spread gossip about it.

Band mates enjoy a special family relationship. We are closer to each other than some married couples. We know each other's faults and weaknesses. We sometimes watch each other fail. The appropriate response to that failing is to protect the one who failed while at the same time addressing the problem. Treating each other respectfully even during times of utter failure, loving as you would like to be loved, is essential to maintaining a solid band ministry.

Father, give me grace to show love when my brother fails.

July 3
The Lord Opens Hearts

"One of them was Lydia from Thyatira, a merchant of expensive purple cloth, who worshiped God. As she listened to us, the Lord opened her heart, and she accepted what Paul was saying."

Acts 16:14

We see here that Paul was doing the preaching and the Lord was opening hearts. This process sums up ministry. We cannot bring people closer to Jesus alone, by our works of preaching, singing, songwriting, or performing. Our work must be done in partnership with the Lord, who works on people's hearts. When we understand our part in God's process we eliminate the temptation for our egos to get out of control. We can preach, sing, perform, and write songs or not. If we choose not to participate in God's process, He will simply use someone else. We are not irreplaceable. Rather, we are privileged to be used by God as He is doing His ministry of changing hearts. In truth, this is not a 50/50 partnership. We are the minor or junior partners.

Neither Lydia nor Paul can take credit for the work God did in opening Lydia's heart. Certainly Paul was faithful to be on the road preaching the best sermon he could. He did his best to choose places to preach that might have the most receptive people to hear his message. But ultimately, God did the work. Often music ministers take on the responsibility for trying to do God's job. When we do not get the results we hoped for, we consider ourselves to be failures. Worse yet, we sometimes take the credit that is due to God when we get good results. Ministries are devastated when we base our success on the results whether the results meet our goals or not. Music ministers are accountable to do our job to the best of our abilities. But God is responsible for the work done on people's hearts.

Father, help me to clearly see my role and then show me how to do my job in a way that will best facilitate Your ministry.

July 4
Praying for Authorities

"I urge you, first of all, to pray for all people. Ask God to help them; intercede on their behalf, and give thanks for them. Pray this way for kings and all who are in authority so that we can live peaceful and quiet lives marked by godliness and dignity."

2 Timothy 2:1-2

Many citizens do not want to give thanks for their government because they do not agree with the decisions their leaders make. But that is not what this scripture says to do. So, as Christian leaders, we must lead the people in prayer for our government regardless of how we feel about their decisions in their personal lives or in politics. Today and this weekend many of us will have the opportunity to do so at our gigs, but some of us will refuse. Others of us will pray for the leaders to change their politics to our personal viewpoints. But that is not how this scripture says to pray. Christian music ministers must live up to our calling to lead people to pray correctly for our rulers.

Notice the guidelines given in verse one: ask God to help them, intercede on their behalf, and then give thanks for them. We can do all three of those things without agreeing with our government's policies or our leaders' voting record. We can also do all three of those things respectfully, without any negative comments about the person or their political views. We do not need the person in office to vote and act as we would if we were in that position before we pray for them. God can use them as they are right now to enable us to live peaceable, quiet lives marked by godliness and dignity. We can pray that God will use our government officials to do so. Christian music ministers can set an example to all Christians by publically leading them to pray this way whenever the opportunity arises.

Father, give me the wisdom to know how to pray for my government. Teach me to lead Christians to pray for them.

July 5

Fear vs. Faith

"But when Jesus heard what had happened, he said to Jairus, 'Don't be afraid. Just have faith, and she will be healed.'"
Luke 8:50

The opposite of fear is not courage, it is faith. Fear is the enemy of belief. Often it takes courage to believe, but that courage is only a tool to get to the goal of belief. Eradicating fear from our hearts is critical because fear hinders most of the work that God wants to do through us and for us.

Fear encourages us to choose safety and security. When we are safe and secure we can avoid fear, hiding it in our hearts, rather than confronting it. Risk of any kind involves faith. Creating art and then putting it out in front of people is very risky. The questions "How will it be accepted? What if we make a mistake? What if my music is not good enough? What if I am not good enough? Will we look foolish?" plague all artists. The way to overcome these fears is to meet them head on, not avoid them by simply never putting ourselves and our music out there. Do we believe God has called us to music ministry? If so, we can have faith that He will use us in that ministry regardless of all the other questions and fears that may come against us. If we know that we are doing what God has called us to do and we are walking with Him in that calling, we can be sure that His plan will be accomplished. The questions do not disappear, they simply lose their power to paralyze and stop us.

What do we dare to believe God for? Whatever it is, it is certainly much less than He is willing to do. Just as Jesus walked with Jairus to his home, Jesus will walk with us through fear into belief. To be truly effective music ministers, we must choose to confront the fear, take the risk and move into belief.

Father, thank You for Your perfect love, which casts down all fear. Give me the courage to believe in my calling.

July 6
Battling to Love

"Do not seek revenge or bear a grudge against a fellow Israelite, but love your neighbor as yourself. I am the LORD."
Leviticus 19:18

Humans are constantly trying to out maneuver each other. Most of us will do anything we can to stack the laws of supply and demand in our favor. We want more and we are willing to bend the rules a little to get it. In today's market there are more Christian musicians than there are places to play. So, it is fairly common to see bands and soloists trying to manipulate the booking system in their favor. The goal is to get better shows and to get the best time slot at each show. This is supposed to give better odds at increasing the fan base and solidifying a solid music career. Most musicians believe this competition and slightly black hat tactics is a healthy part of doing business. What happens when you or your band is the recipient of this manipulation? How do you respond when your ministry is bumped for another band? What do you do when you have donated your time, equipment, and services only to discover that the recipients of your donation were talking poorly about you?

People are going to say and do things that hurt. They are going to put you and your ministry down in an attempt to build them and their ministries up. It is an unfortunate fact of life. We cannot change their actions but we must be careful of our response. The most important element to the success of our ministry is the favor of God. To receive that favor and blessing, we must be love warriors. This battle begins with God's command to not hold a grudge and ends with God's command to love the offending party as we love ourselves. We must battle to love in every circumstance simply because God commands it.

Father, help me to go beyond forgiveness into demonstrating Your love, especially when my ministry is slighted.

July 7
Borrowed Equipment

"But as one of them was cutting a tree, his ax head fell into the river. 'Oh, sir!' he cried. 'It was a borrowed ax!' 'Where did it fall?' the man of God asked. When he showed him the place, Elisha cut a stick and threw it into the water at that spot. Then the ax head floated to the surface."

2 Kings 6:5-6

One of the men in the school of prophets borrowed an ax to help do the work of building a bigger meeting place. Notice that when the ax head fell off the handle into the water, the man was not rebuked for borrowing the ax. Elisha's only concern seemed to be making sure that the person who lent the ax received it back. In fact he was so concerned about the return of the tool that a miracle was done to ensure the owner did not receive only the handle—a broken tool.

It makes sense for musicians to borrow (or rent) equipment from time to time. God does not seem to have a problem with the borrowing; but we must be as concerned as Elisha was about returning the equipment in good condition. When we forget to return equipment or return broken or dirty equipment, we give people a reason to look down on Christians and our ministry in particular. When we borrow a vehicle, we should leave the gas tank full with the inside and the outside cleaned. If we borrow an instrument or gear, we should return it in better condition than we received it. Borrowed equipment that is damaged while in our possession should be repaired or replaced (at our expense) in a timely manner. Returning borrowed equipment in excellent condition is a way to demonstrate our gratitude, ensure that we will be welcome to borrow again and be an example of the love of Christ.

Father, remind me now of gear I have that should be returned or any restitution I need to make for things I have broken.

July 8
Waiting for You

> *"So the LORD must wait for you to come to him*
> *so he can show you his love and compassion.*
> *For the LORD is a faithful God.*
> *Blessed are those who wait for his help."*
> *Isaiah 30:18*

This verse talks about Israel wanting to get help from the Egyptians instead of only trusting in God. Who in their right mind would ally themselves with their former oppressors and enemies after being rescued from them? We would, we do it all the time. We finally get out from under credit card debt and the next time we want some new equipment we charge it. Then, when we want to go on a tour, we charge that too. Finally, when we need more merchandise to sell on the tour, we charge that as well. Soon, we are right back into the credit card debt we fought so hard to get away from. We did it all in the name of ministry. While some of our intentions may have been good, this kind of behavior should cause us to wonder how much we are really trusting God with our ministry. So, God does what a loving Father must do: teach us how to fully trust Him by letting us create our own messes and wait until we come to Him and ask for His help to clean it up.

At some point we must stop trying to get ahead in ministry by running ahead of God. When God wants us to do something He will make a way for us to do it. When a way is not made we must consider that perhaps God is not asking us to do whatever it is. Most likely it is something we want to do ourselves and we will make a mess if we go ahead and do it. There are certainly times when God will ask us to stretch and step out in faith. But He will generally not ask us to do that by trusting in someone or something else other than Him.

Father, give me discernment of my own heart to know when I am doing what I want by trusting someone other than You.

July 9
Bad Business Deals

"'If you let them go with your troops into battle, you will be defeated by the enemy no matter how well you fight. God will overthrow you, for he has the power to help you or to trip you up.' Amaziah asked the man of God, 'But what about all that silver I paid to hire the army of Israel?' The man of God replied, 'The LORD is able to give you much more than this!'"
2 Chronicles 25:8-9

King Amaziah made a mistake and hired men from the army of Israel when he should not have. A man of God let him know about his mistake and counseled him to get out of the deal. The gist of the Godly man's message: please God. Even if it costs you money to get out of a bad deal—do it, because God can make up the financial difference. But if you do not do what pleases God, you will fail and lose your money.

Musicians sign contracts all the time. But they are not all good or Godly contracts and they are not always made with people God wants us to be involved with. What do we do when we realize we have made a mistake in a business deal? Please God, no matter what the cost. We should start with prayer and then seek the counsel of Godly people to determine what God would have us do. The answer and steps to take are not the same in every circumstance. Sometimes God would have us honor the contract and other times he would have us buy our way out. But He will always ask us to walk with honesty and integrity. Notice that King Amaziah did not kill or harm the men he had wrongly hired in any way. In fact, he let them keep the payment for work they did not do in an attempt to amicably break the contract. Regardless of the circumstances, we must treat people with respect. But we can respectfully decline if that is the way God leads us. We can trust Him to make up the difference.

Father, give me wisdom and Godly advice in business deals.

July 10

Saying & Doing

"So why do you keep calling me 'Lord, Lord!' when you don't do what I say? I will show you what it's like when someone comes to me, listens to my teaching, and then follows it. It is like a person building a house who digs deep and lays the foundation on solid rock. When the floodwaters rise and break against that house, it stands firm because it is well built."

Luke 6:46-48

The Christian music industry requires a certain amount of hype to capture the attention of an audience and sell music. Of course, the hype we like to hear most is stories about how much this music has already affected people. Christians want to hear how their favorite artists are changing the world by bringing people closer to Jesus. Unfortunately, many artists do not truly have this kind of impactful ministry, so the marketing hype often tends to be exaggerated. Instead of asking what artists need to do to attain an impactful ministry, we ask how we can market the little ministry we have. In the end, our marketing says that our ministry is submitted to God but our lives do not show it.

When we continually ask God how to have a ministry that advances His kingdom and then do what God says, the way He wants it done, and when He wants us to do it, the results are a solid ministry foundation. The ministry will stand through the storms. This kind of obedience is not the easy or quick route to music ministry, but it is the long lasting, unshakable route. The ministry that is determined to do things God's way cannot help but yield results that will impact the world for Jesus. Then the marketers will have ministry stories that are true and real to use because the world will be changed by our music and ministry.

Father, I submit to Your plan for my ministry. Show me what You have for me to do and I will do it. Reveal exaggerated marketing of my ministry so I can correct it.

July 11
Praying for Partners

"Whenever I pray, I make my requests for all of you with joy, for you have been my partners in spreading the Good News about Christ from the time you first heard it until now."
Philippians 1:4-5

In the business world, partners have gained a bad reputation. We are always seeing on TV shows and hearing in the news about partners who took advantage of each other to steal the company or its money. It seems like everyone is trying to get ahead, even if it means hurting people who used to be friends.

Band mates are partners in ministry, and most often partners in business because of the ministry. Hopefully we are partners who bring joy to each other. Most band mates started out as friends. Wouldn't it be great to end up as friends too? The only way this can happen is if we treat each other well, working as a team in ministry. Determine not be the person who advances their personal career at the expense of the other people in the band and the band's ministry. There is no need to put down the team in order to be a superstar. This brings joy to no one and God will not honor it. When the stress levels rise and the situations are demanding, we often let the team down by allowing our tempers to flare and our attitudes to show. Apologies can and should be given, but the damage is done. God forgets our sin, but people have memories they cannot simply wipe clean. It is far, far better to be praying for each other continually and to guard our hearts from falling into acting poorly towards our partners. When a band member leaves your band, do they look back on the memories with joy? Do they pray for you, not begrudgingly, but with joy? Pray continually for your partners now and you will have people to joyfully pray for you forever.

Father, correct my attitude towards my partners as needed. When they think of me, let it bring them joy.

July 12
A Job Well Done

"Pay careful attention to your own work, for then you will get the satisfaction of a job well done, and you won't need to compare yourself to anyone else."

Galatians 6:4

"They should have done that better." "Why did they get to play that show and we didn't get called at all?" "Our stage show is much more fun than theirs." "We had to loan them our equipment because they forgot to bring what they needed." Beware of subtle comparisons. There is always someone else who can say similar things about you and your ministry. There will always be another band, another artist who is better at any given thing than you. Comparisons can leave you feeling bitter.

In this time where there are so many resources and there is not one established way to accomplish music ministry, it is especially important to stay focused on our own work. No two ministries are going to do things exactly the same, nor should we. This does mean that we will have to try many new ideas and most likely will fail frequently in the effort. While each ministry is trying to find our own path, we must work harder than ever before. We have our hands full simply doing what God has for us to do in the timing He wants us to do it. While we certainly must make time to learn from each other; we do not have time to waste on comparisons or criticism. We must stay focused.

At the end of the day we can either go to bed with a feeling of failure and bitterness caused by comparisons, or knowing that we have done our best and worked hard to advance the kingdom of God. When we stay focused, our minds race in joyful anticipation of what we can do better tomorrow because we learned from the failures and successes of today.

Father, teach me the difference between comparison and learning from another ministries example. Keep me focused.

July 13
Do Unto Others

"Do to others whatever you would like them to do to you. This is the essence of all that is taught in the law and the prophets."

Matthew 7:12

Many Christian musicians say that the bars treat them better than the church, and that non-Christian bands are more supportive towards them than Christian bands. This should not be so. While we all agree that things should be different, that Christians should treat us better, we are obviously not all looking at our own behavior to make things better. It is easy to point our finger at someone else or at a broader organization such as 'the church,' but perhaps the finger should be turned to point at us.

How would we like to be treated by other Christian music ministers? Are we treating the music ministers we play with each gig that way? How do we treat the people who run and serve at the venues we play? If 'things' are going to change, it must start with us. What would we like other bands to do for us? How about sharing contacts for places to play; sharing equipment when needed; keeping extras of things commonly used and forgotten like batteries and Sharpies to give away; helping unload, set up, tear down, and load equipment; staying in the room and participating in every bands sets, especially if the crowd is small. What could we do to treat the venues well? We could thank the sound tech and volunteers, and help clean up the mess after the show. There are probably many ways we could help change the poor reputation of Christian bands and venues. But it all starts with our attitudes, which can be changed through prayer. If we would sincerely, consistently and specifically pray for the success of Christian music ministers and venues, we would treat them like God would treat them—in unconditional and abundant love.

Father, help me to see where I need to change in the way I treat my fellow ministers. Show me ways to do more to help.

July 14
Band Time

"Then Jesus climbed a hill and sat down with his disciples around him."

John 6:3

During this time Jesus' ministry was in full swing. Crowds followed Him wherever He went. But notice that Jesus set aside time for just Him and His disciples: team time. During His ministry we often see Jesus finding time to pray alone. But we also see Jesus spending private time with His disciples, explaining parables, teaching about prayer, and preparing them for the future. This time built His team, showing them how to work together, and laid the foundation for all future ministries.

Christian bands must also set aside time for the band privately. As touring schedules get crazy and life gets more complicated, the pressures in music ministry rise. It is not always convenient to find time to be together. It would be much easier for us to neglect each other, to not make time to discuss problems as they arise. But solid communication, especially during the busiest seasons of ministry, ensures longevity and minimizes the strife within the ministry. There are times when we will simply have to tell other people that the band is unavailable right now because they are spending time together.

Jesus made time together with His disciples a priority throughout His ministry. As we participate in and lead our ministries, we must do the same. Each member of our team must grow individually and together as part of the team. This can only be done by spending time together making decisions, studying, praying, coordinating, and having fun. Friends and fans may not like being told the band is busy in the moment, but in the end they will be admire the teamwork of the band. Successful teams prioritize each other and their time with God.

Father, show us how to grow together as a band. Unite our hearts in ministry and in love for each other.

One Step at a Time

"Late one afternoon, after his midday rest, David got out of bed and was walking on the roof of the palace. As he looked out over the city, he noticed a woman of unusual beauty taking a bath."

2 Samuel 11:2

Everyone knows the story of David staying home instead of leading his troops into battle and falling into sin to the point of murdering Bathsheba's husband. Almost every sermon we hear about this story makes the point that we need to be doing the work God calls us to do, not resting at home. While it is true that David would not have seen Bathsheba if he was where he was supposed to be on the battlefield, it is also true that he did not jump from seeing Bathsheba to immediately murdering Uriah. At first David simply noticed Bathsheba and he let the sin build one step upon another to the point of murder. There were plenty of places in between each step of escalating sin that he could have stopped. None of us starts out with the intention to do any of the "big" sins. We get there one small step at a time.

Christian musicians have an extraordinary number of opportunities to notice an exceptionally attractive person, even when we are doing what we are supposed to be doing in ministry. We know how we are supposed to handle that situation; we simply do not always do it. At first it seems like a little thought which turns into a daydream and progresses from there. Marriages have been ruined and ministries have broken up because the people involved thought they had already gone too far and choose not to turn back, so they kept going. Do not be that person. Stop the chain of escalating sin at whatever link you are currently on. Do whatever it takes to turn around and run back to God before you commit the murder of your ministry.

Father, show me my sin when it is still small. Convict me immediately in increasing strength until I turn back to You.

Unsung Heroes

"God blesses those who are humble,
*   for they will inherit the whole earth.*
God blesses those who hunger and thirst for justice,
*   for they will be satisfied.*
God blesses those who are merciful,
*   for they will be shown mercy.*
God blesses those whose hearts are pure,
*   for they will see God."*
                                        Matthew 5:5-8

The entertainment industry is full of people who are in the spotlight, and those who are not are trying to get there. As a society, we tend to look up to famous people. As musicians, we recognize that it is much easier to sell music and pay the bills as we become more famous. But when we examine famous people in the light of God's word, we see that many of them are sadly lacking. Many have become famous through manipulating, pushing, and even cheating. They do not have God's call on their lives or His character in their hearts. These are not the people we want to emulate, even though at times it is difficult not to be jealous of their status. Unfortunately, status in music ministry is not exempt from this way of thinking. It is often assumed that the Christian musicians who are most famous are also the most Christ-like. They are the people we tend to look up to.

But God has a different measurement of Christ-likeness in ministry, and fame has nothing to do with it. God's heroes are those who are most like Christ and obedient to Him. Some of God's musician heroes are well known; most are not. It's not about where you play, how much you are paid, or who you have played with. True heroes love God so much that they will do anything He asks, whenever and wherever He wants it done.

Father, I want to be Your obedient hero. Show me how.

July 17

The God of Success

"Can people make their own gods?
These are not real gods at all!"

Jeremiah 16:20

What does a successful music ministry look like? Is it defined by large audiences, popularity in social media, music and merchandise sales, or even the number of new converts at our shows? No. We know that successful music ministry is defined by the level of obedience we have to God's plan for our ministry. But measuring levels of obedience is hard to do and hard to communicate to other people. So, we use markers that can be measured to demonstrate that our ministry is growing, and therefore has the favor of God. Flawed logic at best, the favor of God does not always rest most on ministries that are growing or popular. But we persist in using these measures because they can be clearly and easily communicated. Christian musicians are often booked based on the number of fans they are expected to draw at a venue; draw more fans, make more money at each show and play more shows, so we can earn a living doing full time music ministry. It becomes very easy to set our hearts on mini gods, who are not gods at all—popularity and money.

The line between working hard to do our ministry well and making ministry a god is fine, but it is there. It can be defined by looking at why we are working hard—to create a full time job in music ministry, or to please God; to be popular and make money doing something fun, or to be obedient to a Father who loves us. This kind of heart honesty is not easy to do. It is necessary to check from time to time. We do not want to be deceived by the trappings of music ministry or our own hearts. We want to be music ministers who worship the one true God.

Father, reveal my heart to me. Help me remove any gods that are present so I may worship and be obedient to You alone.

Merchandise Reminders

"After the victory, the LORD instructed Moses, 'Write this down on a scroll as a permanent reminder, and read it aloud to Joshua: I will erase the memory of Amalek from under heaven.'"

Exodus 17:14

Joshua had just won the victory against the Amalekites while Moses held up his arms. This day was a turning point for the Jews. It was a day to remember! But our memories are not always as reliable as we would like, so God had Moses create a visual reminder of the victory. Whenever the people had doubts or needed their faith strengthened, they could read the scrolls and be reminded of what God had already done for them.

God works through Christian music ministers at concerts to give His people victories. Fans are brought to know Him for the first time, find release from personal strongholds, and receive a deeper experience with God while we perform. Those victories, the experiences of drawing closer to God, need to be remembered and celebrated. But you and your band cannot stay with fans to remind them daily of what God has done for them. This is why your merchandise is so important: it is a reminder of God's hand at work in your fan's life. When the fan listens to your song, they instantly remember how they felt at the concert. The memory of the experience at your band's concert may be just enough to help a fan overcome a temptation. When they wear your band's t-shirt they are often given the opportunity to tell their friends about their experience at the concert.

Selling merchandise is not about the money, or promoting your music. It is all about reminding fans of their experience with God at the concert and providing them with tools to communicate that experience to their friends.

Father, help me to remember that selling my merchandise is all about reminding fans what You have done for them.

July 19
Qualified?

"It is not that we think we are qualified to do anything on our own. Our qualification comes from God."

2 Corinthians 3:5

The music industry has qualifications for artists that will be signed to a national label. They must have a certain look, play specific styles of music, be in an age range, and have the ability to attract many people. Many musicians work hard to meet the qualifications, but most of us never do. We are often left with feelings of incompetency or inadequacy. Our music ministry sometimes seems like we are settling for less. Fortunately, it is not the music industry who qualifies us for music ministry. Our qualification is simply that God Himself called us to do it. It is up to Him to judge who should be in music ministry and who should not. We must simply follow His call and instructions.

Does meeting the qualifications of the music industry make our music ministry better? Not necessarily. There are many instances in which being a national artist would detract from the ministry we are called to do. For example an artist who is best at connecting one on one with his fans, or an artist who serves an underground market, or even an artist who loves to play shows but does not want to record much. National labels would attempt to pigeonhole these artists into doing what is most marketable. They may play the big stage but they would not be doing the ministry God had planned for them.

God qualifies us to do the specific ministry He has created us to do. That ministry is not a higher or lower calling than national artists on a national label. It is simply God's plan for our lives. Our job is to follow His plan and leading to the best of our ability. If we do that, we are successful music ministers.

Father, help me to refocus to know exactly what You have called me to do. Thank you for qualifying me to do it.

July 20

What Did Jesus Do?

"Those who say they live in God should live their lives as Jesus did."

1 John 2:6

"WWJD: What would Jesus do?" was very popular a few years ago. We saw bracelets and t-shirts with this saying and it inspired us to stop and answer the question before we reacted in any given situation. WWJD helped many people live their lives in a more Godly way, but it also left quite a bit of room for speculation and interpretation based on our idea of who Jesus was and how He acted. Perhaps music ministers would do better to ask WDJD—What did Jesus do?

Christian music ministers are spiritual leaders, whether we want to accept that responsibility or not. People look up to us simply because we are on stage. They look to us as examples of what their faith walk should be like. So, we need to be able to do more than simply speculate on what Jesus might do in a specific situation. We must know the Bible well enough to be able to say, "When this happened to Jesus, He did this. So, I am going to do what Jesus did." Christian music ministers are frequently put in situations that most pastors never have to deal with, especially when we perform in secular venues. The things people say and do can make us very uncomfortable. But Jesus ministered in both the Synagogues and to the Gentiles. He was put in some unusual situations. Studying how He responded and how He turned conversations to lead people closer to God should be a priority in our ministry training. As we study and learn more about what He did, we will be better able to speculate on what he would do in situations that are not covered in the Bible. Ultimately, what Jesus did must be the model for our own ministry.

Father, give me understanding of Jesus' examples of ministry in unusual situations. Guide my conversations to bring people closer to You. Teach me how to live like Jesus.

July 21
Ropes of Love

> *"I led Israel along*
> *with my ropes of kindness and love.*
> *I lifted the yoke from his neck,*
> *and I myself stooped to feed him."*
>
> **Hosea 11:4**

In the country, cats and dogs are often left to run freely in the fields. These animals are frequently injured by other animals and tend to contract more sicknesses than their city counterparts. But, pets in the city are walked on leashes for their own safety and the safety of the people around them. City pets are not exposed to wild animals, so they are not injured by them nor do they contract their illnesses. They are, however, frequently hit by cars and get in fights with other pets. So, animals who live in the city are led by leashes and training. Because of the extra care taken in their training and their ability to walk on leashes, city animals usually get to travel right along with their owners while country animals are left at home. Still, many people believe that country pets have a better life because they have the freedom to run wherever they want and city pets are deprived. Could it be that city pets actually have the better life because they get to spend more time with their owners? If the owner was God, most of us would want to be a city pet.

Musicians tend to be free spirited; we do not like to be reigned in or bound by rules. We feel trapped. But sometimes this trapped feeling is actually God lovingly leading us safely to where we need to go. Leashes may not feel as good as running wild but when God is holding the leash we are kept safe and headed in the right direction. Enjoy the time with God, follow the training, and behave well on the leash so when we get to a place where it is safe to run free God will trust us and allow it.

Father, give me discernment to know when You are leading.

July 22
Let Children Tell Children

"Tell your children about it in the years to come,
and let your children tell their children.
Pass the story down from generation to generation."
                                              Joel 1:3

We know that word of mouth is still the best form of advertising. For example, if you tell a friend about a great restaurant, they are far more likely to try it than if they saw a commercial. But who does the telling is very important because we tend to believe our peers. Using the same example, your friend would be less likely to try a restaurant recommended by your parents than if you told them about it. Why? Because friends have similar values and communication styles. The food may stay the same at the restaurant, but who talks about it affects which aspects of the restaurant are emphasized. Parents may talk about the spices that season the food while the friends might be more interested in the inexpensive price.

This same dilemma occurs when telling the stories of God. The older generation will have a different way of presenting the stories than what will appeal to the younger generation. This is why, as Christian music ministers, we must constantly be encouraging younger Christian musicians to develop their own skills. Our music, our style, and our way of communicating will probably not be the most effective way to tell the next generation. It is our job to find the best way to communicate to our generation. But, we must encourage the next generation to go beyond us in ministry and find the most creative, best ways to tell the story to their peers. We can show them how to draw closer to God and to develop ministry skills. But we must let them tell their generation in their own way.

Father, show me how to train the next generation of Christian music ministers without stifling their creativity.

July 23

Ready to Sing and Rejoice

"Jehoiada now put the priests and Levites in charge of the Temple of the LORD, following all the directions given by David. He also commanded them to present burnt offerings to the LORD, as prescribed by the Law of Moses, and to sing and rejoice as David had instructed."

2 Chronicles 23:18

The rightful king, Joash, was restored to Israel. He and the priest, Jehoiada, brought the people back to God, destroying the temple of Baal and restoring the Temple of God. People had a reason to be happy. The future looked bright once again as the weight of tyranny was removed and replaced with the blessings of following God. It was time to sing and rejoice.

Musicians too had suffered under the previous king; and when it was time to rejoice they were ready to lead the people. Instruments were pulled out and the songs of worship began. But what would have happened if the musicians had become so discouraged that their instruments were lost or damaged? What if they had forgotten how to sing and play well?

It is such an honor to be one of the musicians leading people in worship. We herald in times of rejoicing with our music. We sing the songs of worship that bring people closer to God. We must be ready to sing and rejoice whenever people need it. Everyone experiences the tyranny of hardship and adverse circumstances from time to time but musicians must stay prepared to lead, knowing that a time will come when we will sing and rejoice once again. We must encourage ourselves to stay ready because we have been chosen by God to use music to bring people closer to Him. What an honor; what a responsibility!

Father, I love to lead Your people in songs of rejoicing. Thank You for choosing me to be one of Your musicians! I will keep my instrument ready and my skills sharp so that I can lead Your people to worship You at any time.

July 24
Thankful for Provision

"Then God said to Jonah, 'Is it right for you to be angry because the plant died?'
'Yes,' Jonah retorted, 'even angry enough to die!'"
                                              Jonah 4:9

We get upset when something is taken away, especially if we have come to rely on it. Musicians experience this especially in gigs and donations. "We play that show every year and they always pay us this much," or "They always let us use their room to practice," and the ever popular "They would be excited to be our roadie (without getting paid)," are heard so commonly as to be acceptable assumptions. Christian music ministers must rely on people to help them in order to be able to afford to do the ministry. But when that help is withdrawn, we do not have the right to be angry or to demand explanations. When someone gives us a neatly wrapped gift each day for seven days in a row but no gift arrives on the eighth day, should we be angry? No. We should be grateful for the seven gifts and hold the gift giver in high regard. But that is not how we often treat people who give gifts of time and resources to our ministry.

Just as when the plant died for Jonah, we are often being directed to do something different when the resources in a certain place dry up. Usually, this redirection does not involve physically moving to a different location (but it can). Most of the time God is using the lack to push us to seek something better in that particular area. The provision is available but we cannot see it until we start seeking and moving. If our ministries did not change from time to time we could easy to fall into the trap of "This is how we have always done it." Instead we should praise God for a new direction when something old is taken away. Thankfulness, not anger, is the appropriate response.

Father, thank You for leading us through Your provision.

Uncomfortable Situations

"She came and grabbed him by his cloak, demanding, 'Come on, sleep with me!' Joseph tore himself away, but he left his cloak in her hand as he ran from the house."

Genesis 39:12

Running from any appearance of sin is always a good response. Try as hard as we might to avoid it, Christian music ministers are eventually going to be put into uncomfortable positions with fans. Sometimes fans simply want to get attention and spend more time with us without understanding the situations they create. Other time fans are intentionally placing us in potentially compromising positions. Either way, we can do the right thing and handle the situation as carefully as possible, only to be unfairly accused of inappropriate behavior by the fan or someone else who knows the fan. It is never easy to resolve.

God did not protect Joseph from this situation, so it is rational to believe that He will not always protect us from it either. Why would He allow such things to happen? God used the accusation to move Joseph to where he needed so he could live up to his full potential. Joseph was comfortable in Potiphar's house. But Joseph was destined to save the Israelites from famine. So, he needed access to Pharaoh. God used a false accusation to position Joseph for his future. God's ways of positioning us are not always easy. Joseph went from Potiphar's house to prison before he was appointed to be second in Egypt. We have no record of God telling Joseph why he was in prison. It was probably confusing. Isn't that how we feel when someone accuses us of something that isn't true? Our response must be to realize that God is still in control and seek out His plan. He will use what was intended for harm and turn it to good.

Father, grant me greater discernment to see what You are doing, especially during difficult and confusing situations.

July 26

Being Prevented

"We wanted very much to come to you, and I, Paul, tried again and again, but Satan prevented us."
1 Thessalonians 2:18

Satan prevented Paul from visiting the Thessalonians. Think about that; here is Paul, one of the greatest Christ followers of all time, being stopped from doing something he felt God wanted him to do by Satan. The same enemy opposes us. So, it is to be expected that from time to time we will be stopped from doing something that we feel God wants us to do. Being stopped does not mean we are a failure. It does not mean we are weak. Would we say that Paul was a failure or weak? No. It simply means we have an enemy who fights against us. Being on God's side of the battle does not guarantee that we win every time. We do win the war, but there is still a great struggle going on until the very end. Our enemy does not give up easily.

So, when we are prevented from doing what we believe God has for us to do we must exercise discernment. We should seek the answers to several questions: Is God preventing us, or is it a demonic attack? If it is God preventing us, why? Do we need to make some changes or is it a matter of timing? If it is demonic, what can we do to break their power over the situation? Is our situation a result of our own making? What should we have done differently and what do we need to do now to fix it?

Our ministry is not going to be easy, simply because we are in a war. We can get an idea of the levels of trials we might face by looking at Paul's ministry. We should not automatically make assumptions about the reasons we are being prevented until we have taken time to hear from God. He knows how to win the battles and He will instruct us on what to do next.

Father, show me what is happening n the spirit realm regarding my ministry. Instruct me on how to win the battle.

A Little Laziness

"A little extra sleep, a little more slumber,
a little folding of the hands to rest—
then poverty will pounce on you like a bandit;
scarcity will attack you like an armed robber."
Proverbs 24:33-34

Most people do not get rich because of one lucky winning lottery ticket. Most wealth is built with a lifetime of good work habits. In the same way, most often poverty does not happen in a single moment or because of a single incident. We can invite poverty into our lives by habitually being lazy. People who work a job with a regular schedule and routine do not have as much opportunity to be lazy as artists. We live on an unusual schedule, much of the time without daily deadlines. We are our own bosses and sometimes that means we give ourselves too much freedom to rest. While rest is part of a healthy work ethic, too much rest becomes laziness. Rest and work must be kept in balance but that balance is not an equal amount of time.

Are your goals consistently not being met? Are you living up to your full potential? If not, you may be resting to the point of being lazy. Lazy people do not refuse to work. They simply do not work as hard, as efficiently, or as long as other people. Lazy people do what they want to do when they want to do it, and never seem to have the time to do the more unpleasant things that need to be done. Christian music ministers do not have to live in poverty. But, we may have to work very hard to make ends meet. We must be responsible to hold ourselves accountable to a good work ethic in spite of the challenges of music ministry. We need to work as unto the Lord regardless of whether or not we have a human boss to oversee our work.

Father, show me how I can work better consistently each day, especially since You are my boss in ministry.

July 28
In Front of Jesus

"They couldn't bring him to Jesus because of the crowd, so they dug a hole through the roof above his head. Then they lowered the man on his mat, right down in front of Jesus."
                                                                Mark 2:4

What would you do to get closer to Jesus? What would you do to bring someone else closer to Jesus? The men in this story had to get creative in order to get their friend right in front of Jesus. They had to think about things in a way that they had not previously considered. They were willing to do the unusual, the unexpected. If they had told people ahead of time that they were going to cut a hole in the roof, they would have been laughed at. People who noticed what they were doing were probably concerned about the mess. After all that creative thinking and work, they were not 100% sure their idea would work. But they tried it anyway and got results!

The entire process sounds quite a bit like what Christian music ministers go through to do their ministry. We take chances, because using art to bring people closer to Jesus is risky. Our ideas and our expression of those ideas leave us vulnerable to ridicule and failure. It takes courage to do something different, to cut a hole in the roof or to share Jesus through a new song. Notice that Jesus did not condemn these men for trying something new or for making a mess. In fact, verse 5 says, "Seeing their faith, Jesus said to the paralyzed man, 'My child, your sins are forgiven.'" The man was healed immediately, right on the spot and his sins were forgiven because of their great faith! God honors the courage to act on our faith in whatever form it takes. So, go ahead, be courageous and express your faith using every bit of creativity you have!

Father, thank You for inspiring my creativity. Give me the courage to use my gifts in new and unusual ways.

July 29
Celebrate the Win

"When the victorious Israelite army was returning home after David had killed the Philistine, women from all the towns of Israel came out to meet King Saul. They sang and danced for joy with tambourines and cymbals."

1 Samuel 18:6

Victory is something to be celebrated, and the best celebrations usually include singing and dancing. Too often in the battles of ministry, we forget to take time to go all out and celebrate the wins. Those celebrations are important because they mark a specific period of time in our memories; a time we can look back on during our next battle. We gain courage and strength by remembering past victories when we are mired in a new problem. In our hearts we can say, "Because God has done it once for me (or for our ministry), I can believe that He will do it again." Celebrations help build our faith.

Celebrating as a band binds us together with memories of good times as well as victories won together. Celebrations that include our friends and families build support for our ministry. The people closest to us gain a better understanding of what we do and why we do it. This understanding makes it easier for them to sacrifice time with us during the road trip, practice, or recording session. During the celebration, they have seen that God is working through our ministry and that we value their sacrifices to help us in that work. Celebrations help build the faith of the people who love us.

Most importantly celebrations bring us closer to God because the celebration itself is a way to honor the work He has done through us. When we celebrate a ministry victory, we are not celebrating a win of our own achievements. We are honoring what God has done through us and through our ministry.

Father, remind me to make for room for a celebration party!

July 30
True Ministers of God

"We live in such a way that no one will stumble because of us, and no one will find fault with our ministry. In everything we do, we show that we are true ministers of God. We patiently endure troubles and hardships and calamities of every kind."

2 Corinthians 6:3-4

What does a true minister of God look like? If we examine the lives of the apostles and disciples we see such a variety of lives that we must conclude being a true minister of God is not dependant upon our circumstances, whether good or bad, prosperous or poor, jailed or free. A true minister of God cannot be defined as someone who is paid to work in ministry or as someone who is famous because of ministry. If true ministers of God cannot be defined by their circumstances, perhaps they can be defined by the manner in which they live—the way they respond to the circumstances. Nothing is more telling about our response to circumstances than when we experience trouble and hardship. It is quite easy to patiently endure good times and ease, but bring on the trouble and watch the response.

Are we living up to being a true minister of God? How do we respond in trouble or hardship? Are the people around us encouraged or stumbling because of that response? Can people point to our ministry or our life and find legitimate fault? Most of us can handle criticism because of the Gospel message, but how do we handle criticism of our behavior which does not live up to that message? What happens when people point to our ministry and find illegitimate fault? How do we respond when people do not understand what we do or why we do it, and then criticize us? How do we act when well-meaning Christians do not approve of our ministry? The answers to these questions may tell us if we are acting like true ministers of God.

Father, help me respond with well to difficult circumstances.

July 31
Listening Leaders

"Understand this, my dear brothers and sisters: You must all be quick to listen, slow to speak, and slow to get angry."
James 1:19

Listening is not a quality that most people would list as a top qualification of a leader. But before a leader can address any problem, he must have a thorough understanding of that problem as well as all the surrounding issues it affects. This can only be learned by listening to the people involved. Many times we try to solve a problem quickly and decisively because that is what we think the situation requires. But a great leader will take the time to ask questions and listen to what God says first.

Bands are thrown in to new situations every day. Our environment constantly changes from venue to venue, and the people we work with as promoters and bookers change with them. The way that people and venues do things is different at each place. Because we see so many different methods and situations, it becomes easy for us to judge quickly and make decisions based on those judgments. Out tempers can flare easily because we think we have seen that there is a better way. But what we often forget is that we are seeing only a snapshot, one day or moment in time, of any given situation. We have not seen what has happened before, and so we do not always clearly understand what is happening now. Before we lose our tempers, before we speak our minds, before we judge the situation, we need to stop and listen. Often we will find that we do not clearly understand all the issues involved. Even more often, we will find that we are sticking our nose into someone else's business and should not get involved at all. Being a good leader does not mean solving everyone's problems. It does mean first listening to the heart and spirit of God, before we judge the situations of man.

Father, teach me to listen so I may avoid anger.

Thanksgiving Leads to Praise

"Let us come to him with thanksgiving.
Let us sing psalms of praise to him."
Psalm 95:2

Have you ever noticed how easy it is to tell someone they have done a great job AFTER you experience the impact their work has on your life? You are grateful because they went out of their way to make your life easier, so it is natural to want to praise them. Genuine praise comes easily when we are truly thankful. Praise to our Father can work the same way.

Does your worship seem less genuine when you perform the same songs repeatedly? Has singing songs of praise become a routine performance? Do the technical issues of playing dominate your worship? Is your music technically correct but spiritually dead? It is easy to fall into the routine of performing, leading worship for others but not truly engaging in praise ourselves.

Dead praise can be overcome with thanksgiving. Before your next performance, meditate on how God has changed your life for the better. Consider what God has done for your family and friends and be grateful for His hand at work in our lives. Then, ponder on the greatness of God—how He created and controls the world. After that, it should be easy to praise Him for loving you.

This is a simple concept, but it takes a daily life of discipline to apply it. We do not want to practice the discipline of thankfulness only when we are having a bad day or rough week. By that time it is easier to look at our circumstances and remain numb. Music ministers are called to lead the way in praise, so we must practice the discipline of thanksgiving daily.

Father, help me to do better at leading praise for You. Remind me to practice the discipline of thanksgiving so I can be at the head of the line, leading worship for You.

August 2
The Value of Trials

"These trials will show that your faith is genuine. It is being tested as fire tests and purifies gold—though your faith is far more precious than mere gold. So when your faith remains strong through many trials, it will bring you much praise and glory and honor on the day when Jesus Christ is revealed to the whole world."

1 Peter 1:7

No one likes to going through trials; no one looks forward to them. But trials are valuable because they prove our faith is genuine. What would you be willing to do to have something worth more than gold? How much could you withstand to get something that makes gold look like asphalt? The streets in heaven are paved with gold. There, the faith of a righteous man is far more valuable than gold. How do we prove that we have faith? By withstanding trials. Since faith is so valuable, we should say, "Bring on the trials!"

Perhaps the most difficult trials are not the larger, potentially life changing situations. The trials that we tend to fail more often are the nuisances that never seem to end. We know how we are expected to act during the crisis situations and we generally live up to those expectations. But we often give ourselves a pass when it comes to the daily "smaller" trials such as losing our temper over sound system issues, or not making time to listen to someone when we are in the middle of a ministry task. Trials are not always about the potential to lose something significant in our life. Most often they are about our willingness to lay down our life, often for people we barely know. We do not get to pick and choose which trials we will face or when we will be asked lay down our life. We only get to choose how we demonstrate our faith. Don't waste the opportunity.

Father, help me to see trials from Your point of view. Cause me to recognize my next opportunity to prove my faith.

August 3
New Songs

"Praise the LORD!
Sing to the LORD a new song.
Sing his praises in the assembly of the faithful.
O Israel, rejoice in your Maker.
O people of Jerusalem, exult in your King.
Praise his name with dancing,
*   accompanied by tambourine and harp.*
For the LORD delights in his people;
*   he crowns the humble with victory."*
                                    Psalm 149:1-4

Has church become boring? Are services so common that they have begun to run together? One of the dangers in the freedom and prosperity we experience in our western culture is that we take church for granted. One reason new songs can be difficult to write is that our passion for the church has dried up. Most of our songwriting is inspired by an emotional response to an experience. But when we stop experiencing God in church, we lose our inspiration to write new songs of praise for the church.

How do we regain our passion and our inspiration? We must engage our hearts to truly appreciate what we have. Be grateful for the building that keeps us comfortable; we are not sitting in the hot sun for service, as many believers in other countries do. Thank God that the pastor is preaching and not in jail, nor is his family being threatened. Rejoice in the fact that we do not have to sing quietly so our neighbors won't turn us in to the police. Remember those who have given their lives to preserve the Bible that we hold in our hands today. Refuse to dwell on the faults of people attending church. Rejoice that they set aside time to praise God with us in the faithful assembly.

Father, reignite my passion for Your bride. Inspire new songs as I remind myself of all I have to be thankful for in church.

August 4

Who Do You Know?

"Do not get involved in foolish discussions about spiritual pedigrees or in quarrels and fights about obedience to Jewish laws. These things are useless and a waste of time."

Titus 3:9

In the New Testament church some believers were saying they followed Paul, or that Peter baptized them. Others were still citing their standing in the hierarchy of the Jewish synagogue. These were their religious pedigrees—who they knew, who they worked with in ministry, and how much they had studied. Not much has changed since that time. We still talk about which denomination is better, which label is more spiritual, and who we have worked with that is famous in Christian circles. Worship leaders have become the new rock stars and working with the right one can open the right doors for our careers. We even allow which rules people do or do not follow to determine who we think is more Christ-like.

While there certainly is a time to check resumes and references, this scripture reminds us that who and what we know on earth is not nearly as important as how well we know our Father in heaven. We do not have time to waste on proving we know all the best people in order to advance our career or spiritual standing. We must stay focused on actually doing our ministry. If we take the time to go all out in seeking after God and then do all the work involved in our ministry, we will not have time for much else, including the politics of keeping track of spiritual pedigrees. When we stay focused on seeking and serving God, we can count on Him to expand our ministries to be the most effective possible for His kingdom. We do not need spiritual pedigrees; we need to know God.

Father, show me the useless things I spend too much time on so I have more time for You and Your work.

Accomplished Musicians

"All these men were under the direction of their fathers as they made music at the house of the LORD. Their responsibilities included the playing of cymbals, harps, and lyres at the house of God. Asaph, Jeduthun, and Heman reported directly to the king. They and their families were all trained in making music before the LORD, and each of them— 288 in all—was an accomplished musician."

1 Chronicles 25:6-7

The musicians in the Temple were so important that their leaders reported directly to the king. All 288 of them were trained, accomplished musicians. Apparently the king put great emphasis on their training and expertise, so much so that he took time from his political schedule to check on the musicians. God places the same importance on us, our training, and our expertise. We represent God to many people who otherwise do not know Him. Why would he want to use people who consistently choose not to work towards being the best?

Christian music ministers have much more to do than ordinary musicians. We take care of the ministry as well as the music. But in our busyness, we must not neglect daily practice on our instrument. We may never be the best in the whole world at any one instrument, but we must strive to improve to the point of being an accomplished musician. Unfortunately, there is no way to get to this level except to learn the basics, practice, and then move on to greater and greater expertise. This kind of training takes self-discipline and prioritizing the importance of having an effective daily practice time. It is not always fun, but it is required in order to move up to the next level of music ministry. God wants to use us, so He wants us to be the best.

Father, show me ways to make my practice time more effective. Teach me to be the best I can be at serving You.

August 6

Popular Ministry

"For the world offers only a craving for physical pleasure, a craving for everything we see, and pride in our achievements and possessions. These are not from the Father, but are from this world. And this world is fading away, along with everything that people crave. But anyone who does what pleases God will live forever."

1 John 2:16-17

All Christian music ministers are keenly aware of the temptations of the entertainment industry. We know that we should not dress immodestly, sing inappropriate lyrics, or otherwise act like many secular musicians because we are representing God. Most of the time we do a pretty good job of staying away from those problems. But we face an entirely different set of issues as Christians. Our temptations can come by desiring position and power within the Christian music industry. We want to know the right people and we want to be one of the artists that attract industry professionals. The real problems come when we are willing to do anything to make that happen. We start emphasizing our achievements in ministry more than Jesus. Along the way we become more concerned about marketing our ministry to get better exposure than about doing the work of bringing people closer to Jesus. The difference is subtle, so many people are not able to look at us and see that there is a problem. But our hearts give us away.

Only by staying completely focused on pleasing God can we survive the temptation of lusting after more popular ministry. Like money, more popular ministry in and of itself is not evil; the lusting after it is. Which do you choose to do more of when you have extra time: working towards gaining music exposure, or spending more time in the presence of God? That choice might be one indicator of your heart.

Father, forgive my ambition for popularity over pleasing You.

Generous Art

"The generous will prosper;
those who refresh others will themselves be refreshed."
Proverbs 11:25

Christian music ministers are frequently frustrated when hearing sermons or reading verses about being blessed when we give. Many of us do not have extra money to give because we spend it on our ministry. Some of us feel guilty when we do not give, and we do not expect to be blessed because of our lack of giving. How are we supposed to be generous and refresh others when we have no money to give? We give ourselves in the form of our art, our music.

We have all seen musicians who play every note correctly but do not give anything to their audience. We leave feeling uninspired if not bored. Then there are other musicians who, while they may not play as difficult pieces or play as technically correct, leave us feeling that we have connected with God. These musicians are completely engaged with us, with the music, and with worshipping God. They risk showing us a part of themselves through their music. They are truly doing art. Their art refreshes our spirits. This is how we can give and give generously: we can pour ourselves into our music and the worship of our God so much that other people cannot help but be refreshed. This kind of giving is more than throwing a few extra coins into the offering; it requires us to risk giving everything we have, all of our heart all of our being, through music to refresh others. It requires experiencing our relationship with God in front of and with the audience. We are not giving from our excess, but risking ourselves in giving sacrificially. God loves this kind of a generous giver. He blesses our generous giving because it is more than just money—it is our hearts.

Father, give me the courage to be a very generous giver.

August 8

It's About Him

"And then I heard every creature in heaven and on earth and under the earth and in the sea. They sang:

> *'Blessing and honor and glory and power*
> *belong to the one sitting on the throne*
> *and to the Lamb forever and ever.'"*
>
> *Revelation 5:13*

All creation sings praise to God! Christian music ministers are extremely privileged to be able to lead worship. We are not just some rock star promoting our own music. We do not sing to honor a human dignitary at a special event. We do not sing only to express our own creativity. We sing to lead people in the worship of the Creator of the universe. Our status is higher than a rock star, more important than a dignitary, and more influential than an artist. We are Christian music ministers, honored by God to lead people in His worship.

The fact that what we do is not based on us or who we are should give us great confidence. We do not have to draw attention to ourselves, our creativity, or our shortcomings. The whole ministry is not on us; it is on God. We do not have to bear the responsibility for how it all turns out as long as we are following Him. So, we can be free to worship with our whole heart! God has given us status and privilege in Him without the full weight of everything being built around us. What an amazing God we serve! He loves us so much as to give us the best gifts without the negative aspects that could hurt us. The God of the universe honors us as His obedient children and covers us as a loving Father. We can certainly bless Him with our worship.

Father, help me to remember that worship is not about how well I perform and to lead worship with my whole being. Thank You for not making this ministry revolve around me.

August 9
Giving Up

"And everyone who has given up houses or brothers or sisters or father or mother or children or property, for my sake, will receive a hundred times as much in return and will inherit eternal life."

Matthew 19:29

Christian musicians could have larger homes, better possessions, and more time with our families if we would be willing to get a "regular job" that "paid us what we are worth" and did not require us to travel so much. So, many of us view this verse as a promise to repay what we have given up. That promise is true. But what, exactly, have we given up? It is possible to "not have" houses, brothers, sisters, father, mother, children, or property but to still be consumed or controlled by them.

In order to "give up" something we must completely submit its influence on us to the Lordship of Jesus. That does not mean we cannot allow ourselves to be influenced by them. It does mean that we must hold their influence up in submission to God's influence on us. To give up our family, we must compare our entire family culture (the way we think, how we do things, what we think is right) to God's culture (the way He thinks, how He wants things done, and what He thinks is right). We must leave behind whatever aspects of family culture do not line up with God's culture. We have been raised with our way of thinking, so it is not easy to differentiate between what is truly God's way and what is simply the product of our environment. Examining the things that have influence or a hold on us allows us to see things from God's point of view more clearly. This process allows our thinking to change to God's thinking, which is truly giving up something. When we think like God, we will act like God, and then anything is possible!

Father, show me everything that has influence over me that is not You so I can give it up. Change my thinking to be Yours.

Who is the Celebrity?

> *"Listen, you kings!*
> *Pay attention, you mighty rulers!*
> *For I will sing to the LORD.*
> *I will make music to the LORD, the God of Israel."*
> *Judges 5:3*

Deborah sang this song after defeating an enemy that ruthlessly oppressed the Israelites for 20 years. The victory was unusual because it was led by a woman. The woman was unusual because she was a judge. Women simply did not hold those kinds of positions or instigate battles in the Jewish culture at the time. Deborah must have been a celebrity. But notice that this song is not about how great Deborah was or about how greatly God worked through her. This song is about what God has done and how great He is. Deborah's only reference to herself is her commitment to Him. God is the celebrity in this song.

Christian music ministers can follow Deborah's example. We have a certain amount of celebrity status simply because we are musicians. People recognize us because we are up front, on stage. We may even hold positions within the church or the music community. But no matter how unusual or important other people think we are, we must consistently place the focus back on how great God is. We simply serve Him; we are human just like everyone else. We do some things really well and fail miserably at others. So, we cannot afford to allow people to place their faith in us. We can ask people to follow our example in our commitment to God. We can point out to everyone how God has worked in our lives. We can and should celebrate the victories of God but we must be very careful not to take God's glory for ourselves.

Father, examine my heart and show me where I take some of Your glory for myself. I want to lead people to follow You.

August 11
Enthusiastic Creation

"So, my dear brothers and sisters, be strong and immovable. Always work enthusiastically for the Lord, for you know that nothing you do for the Lord is ever useless."
1 Corinthians 15:58

Working a secular job can feel useless at times. In fact, some employers go out of their way to make sure employees feel useless so they will not feel justified in asking for a raise. Most employers do not want employees to do anything other than their specified job in the specified way. In other words, they do not want employees to work with creativity and enthusiasm because it will upset they system. We should not confuse working for God with working for a typical employer.

God loves us to think out of the box, to come up with new ideas and creations. Creativity is at the core of His being. Part of the problem with our creativity is that it does not always work; it is not always as successful as we want it to be. But God gives us permission, even encourages us, to try anyway. It takes courage and strength to risk working for God because He wants us to be fully engaged in the process. This means God does not usually prescribe the exact way we should do the work. He allows room for us to think creatively and come up with new ideas and methods. Some of those are bound to fail, but God uses our failures and mediocre attempts. He does not waste any of our efforts. This verse should give us the freedom to use all of our talents and abilities in new and innovative ways in music ministry because we know God will find a way to use them. We can find strength and remain immoveable in our calling as music ministers and continue to work with enthusiasm, fully engaged in the work, because we know that God uses everything we do for Him!

Father, thank You for the freedom to create and the knowledge that You use my work to further Your kingdom!

August 12
Popularity Competition

"When the victorious Israelite army was returning home after David had killed the Philistine, women from all the towns of Israel came out to meet King Saul. They sang and danced for joy with tambourines and cymbals. This was their song:
'Saul has killed his thousands,
and David his ten thousands!'"

1 Samuel 18:6-7

This song made Saul angry. David was a rising star; Saul was already the king but was worried that David would surpass him. He was jealous because David was becoming the most popular person in the kingdom. This jealousy was the beginning of Saul's demise. Eventually, he lost everything.

Christian music ministers face the possibility of becoming jealous at almost every show. There is always some other band or musician who seems to be more popular than us. They are gaining fans exponentially and their career is on the rise. They play out far more than us and sell more merchandise. After the show everyone is gathered around their table, waiting to talk to them. Or, worse yet, we used to be the popular band but now a new band is stealing our popularity. How do we react? We can learn from Saul or we can be like him. If we choose the path of jealousy, we will eventually forfeit our entire ministry. But if we choose to act like David, we will be a person after God's own heart. Look at how David treated Saul: he served in his army and household, doing everything he could to make Saul successful and prosperous. Even after Saul declared war against David, David still respected his office as king and refused to kill Saul. Are we treating other Christian bands with respect? Are we doing all that we can to help them be as successful as possible?

Father, remind me that I am not in a competition with my brothers. We serve You together to advance Your kingdom.

August 13
Safety First

"Do not stand idly by when your neighbor's life is threatened. I am the LORD."

Leviticus 19:16b

Life threatening situations are always frightening and often devastating. We see stories in the news about entire families and towns being affected when someone is lost. Life threatening situations do not only occur when one person threatens to kill another. More often, they look like accidents. Unfortunately, many of those situations could have been avoided. Too many of us take shortcuts without considering the potential consequences. Bands sometimes play in the seedier areas of town, and we generally know to watch out for equipment theft and to protect ourselves personally in those areas. But we are not usually as good at watching out for more common problems: drivers that fall asleep, and fires.

At the end of the day it is just too easy to fall asleep in the back seat on the way home from a gig and let someone else drive. When everyone in the vehicle does this, the driver is left to try to keep himself awake. Are a few extra hours of sleep worth yours or anyone else's life? People's lives are threatened, both in your vehicle and in the vehicle you could potentially hit, when no one stays awake to talk to the driver all the way home.

Fires can easily occur when we do not maintain and use the correct equipment, both in our vehicles and our gear. 'Being poor' is not an excuse to use broken cords or poorly maintained gear. 'Just because we can' is not an excuse to use equipment (especially pyrotechnics and candles) that does not have the appropriate fire rating for the venue. Bands work with electricity at every show. It is our responsibility to demonstrate love for others by using it correctly and safely.

Father, forgive me for not considering how many people I could be putting at risk by taking chances with safety.

Controlling Success

"Then he said to me, 'This is what the LORD says to Zerubbabel: It is not by force nor by strength, but by my Spirit, says the LORD of Heaven's Armies.'"

Zechariah 4:6

We can do all the right things in ministry and still not succeed in God's eyes. There are many books written about how to make your ministry better, larger, and more dynamic. There are more books written about how to succeed and earn a good income in the music industry. Include the blogs and assorted websites, and we are deluged with information about how to succeed in music ministry. We should read and apply as much of the available information as possible. We should work diligently. But in the end, if we are not carefully walking in synchronicity with what God is doing in our ministry, we will fail. God's Spirit, not our strength, gives us victory. God's Spirit, not our hard work, actually accomplishes the work of the ministry.

So, why do we stress so much? Because we are not allowing God to be in control. Every time we worry about money instead of asking God what He wants us to do, we are taking the responsibility upon ourselves to provide for our ministries. Every time we are discouraged because we have not booked enough good shows, we are taking it upon ourselves to decide which ministry is important enough to do. Whenever we are upset because of the number of ministry problems we have to constantly fix, we are taking over God's responsibility to provide for, heal, and protect. Before we act we need to ask: is this God's job or mine? Am I doing this job as He wants it done? When God is in control we may still do the same tasks, but we are not stressed—we walk in peace knowing that God gives the victory.

Father, my ministry is so important to me that I wrestle for control over it with You. Remind me who the better leader is.

August 15
Ministry in Trials & Sorrow

"I have told you all this so that you may have peace in me. Here on earth you will have many trials and sorrows. But take heart, because I have overcome the world."

John 16:33

Christian music ministers are not immune from trials and sorrows. One of the most difficult things we have to do is to perform on stage, and then do ministry off stage during times of trial or great sorrow. The audience, our fans, seems to demand too much at a time when we need comfort ourselves. We can grow bitter about being required to minister, we can avoid ministering, or we can minister while we are hurting. We want to continue our ministry, but truly ministering while we are hurting requires that we experience the overwhelming, supernatural peace of God. Peace during sorrow and trial is freely given by God, but not always so easily received by us.

Knowing ahead of time that Jesus said we will experience trails and sorrow helps us to remember that His love for us is not based on our current circumstances. The trials and hardship we experience is not a sign of His disapproval of our lives and our ministry. We have not necessarily done anything wrong. In fact, most often trials and hardships seem to come when we are doing many things right. In our emotions we may cry out, "God why is this happening to me? Haven't I been serving You well?" But in reality, how well we are doing in our ministry is not reflected in trials and sorrow that comes our way. This knowledge allows us to have peace, the peace that comes from knowing our relationship with God has not changed because trials and sorrow have come. This peace, a result of consistently walking in the love of God, allows us to minister in any circumstance.

Father, overwhelm me with Your love in the midst of the next trial or sorrow that comes my way. Teach me to have peace.

Where's Your Focus?

"So we don't look at the troubles we can see now; rather, we fix our gaze on things that cannot be seen. For the things we see now will soon be gone, but the things we cannot see will last forever."

2 Corinthians 4:18

There will always be problems in ministry: equipment and vehicles are going to break down, band members will struggle to get along with each other, the workload will be more than anyone wants to handle, and there will always be financial stress. We can get overwhelmed on any given day with the amount of work to do and decisions to make. Ministry is not easy. We can constantly think about the problems and the next thing we need to do, but that will leave us exhausted. If we keep that focus, eventually we will come to the conclusion that it just is not worth it and decide to quit doing music ministry. Of course, we tell ourselves that we would never do that because we are called to music ministry. But many musicians have done it before us; everyone has a breaking point. It is unrealistic to think that our enemy would not push us in the direction to get us to quit.

The way to defeat the enemy and to keep from quitting is to keep a check on what we fix our eyes on. We must deal with the troubles we have now, but we simply cannot afford to keep our main focus on them. We absolutely must fix our eyes on the unseen—Jesus and His kingdom. How can we tell when we are out of focus? When the troubles upset us, when we lose our temper and our peace, when we are so busy that we do not make time for relationship with God. During these times we may be fixing ministry problems, but we are actually playing into our enemy's hand and allowing him to win. If we catch ourselves doing this, we must refocus quickly back on our Father who loves us.

Father, immediately convict me when I focus on the troubles. Keep my spirit finely tuned to staying focused on You.

Biblically and Legally Right

"When they tied Paul down to lash him, Paul said to the officer standing there, 'Is it legal for you to whip a Roman citizen who hasn't even been tried?'"

Acts 22:25

The Bible is very clear that we are not to sue other believers in court. But it also has several examples, like this one, where Godly people use the law to defend themselves and others from the unlawful behavior of ungodly people. How should we use the law when it comes to music issues such as copyrights, royalties, and breach of contract? Do we have to simply live with whatever people and companies do to us? What about our responsibilities to live up to the contracts we sign? Legal questions and Biblical morality can be quite confusing and do not always agree with each other. How do we know what to do? We can simply view the situation from God's perspective. How will other people, especially un-believers, perceive God as a result of our actions? People and their relationships with God are always more important than us winning or losing.

We must use every tool in our arsenal to bring people closer to Jesus. When it comes to law, we must use it when people are being hurt, but we cannot use it to hurt others, especially other brothers and sisters in Christ. In times of anger and offense this line is difficult to discern. So, before we take any legal action, we must refocus back on Jesus. If the reputation of Jesus is besmirched by our actions, our actions are Biblically wrong even if they are legally right. If the reputation of Jesus is besmirched by our inaction, our inaction is wrong even if it is legally right. It's not about who has the best case to win in court. It is about who will do whatever it takes to please God.

Father, give me the courage to stand up for the rights of others and to lay down my own rights for You.

August 18

Turning the Tables

"For God has not given us a spirit of fear and timidity, but of power, love, and self-discipline."

2 Timothy 1:7

Fear is the one greatest thing that will keep us from doing what God wants us to do. Timidity will cause us to hesitate and procrastinate, often until it is too late. Fear and timidity are the two most powerful forces that hinder ministry. God did not create us to operate this way.

Creating and performing music is risky. We are never sure if we will please fans or not. There is always the potential to mess up in a big way. This risk can be an opportunity to fall prey to fear and timidity. Or we can use the scariness of it all to motivate us to operate in God's power. Fear that has been faced down and timidity that has been lost to action are inspirational to future victory because they demonstrate our power to overcome them. Are you facing fear now? Remember the last time you faced it and won! Are you timid now? Remember the last time you overcame it and how well things turned out!

Love can be a great motivator to overcome fear and timidity. We have all heard stories about people who have done heroic deeds because someone they loved was in danger. We can use this same principle. The love of people will cause us to do things we would otherwise not have the courage to do. Are you afraid to do a particular ministry task? Think about the people it will affect. Are you timid about risking exposing your art and yourself? Think about the impact it will have on the people God loves. It takes self-discipline to consistently face fear and timidity. But God has given us that too! We use self-discipline to recognize when we need to inspire ourselves with power and motivate ourselves with love. God created us to be overcomers!

Father, show me where fear and timidity are hindering my ministry. Teach me to walk in power, love and self-discipline.

August 19

Signs of the Times

"When you hear a sound like marching feet in the tops of the poplar trees, be on the alert! That will be the signal that the LORD is moving ahead of you to strike down the Philistine army."

2 Samuel 5:24

David defeated the Philistine army once using God's plan, but they came back. David could have implemented the same plan but because he was wise, he went back to God and asked what he should do this time. God gave him a different plan. The first time, God told David to go out and meet the enemy head on, and they won. But the second time, God told David to wait for a signal and then attack the enemy from behind. What if David had relied on his past experience and used the first plan the second time? The enemy would probably have known exactly what he would do and would have been prepared to defeat him. This story illustrates why we need to be consistently asking God for His plan and His timing as we lead our ministries. Relying on our past experience is not enough to be successful.

As the saying goes, "timing is everything." Implementing God's plan at the wrong time can be devastating. The modern church has often viewed asking God for a sign as evil. It is not. Asking God for a sign and God giving signs is throughout the Bible. Testing God by asking for a sign is wrong, but asking God for a sign so that we may be clear about His direction and timing is not. It is a heart issue: are we asking God for a sign in faith so that we may walk in complete obedience to Him, or are we asking for a sign in a defiant attitude? It is critical that we know God's timing for the seasons and activities of our ministry. He is willing to show us His plan and His timing for that plan. We must listen carefully and act when He leads us in the way He leads us.

Father, show me Your plan for this ministry and when You want me to implement it. Give me wisdom to seek You.

August 20

The Lord Has Helped Us

"Samuel then took a large stone and placed it between the towns of Mizpah and Jeshanah. He named it Ebenezer (which means "the stone of help"), for he said, 'Up to this point the LORD has helped us!'"

1 Samuel 7:12

Visual reminders and stories of a past victory can be great encouragement to us. When we are discouraged by present circumstances, it is right to remember how God triumphed for us in a similar circumstance. Throughout the Old Testament there are many stones set up and altars built in honor of a successful battle. But the stone Samuel set up here is different. It was not a stone of remembering one victorious battle; instead it was set up to remember everything God had done up to that point. He had been with them through many battles, as well as all the times in between. God was present and had helped them through times of distress, sickness, temptation, victory, wealth, disobedience, and when it seemed like nothing was happening or changing. God was present and helping in every aspect of their lives. This stone was set up to remind the people that surely, if God has endured through all of history with us, He will not abandon us now.

Often our most challenging times are not during great battles or feats or heroism. Many of us are more easily defeated by the in-between times of everyday life. The self-discipline to consistently do what we need to do to be healthy, the courage to make even small choices with integrity, the ever present struggle to walk in love, and feelings of insignificance can wear us down to utter discouragement. It is then that we need to remind ourselves most of everything that God has done up to this point, not just the spectacular wins. Perhaps God's greatest victory in the lives of most artists is to carry us through the mundane.

Father, give me inspiration to live this day well with Your help. Bring back memories of days we have been together.

August 21
Results from Obedience

"'Master,' Simon replied, 'we worked hard all last night and didn't catch a thing. But if you say so, I'll let the nets down again.' And this time their nets were so full of fish they began to tear!"

Luke 5:5-6

Simon had already worked hard, with all the right equipment, and at what should have been the right time and the right place. But still, he had nothing to show for it. Many of us experience the same lack of results in our ministries. We play show after show, write and rehearse song after song, and our audiences stay small. After a while we ask ourselves if music ministry really is what God has called us to do.

To find the answer, we should start by examining our obedience. Answer who, what, when, where, why, and how in light of what God wants for you. For example: Who has God called you to minister to? Simon was a fisherman who became extremely successful when he changed his focus from fish to men. What has God called you to do? Simon was called to lead the church, not run a fishing company. When should you take the next step toward your calling? Simon did not immediately start running the church; he took the next step by obediently casting his nets again. Where are you called to minister? Simon started out in the correct location, but eventually he was required to follow Jesus and then to relocate to Jerusalem. Why are you in ministry? Simon's motivation most likely was not the notoriety or money that came with leading the church; he simply wanted to be with Jesus. How should you go about ministry? Simon did exactly what Jesus asked—leave everything and follow Him. Most often, lack of ministry results can be traced back to lack of clarity and/or obedience in one or more of these areas.

Father, show me where and how I can follow Your plan for my ministry more closely.

August 22

Choosing Your Team

"One day soon afterward Jesus went up on a mountain to pray, and he prayed to God all night. At daybreak he called together all of his disciples and chose twelve of them to be apostles."

Luke 6:12-13a

Jesus did not randomly choose the apostles. Many people chose to follow Jesus. Some of those people chose to support His ministry by voluntarily helping and/or giving money. But out of all those people, Jesus only chose 12 to be in His closest circle. Jesus prayed all night before the final choice was made. Most likely, this was not His first conversation with the Father about who to choose. But the final decision was important enough to bring Jesus to many hours in prayer. Are we that careful when choosing whom we will work with in ministry?

Many band issues occur simply because we have chosen the wrong people to work with—either as band members, our professional team, or business partners such as labels and studios. Too often our heart to do great things in ministry gets ahead of our wisdom and discernment. Of course, we should avoid partnering with evil people. But most often the "wrong people" are not evil; they simply are not the best match for us at the time. Saying "no" to a potential new band member, manager, or label is not a bad thing. But, saying "yes" without wisdom or discernment can lead us out of God's plan for our ministry. The key is not to rush ahead of God because we see what looks like a great opportunity. We must choose our partners as carefully as Jesus chose His apostles, with much prayer. Getting God's advice is worth waiting for, even if we lose the person we thought was perfect for the position.

Father, I want to do great things in ministry, but I cannot do it alone. Send me the right people at the right time. Give me the wisdom and discernment to recognize who they are.

August 23
Not All At Once

"But I will not drive them out in a single year, because the land would become desolate and the wild animals would multiply and threaten you. I will drive them out a little at a time until your population has increased enough to take possession of the land."

Exodus 23:29-30

Many artists wonder why God allows us to struggle along, slowly building our careers and ministry. He could, after all, orchestrate the circumstances to make us an overnight success. One answer to God's perceived inaction might be found in this verse. Here, God is promising to drive out the enemies of the Israelites so they could expand and take over all the land He had promised them. But look how He clearly says that He will not do it all at once because the Israelites would be threatened.

Building our ministry a little at a time is not as exciting as becoming an overnight success. But many overnight successes do not stand the test of time. Often they fall apart personally and so we never hear from them after their first national release. The pressure on the unprepared is unexpected and intense. God does not want that for us. He wants us to succeed. He wants us to be established with a solid foundation in Him. Then we can do the ministry He has called us to do without giving in to the pressure and inflicting damage on ourselves or others. God is protecting us from threats and training us for greater future ministry by increasing our ministry only a little at a time. It is difficult not to be impatient with the process because we always think we are ready for more before we really are. But God knows the future and He knows what is best for us. So, instead of questioning, we should thank Him for looking out for us and for taking the time to train us for success.

Father, give me as much ministry success I can handle and train me for more. Thank you for not giving me too much.

The First Step

"Always be joyful. Never stop praying. Be thankful in all circumstances, for this is God's will for you who belong to Christ Jesus."

1 Thessalonians 5:16-18

These verses are nearly impossible to do all the time. There are simply some circumstances that do not encourage us to be joyful or thankful—when our vehicle breaks down on a road trip, when we are lost and late for a gig, when we do not have enough money to repair broken equipment, or when we have just made a huge mistake on stage. Who wants to be joyful or thankful about any of that? Many times we do not even want to pray because we know we will just end up complaining to God.

Christian music ministers have an advantage in these difficult situations—we know how to worship in song. Worship breaks through our focus on the situation and refocuses us back on God. Because the words and melodies of the songs are so familiar to us, we can sing them almost automatically, even when we do not feel like it. The words change us, even when we start singing simply out of habit. Our circumstances are much easier to change after we have changed. Sometimes God will intervene and sometimes we will simply be in a position to think more clearly to solve the problem. Either way, focusing on God's greatness and love for us instead of the problem is the place to start, and worship will get us refocused.

We do not have to feel joyful or thankful; we do not have to feel like praying. We do have to choose how we will respond to situations that cause us not to feel joyful, thankful, or like praying. We can respond in a way that moves us away from God or we can respond in a way that brings us closer to Him. Singing worship songs is always a step toward Him.

Father, when I am in difficult situations, remind me that how I respond is more important than the actual circumstance.

August 25
Get What They Pay For

"Your scales and weights must be accurate. Your containers for measuring dry materials or liquids must be accurate. I am the LORD your God who brought you out of the land of Egypt."

Leviticus 19:36

In Biblical times many different kinds of goods were sold by their weight. A merchant would negotiate with the buyer for a price based on that weight. This is very much like how we sell produce by the pound today. One way the merchant had to cut his costs a little and cheat the buyer was to use scales that were not quite balanced or containers which claimed to hold a certain weight but were actually slightly smaller, so the buyer would think he was getting more than he actually received. The merchant would keep small amounts of the product from each transaction, eventually selling more than he actually had. Technology and regulations has now made it almost impossible to cheat at weighing merchandise. But this principle still applies to us today. Are we giving the people who pay for our services and merchandise everything we said we would?

Some Christian bands feel that because they are a ministry, it is OK to deliver less than what the buyer anticipated, especially since we rarely are paid well. We consider this to be hype or good salesmanship. But the principle in this verse would imply that we need to do everything we said we would do without leading the buyer to believe they are getting more than what they actually receive. When we are booking shows, do you exaggerate the number of people who will probably show up to see you? Is your press kit fairly representing your ministry? Did you cut corners on the quality of your merchandise? Be honest in your business dealings because you represent God.

Father, reveal the ways that I am not being honest in my business dealings. I want to represent You with integrity.

August 26

Speak Up for the Oppressed

"Speak up for those who cannot speak for themselves;
ensure justice for those being crushed."
Proverbs 31:8

Many Christian bands partner with a nonprofit organization to raise awareness for a cause. This is a win-win situation. The organization receives more recognition and donations than it would have without the band's partnership; the bands usually receive a small payment for their fundraising efforts plus a few extra booking leads with churches that support the organization. These kinds of partnerships go against the training of the world, which says that for someone to win someone else has to lose. In God's kingdom, doing what is right often causes everyone to win. The people who receive services from the organization win, the organization receives more money than it would otherwise so it wins, and the people giving the money are blessed to give—all because the band does what is right and speaks up for the oppressed.

Some people have said that the band is wrong for taking payments for their efforts. People who say that do not realize that most nonprofit organizations spend a significant amount of their income and staff time raising enough money to pay their bills. It is far more cost effective both in freeing up staff time and in money it costs to do fundraising for them to work with bands. Bands have access to people the organization normally would not. So, do not let uniformed opinions sway your decision to help the oppressed. Doing what is right should create a win-win situation for everyone—including your ministry. Research the best organizations to work with carefully and then do your very best to use the bands platform to speak up for the oppressed.

Father, guide our decision about which organizations to work with when we are speaking up for the oppressed.

Listening

"At this, Abram fell face down on the ground. Then God said to him, 'This is my covenant with you: I will make you the father of a multitude of nations!'"

Genesis 17:3-4

Wouldn't it be great to hear a promise like this from God about your ministry? We would all love to have God promise us that our ministry will impact people for generations to come. So often we focus on the last part of these verses. But look at Abrams position—on his face before God. This position signifies reverence and submission. In other words Abram was physically demonstrating that God's presence was more important than anything else going on in his life. God was speaking and Abram was listening with all his being, blocking out all other distractions, intent on doing whatever God said.

If we expect to hear God's promises about our ministry we must spend time in submitted reverence with God. We must listen. We must place a priority on taking the time to listen and then we must remove everything that would distract us, so that we can hear clearly. Learning to listen does not occur quickly. It takes practice and time. So often, we want to hurry up and be doing something, anything. We want to speed up the process, to catapult over the tough places and move on to the next thing. We see what we think is the end goal and we want to go for it. But that is not God's way. He desires relationship with us far more than achieving our goals. In that relationship we must acknowledge our proper place: to always be longing to hear what He has to say and to make the time to hear Him say it. It would be such a shame to lose out on a blessing for our ministry because we were too busy doing ministry to listen to God.

Father, I desire to hear You speak more than anything else. Teach me to listen to hear Your voice clearly and frequently.

August 28
Motivated by Compassion

"Jesus saw the huge crowd as he stepped from the boat, and he had compassion on them because they were like sheep without a shepherd. So he began teaching them many things."
Mark 6:34

At this point in ministry, Jesus and His disciples were exhausted. Just a few verses prior to this one Jesus said, "Let's go off by ourselves to a quiet place and rest awhile." Because there were so many people coming and going, neither Jesus nor His disciples had time to eat. But when they left by boat, people followed them. Tired, hungry, and ready for a rest—what motivated Jesus to continue to do ministry? Compassion. Compassion is identifying with the distress of others and doing something about it. Feeling compassion causes us to act compassionately. This feeling and action is one of the main characteristics of Jesus' ministry.

Christian music ministers are often tired and hungry. We tend to work very long days (and nights) and do not get fed at regular intervals. Sometimes it is very difficult to spend time talking to yet another fan at the end of a gig when all we want is food and a bed. How do we motivate ourselves to push through, to stay completely engaged in ministry until there is no more ministry to be done? We can be like Jesus: look at the people, feel compassion for them, and then act on that compassion. We do not know the circumstances of our fans' lives. It could be that the kind words they receive from us will be the only kindness they experience all week. Our ministry could prevent their suicide or their harming another person. We never know fully what God has done through us. We do know that God has called us to represent Him on earth and that Jesus showed compassion.

Father, move me with compassionate love. Break my heart for people. Give me Your words to say to bring them life.

Plotting to Get Ahead

"He replied, 'As you know, the kingdom was rightfully mine; all Israel wanted me to be the next king. But the tables were turned, and the kingdom went to my brother instead; for that is the way the LORD wanted it. So now I have just one favor to ask of you. Please don't turn me down.' 'What is it?' she asked. He replied, 'Speak to King Solomon on my behalf, for I know he will do anything you request. Ask him to let me marry Abishag, the girl from Shunem.'"

1 Kings 2:15-17

Adonijah (one of the sons of David) admitted that the Lord wanted Solomon to be king. But he would not submit himself to God's plan. Adonijah plotted to put himself on the throne instead of Solomon. He rallied people behind him by acting like he was king while David was still alive. He was a master of political intrigue. Even after Solomon was declared king, Adonijah asked for the one girl's hand in marriage that would strengthen his position to be able to overthrow Solomon. Did God have a plan that would have blessed Adonijah without him being king? Absolutely. But Adonijah was not satisfied with God's plan and he was willing to hurt Solomon to get ahead.

What are we willing to do to get ahead in the music industry? Who are we willing to step over to get to where we feel we need to be? Do we manipulate shows for 'the best' time slots? Do we infer things about other bands to build our band up? We need to learn from Adonijah. God places people and ministries where he wants them to be. Our goal must be to stay in line with God's plans rather than trying to get ahead through our schemes. Submitting to God's plan will always involve us blessing our brothers rather than competing with them.

Father, I want to pursue only Your plan. Show me where I am scheming to get ahead so I can repent.

August 30
Kingdom Building

> *"May your Kingdom come soon.*
> *May your will be done on earth,*
> *as it is in heaven."*
>
> **Matthew 6:10**

When we say "Your kingdom come," we must understand the necessity of our kingdom being undone. Two kings cannot reign on the same throne at the same time. So, in order for God's kingdom to reign, for His will to be done on earth, our kingdom and our will must be thwarted. Every time we pray this prayer, we are saying that we want to die to ourselves so that that God will prevail; a lofty spiritual principle that affects us daily.

Music ministers have the opportunity to build mini kingdoms. Simply by being on stage we are lifted to a position of respect and admiration. Our fans' admiration leads us to a trap of false pride and power; the bigger our fan base, the bigger our kingdom and the larger the trap. We must wrestle daily with remembering whose kingdom we are trying to build and who is King. One of the best ways to gauge where we stand in that battle is our level of peace. Are we satisfied with the level of ministry God has given us or do we constantly strive to get "better shows"? Are we doing the very best we can with what we have been given, or have we thrown up our hands in frustration saying that we cannot possibly grow the ministry with these tools? While it is certainly part of our job to plan for growth and to purchase the equipment we need to facilitate that growth, we have gone too far when our disgruntled attitude causes us to lose out on today's ministry opportunities. Our dissatisfaction can show us that we are attempting to build our ministry, our kingdom rather than coming into line with God's will to build His kingdom. We must die so that God's will can be done in us.

Father, reveal to me wherever and whenever I am building my own kingdom. Help me to die to myself so I can do Your will.

August 31
Dangerous Strongholds

"One day the prophet Gad told David, 'Leave the stronghold and return to the land of Judah.' So David went to the forest of Hereth."

1 Samuel 22:5

A stronghold is a place where people can run to in times of trouble, hide, defend easily, and rest. It is often used as a defensive position in between battles. Strongholds can be a good thing to have and a great place to be. But if the occupants stay there too long, it is very likely the enemy will discover where they are and attack. Staying in a stronghold too long can become stifling as all the warriors enjoy the comfort of too much sleeping and eating. Even if the enemy does not discover where they are, the occupants can become lax in their battle and begin to lower their defenses. The warriors become weak.

God brings people through seasons of being in strongholds, safe, sheltered, and comfortable. He also brings ministries through stronghold times. These are the fun, exciting, and successful times that everyone wants to remain in forever. But, eventually we must leave the comfortable situations we have grown accustomed to and fight our way to the next level. It is not easy to push forward. It is much easier to stay where we are. Even more difficult is to decide when we are to stay, when we are to move on, and where we are to move on to. No two situations are the same, so relying on our past experiences or what other people have done will not guarantee that we will be in the right place at the right time. We must be led by God. It is interesting in this verse that David was directed to go to Judah, which means praise. From there God directed Him to other, new battles. Perhaps we also need to start in the place of praise when we need discernment for the direction of our ministries.

Father, I must have Your wisdom to know when and where this ministry should go next. Show us Your plan.

September 1

Regardless of the Results

"Shadrach, Meshach, and Abednego replied, 'O Nebuchadnezzar, we do not need to defend ourselves before you. If we are thrown into the blazing furnace, the God whom we serve is able to save us. He will rescue us from your power, Your Majesty. But even if he doesn't, we want to make it clear to you, Your Majesty, that we will never serve your gods or worship the gold statue you have set up.'"

Daniel 3:16-18

What happens when we take a stand for God and then do not get the results we were expecting? What do we do when it seems like God has let us down, especially after we sacrificed for Him? The correct answer, of course, is very clear to us until we actually face the situation. When we do not get the anticipated results, we start questioning our actions. While results can be an indicator to help us find the best direction for our ministry, making decisions based exclusively on results is dangerous.

Discernment about what God is saying regarding the decisions we need to make is the key to doing His will. Sometimes the decisions are obvious because they either fall in line with or violate God's perfect will, such as not worshipping false idols as commanded by the king. Other times the decisions are not as obvious because our own rationalizations come in to play. For example, what if not many people came to our shows? Gaining a large fan base requires the band to be popular, and so we decide to switch music styles to play what is most popular. This may not be God's will for us at all; it may even thwart His plan for the success of our ministry with a particular target audience. It seemed logical to us, but because we did not exercise discernment, we bowed down to the idol of popularity. We must clearly hear God's directions before making decisions.

Father, help me to focus on Your plan, not on the results.

September 2
Gifts to Help

"God works in different ways, but it is the same God who does the work in all of us. A spiritual gift is given to each of us so we can help each other."
1 Corinthians 12:6-7

God has not gifted everyone to be a musician. You can often pick musicians out of a crowd because of how they look and act even when they do not have an instrument in their hands; they are showing some of the symptoms of their gifting. In the same way, other people show some of their gifts by how they look and act. Paying attention to other people's gifts is one of the best ways to find the right people to help your ministry.

Many ministries make the mistake of hiring a friend. We also tend to hire people that are similarly gifted to ourselves. This person may not have any of the gifts needed for the particular job that needs to be done. Often what we really need is someone completely different from us in gifts and personality. If we were good at doing the job needing to be done, we would not be looking for someone else to do it.

When looking for someone to help with your ministry, start by defining the job that needs to be done. Then identify the type of gifts and personality that a person should have to do that job really well. After that, pay attention to the people who already support your ministry. It is probable that the person you need is already involved. Identifying the specific gifts that people have been given by God and matching those gifts to the work that needs to be done will give the person hired the greatest opportunity to succeed. They will be doing what God has called and gifted them to do. Choosing the wrong person, based on their need, your friendship, or your need to fill a position quickly will set them up to fail and cause friction within your ministry.

Father, make me aware of other people's gifts so we can mutually help each other.

September 3
Deadly Weapons

> *"Just as damaging*
> *as a madman shooting a deadly weapon*
> *is someone who lies to a friend*
> *and then says, 'I was only joking.'"*
> Proverbs 26:18-19

Most bands joke around with each other. We build relationships and camaraderie by playing together. But, covering up a lie by saying we were joking is not the same thing. The problem is that we lied in the first place. Then we lied again by claiming it was a joke. We might be able to get away with it with people who do not know us well, but band mates know each other better than the closest friends. We know when each other is lying. We know it is wrong to do, but sometimes do it anyway in an attempt cover embarrassment and to save face.

Vulnerability between band members is critical because we do not simply work together—we are ministry partners. Trust is one of the most important traits in band relationships. Lying destroys trust, and then trying to cover it up proves that saving face is more important to us than our friendship. Unfortunately because of the friendship and the drive to create a successful band, band members may put up with the lying for a while. So, the liar thinks they have gotten away with something and continues to lie. Eventually people will be hurt, sometimes to the point that the relationship cannot be saved.

If we saw a madman shooting a deadly weapon, we would take action to stop it. We need to do the same with band members who lie. Of course, we need to confront the issue with love and sensitivity, but we must stop the lying to keep all the people involved in the ministry from being wounded.

Father, help me to recognize and to confront lying. Give me to courage to protect our friendships and the ministry.

September 4
Remain in Fellowship

"But you have received the Holy Spirit, and he lives within you, so you don't need anyone to teach you what is true. For the Spirit teaches you everything you need to know, and what he teaches is true—it is not a lie. So just as he has taught you, remain in fellowship with Christ."

1 John 2:27

We generally know what is true and right to do. But as we mature in our faith, we tend to start thinking that the basic disciplines do not apply to us because we have the faith to believe for the exceptional. So, we create messes, then we wonder why God did not back us up with the exceptional result. But, exceptions are just that: unusual, not normal results. There will be times when God does the exceptional in our ministry, but it will not be the normal way we should live. We simply cannot view ourselves as the exception for everything. Most of the time, God works through the natural laws and principles He set up.

How do we know when God is going to do something exceptional? We discern what He is saying. The Holy Spirit has already spent a great deal of time teaching us God's laws and principles. We can trust that what He has taught us is true in our specific circumstance. For example, we know that debt is not God's best for us. So, when we want new equipment and do not have the money, it is best to assume that we should not charge that equipment. We apply the Scripture we already know rather than assuming we are the exception. It could be that God does want us to have the equipment but He is making another way for us to get it, such as a gift or a fundraiser. This is why we must remain in fellowship with Him—not to make ourselves the exception to the rule but to clearly hear God's plan for what He wants to accomplish through us and how He wants to do it.

Father, help me to apply Your principles that I already know and listen to how You want to accomplish Your work in me.

September 5
Ambition & Contentment

"Not that I was ever in need, for I have learned how to be content with whatever I have."

Philippians 4:11

Ambition can be a good characteristic, but when it is taken too far it can kill a ministry. We have heard the sermons about living in a first world country vs. a third world country. We know that we are among the richest people on earth so we should be content with the things we have and even give more. But have you ever heard a sermon about being content and fully engaged with the ministry God has placed you in right now? In the western world we do not hear much about that because we are trained to always aspire to do more. How many ministry opportunities have we lost out on, how many people could we have helped, but we did not because we were chasing a bigger dream at that moment? How often are we playing the political game when we should be ministering?

Band members are particularly tempted with this issue because there are many more bands than there are places to play. After the show we have a tendency to make sure we socialize with the promoter or booker. While this is not necessarily bad, after the show is our prime time to minister to fans. Do we always meet the needs of every person in the room before we attempt to get re-booked? Do we seek out the hurting, or do we seek out the promoter? How do we act if there is a talent scout in the room? This ambitious attitude of constantly focusing on expanding and moving up the ladder rather than being content to pursue ministry with the people right in front of us permeates many aspects of our ministry because it originates in our hearts. Our hearts need to change.

Father, do not let my heart deceive me. Show me every area that I fall short of pure motives for doing Christian music.

September 6
Stories to Grow Faith

"We think you ought to know, dear brothers and sisters, about the trouble we went through in the province of Asia. We were crushed and overwhelmed beyond our ability to endure, and we thought we would never live through it. In fact, we expected to die. But as a result, we stopped relying on ourselves and learned to rely only on God, who raises the dead. And he did rescue us from mortal danger, and he will rescue us again. We have placed our confidence in him, and he will continue to rescue us."

2 Corinthians 1:8-10

We have easy access to everything we need and most of the things we want. So, we know what it is to rely on ourselves. In fact, we are taught that being self-reliant is a very good thing. But God's plan for us is to trust Him to be in control of every aspect of our lives and ministry. Although it goes against our very nature, Christians must make an effort to learn to rely on God.

God helps us along in the process by allowing us to be placed in situations that are out of our control, which we cannot fix by ourselves. Often those situations seem like hindrances to our ministry: our vehicle breaks down in the middle of nowhere, equipment malfunctions, band members get sick at the last minute, we run out of gas money, and key shows on a tour get cancelled. Situations that are out of our control teach us to rely on God. These situations may be emotional, extremely difficult, uncomfortable, and even embarrassing at times. But, we can go beyond simply growing in faith ourselves by using those stories to encourage other people, just as Paul did in these verses. It is important to tell these stories. We can encourage our fans and members from other bands to grow in their reliance on God with our stories of learning to rely on God and God rescuing us.

Father, teach me to rely on You instead of myself and how to share the stories of Your faithfulness to encourage others.

September 7
Worthy Sacrifices

"If you refuse to take up your cross and follow me, you are not worthy of being mine."

Matthew 10:30

God often asks us to sacrifice more than what we want to do. Christian music ministers are constantly asked to live on others people's schedules; we work hard to make it to gigs on time only to find that the venue is not ready for us. "Hurry up and wait" is a way of life. We are paid little for our services and then asked to go over and above in ministry. People steal from us with illegal downloads and the same people ask us to pray for them. There is never enough money, or time to spend with our family and friends. Music ministry is hard. We must continually die to what we want and think is best for the privilege of playing in less than ideal circumstances. We have to spend our own money and take time away from our family to do ministry. It is no wonder we sometimes have bad attitudes. We sacrifice more than most people imagine.

We could constantly think about all the sacrifices we make. We could bring them to God's remembrance every time we pray. We could use our sacrifices to justify our worthiness in our minds. Or we could simply ask, "Is God worthy of the sacrifices He asks me to make?" Suddenly, our sacrifices do not seem so large. Our God laid down His life for us, so He is more than worthy of any sacrifice He may ask of us. Anything we do cannot possibly make us worthy enough to be in His presence. He must give us His worthiness so that we can have relationship with Him. "When we display our righteous deeds, they are nothing but filthy rags" (Isaiah 64:6b). So, how do we endure hardship, continually die to our own desires, and sacrifice with joy? We remember that He is worthy of anything we can do for Him.

Father, remind me to focus on Your worthiness rather than my sacrifices. Show me what more I can do for You.

September 8
The Lord is Here

"For you said, 'The lands of Israel and Judah will be ours. We will take possession of them. What do we care that the LORD is there!'"

Ezekiel 35:10

Edom wanted Israel and Judah. It looked like an easy conquest, because at that time their land was desolate as a result of Israel and Judah not completely following God's commands. Edom did not care that God considered the Jews to be His people; they did not care about God at all. So, Edom lost the battle when God rose up and defended His people.

Consider how much this situation is like our own situations at times, especially in ministry. We are called to be God's chosen people, His music ministers. But we do not always walk in obedience to Him. We often fail to do ministry in the way He wants, when He wants, and with pure motives. We reap the consequences of our disobedience, often in circumstances that could have been better. So, our ministry sometimes looks desperate—like desolate land, an easy conquest, to other people. They concoct schemes to take advantage of a band that needs money. They attempt to buy equipment for pennies on the dollar, pay us nothing to play shows, and offer bad contracts. It is nice to know that God defended the Jews even as He was disciplining them. Time after time they did not live up to His expectations, and time after time He rescued them. We might make many mistakes in our ministry that do not bring honor to God. Our ministries may appear week because we reap the consequences of our sin. But God is still present. Our enemies might not take God into account by respecting us because we belong to Him. But God will always claim us as His own children. We do not have to fall prey to our enemy, even when we sin and make mistakes in ministry, if we run to our Father.

Father, I am humbled that You stay with me even when I sin.

September 9
Faithfulness and Betrayal

"Give the following instructions to the people of Israel: If any of the people—men or women—betray the LORD by doing wrong to another person, they are guilty."

Numbers 5:6

"Betray the Lord by doing wrong to another person"—that is strong language. As we read further along, we discover that doing wrong to another person is not limited to physically harming their body, but includes harming them in any way. How would we act differently if we truly believed that harming any other person was betraying God? We would live much more carefully and thoughtfully as we considered the impact of our lives even on people in other countries that we will never meet. Donating to missions, living green, and buying local are some of the more popular applications of making sure that we do not harm other people. Those smaller decisions matter, but what about the larger decisions we make? Does withholding our gifts and not living up to our full potential in Christ hurt people?

While the Old Testament laws certainly would not have required us to make restitution, not living up to our potential can hurt people who we could have led closer to Jesus. When we do not help people because we are bowing down to the idols of selfishness, laziness, or self-absorption, we are betraying God. Every unwritten song, every gig we did not play, every prayer we did not pray, every encouragement we did not give had the potential to change a life. On the flip side, every time we help another person we prove our faithfulness to God. Do we want God to know us as an adulterous, betraying wife or as a faithful wife who looks for ways to demonstrate her love?

Father, burn into my heart that how I treat people is I how I treat You. Show me how to use every part of my being to help people by living up to my full potential in You.

September 10
Relationship and Ministry

"Though the fig tree does not bud
and there are no grapes on the vines,
though the olive crop fails
and the fields produce no food,
though there are no sheep in the pen
and no cattle in the stalls,
yet I will rejoice in the LORD,
I will be joyful in God my Savior."
Habakkuk 3:17-18

There are several reasons why trees do not bud, grapevines do not have grapes, crops fail, and animals die. Sometimes it is simply not the correct season for crops to produce or animals to reproduce, or other times it is a result of drought or poor management. Christian music ministries can experience similar situations: no money, no shows, no new music, or no fans. The reasons for those experiences can also be similar: it is simply not God's timing, some extraordinary circumstance is affecting our ministry, or poor management. We must deal with these kinds of problems from time to time, often repeatedly throughout our ministry. As we are going through the problems, are we still rejoicing and joyful in the Lord?

Most of us find this extremely difficult to do. Because we work for the Lord, we have a hard time separating our personal walk with Him from His ministry. We love doing His Christian music ministry and He loves for us to do it. But that is not the same as our love for Him and His love for us. Doing the work is a result of, not the same as, personally experiencing the love. We can rejoice and be joyful in spite of the problems that occur in ministry because our relationship with Him remains intact.

Father, Your love is the most important aspect of my life. Cause me to seek out Your love during problems and troubles.

September 11
Light Winds

"When a light wind began blowing from the south, the sailors thought they could make it. So they pulled up anchor and sailed close to the shore of Crete."

Acts 27:13

The soldiers were attempting to transport Paul to Rome. They had already had a difficult time because the winds were against them. Light winds from the south were exactly what they wanted and needed to complete their task. There should have been nothing wrong with following the wind, according to the captain of the ship it was the right thing to do, except that Paul had already warned them not to do it. What does sailing have to do with us? We all want smooth sailing with light winds and beautiful days. But how many times have we gotten what we thought we wanted, what seemed logical to do, only to have it blow into a disastrous storm? How can we avoid that?

Christian artists are constantly being told what is right to do. Some of the advice genuinely seems good and logical for our situation. But we cannot simply apply what we think is right without consulting with God first. We must be led by God even when applying what is logical and reasonable to do. The biggest problem we have with being led by God is when we listen to our hearts instead of being guided by the Spirit. It is very difficult to hear clearly from God when our hearts desire something very strongly. Then, when logic also lines up with what our hearts desire, we have a tendency to go ahead. When we see a light wind, our hearts desire is to go in the direction of the wind, logic and our counselors tell us to go ahead—that we can make it. In this situation, the test is not in what we decide to do; the test is if we can set it all aside and inquire of God before taking action.

Father, lead me by Your Spirit. Teach me to follow the peace that comes from Your Spirit rather than following my heart.

September 12
Remain in Me

"Remain in me, and I will remain in you. For a branch cannot produce fruit if it is severed from the vine, and you cannot be fruitful unless you remain in me."
John 15:4

Just as a branch cannot produce fruit without the vine, we cannot expect results from our ministry without the presence of God. God's presence works on the hearts of people. We can do the tasks of ministry and relate our experience with Him, but we cannot change hearts. It is the vine which creates and produces fruit. The branch allows the sap of the vine to flow through it and support the new fruit. We must allow God's presence to flow through us so we can nourish and support those we minister to.

The key to having God's presence in our ministry is found at the beginning of this verse, "remain in me." Remaining in God is a moment-by-moment choice. The instant we decide to step out in our own power, we have chosen to move away from Him. It is a heart issue that most of the time will not be detected by other people right away. We can do the works of ministry without God's presence simply because we already know the right tasks to do and the rights words to say. We may even be able to work the system well enough to become successful and famous. But the power of God's presence will not follow us and our ministries will have no fruit. Remaining in God as a choice is much more difficult to do when we already know what we need to do in ministry. Relying on His presence daily after we have attained a measure of success in ministry is the mark of a mature Christian. Pushing toward Him and striving to run after His presence daily is the mark of a ministry that will be used to produce an abundance of fruit!

Father, give me a hunger to seek Your presence. Increase my thirst for You. Flow through me as I do Your ministry.

September 13
Use All Your Gifts

"In his grace, God has given us different gifts for doing certain things well. So if God has given you the ability to prophesy, speak out with as much faith as God has given you. If your gift is serving others, serve them well. If you are a teacher, teach well. If your gift is to encourage others, be encouraging. If it is giving, give generously. If God has given you leadership ability, take the responsibility seriously. And if you have a gift for showing kindness to others, do it gladly."

Romans 12:6-8

Christian musicians are often extremely gifted people. The gift of music stands out because people see it every time we play. Our musical talent is so prominent that many people cannot see beyond the one gift. So, we frequently get pigeon-holed into only doing music. But God has most often given us more than one gift, talent, or ability. It is not enough to use only the gift of music well to the detriment of developing our other gifts.

Picture a child opening his presents at a birthday party. There is always one toy that gets immediate attention. This toy is played with even before all the other gifts are unwrapped. The gift givers know that eventually all the gifts will be opened, but their gifts may be stored, unused in a toy box. Whenever a gift is given but not used, the gift giver experiences disappointment. Is that how we want to treat our ultimate gift giver, God?

God does not randomly give gifts. He chooses which gift to give each person carefully. When God gives gifts, it is for the benefit of the whole body of Christ. If we are not using all the gifts He has given us, the body is missing out. Be an excellent musician, but do not allow yourself to be defined only by your gift of music. Use all your other gifts just as excellently.

Father, thank You for Your gifts to me. Show me how to use all of them well to help grow Your kingdom.

September 14
Sabbath was Made for People

"And let us not neglect our meeting together, as some people do, but encourage one another, especially now that the day of his return is drawing near."
Hebrews 10:25

Some Christians use this verse as an argument for why members of Christian bands must be in church every Sunday morning. Even if we do not interpret the verse exactly that way, it often leads Christian band members to feel guilty for not being in church and to feel judged by church-going people. Band members are pressured to turn down late night gigs on Saturdays or to go to church Sunday morning with little or no sleep Saturday night. Often, these same band members are expected to play on church worship teams Sunday morning. It is a tough way to live—choosing between judgment, guilt, and sleep.

Look at the center of this verse: "but encourage one another." Are the guilt, judgment, and lack of sleep encouraging? Perhaps instead of giving in to expectations and judgment we should be applying Mark 2:27 "Then Jesus said to them, "The Sabbath was made to meet the needs of people, and not people to meet the requirements of the Sabbath." Of course, it is best to attend church regularly and we should volunteer and help out using all our gifts and skills, but not at the expense of our personal Sabbath's rest. Meeting together and encouraging one another does not only happen in church on Sunday morning. We must stay in fellowship with God and with His people, but we also must allow ourselves time to rest. Finding the appropriate balance between church and band ministry is a personal decision for each band member. That decision must not be made based on other people's expectations, but on our relationship with God. He will lead us to do what we need to do, when we need to do it.

Father, speak clearly to me about my church involvement and attendance. Give me wisdom to know when to rest.

September 15

Timing is Everything

"Now Sarai, Abram's wife, had not been able to bear children for him. But she had an Egyptian servant named Hagar. So Sarai said to Abram, 'The LORD has prevented me from having children. Go and sleep with my servant. Perhaps I can have children through her.' And Abram agreed with Sarai's proposal. So Sarai, Abram's wife, took Hagar the Egyptian servant and gave her to Abram as a wife. (This happened ten years after Abram had settled in the land of Canaan.)"

Genesis 16:1-3

We are always in a hurry to see the promises of God happen in our lives and ministries. We want to see God's hand at work so badly that when it does not come to pass right away we wonder if we have done something wrong, or if we are somehow inadequate for God to work through us. We often think there is something more we could or should be doing. So, in our desire to see God working in our lives, we try to help God. As Sarai experienced, the results of our efforts can be devastating.

When God makes a promise or gives us an idea of what He wants to do through us, the end result does not usually occur immediately. God gives us a vision of the future to inspire us and give us courage and determination through the difficult times. God seems to savor the process of having relationship with us while we are preparing for our future. We tend to want to achieve the end results instantly, whether we are prepared or not. But God wants us to build a solid foundation now so that we will not fail in the future. We are often in a hurry to get to the future and we arrive unprepared. We lose some of God's best blessings this way. We do not have to be in a hurry; we do not have to get ahead of God. We simply have to walk with Him.

Father, reveal where I am using my own efforts to get ahead of You in my ministry. I want only Your will in Your time.

September 16
The True Riches of Heaven

"If you are faithful in little things, you will be faithful in large ones. But if you are dishonest in little things, you won't be honest with greater responsibilities. And if you are untrustworthy about worldly wealth, who will trust you with the true riches of heaven?"

Luke 16:10-11

The concept of these verses is easy—faithful in little, faithful in much and vice versa. But, have you considered what the true riches of heaven are? This verse implies it is more than worldly wealth. Imagine being quite wealthy by the world's standards. Then, consider how much more the riches of heaven must be. This begs the question, "What does God value more than all the wealth of the world?" The answer to this must be the "true riches of heaven." There is only one time God paid for or purchased anything—when Jesus died on the cross. What did He buy? People. Could it be that human beings are the "true riches of heaven"? Are people the thing that God places more value on than anything else? Jesus' life and death would suggest that the answer to that question is "Yes".

Now look at how you have been faithful in what God considers the little things: how you handle money, how truthful you have been, how you use your talents. Then look at the number of people God has entrusted to your care, the true riches of heaven. There is probably a direct correlation. Do you want your ministry to expand? Do you want to impact more people's lives? It starts with being faithful in "the little things," proving your trustworthiness with worldly wealth. Continue to be reliable and honest in your current responsibilities, and then you will be given more people to love and lead.

Father, I want You to be proud of me, my faithfulness, and my honesty in little things. Show me where I need to improve so that I can expand my ministry to impact more people.

September 17
Don't Give Up

"Five different times the Jewish leaders gave me thirty-nine lashes. Three times I was beaten with rods. Once I was stoned. Three times I was shipwrecked. Once I spent a whole night and a day adrift at sea. I have travelled on many long journeys. I have faced danger from rivers and from robbers. I have faced danger from my own people, the Jews, as well as from the Gentiles. I have faced danger in the cities, in the deserts, and on the seas. And I have faced danger from men who claim to be believers but are not."

2 Corinthians 11:24-26

Paul was a man who certainly knew about persistence. Most of us will never endure the hardships he went through to preach the Gospel. We all have hardships in ministry. Sometimes they are financial, but often they are difficult circumstances and people. Our hearts get broken, our bodies get tired, and our spirits get weak. It's all part of serving God.

Look at Paul's life and you will see that God was doing something with each hardship he endured. Sometimes He sent people to help Paul, other times angels. Still other times He arranged circumstances to benefit the furtherance of the Gospel. But through it all, God was participating in Paul's ministry.

Secular musicians may live the rock star life of parties and fun, but as Christian music ministers we expect times of trials and hardships. Musicians find another line of work when the fun and parties are over. Christian music ministers don't quit because our ministry has been tempered through difficult times. We have experienced God's hand actively working in our ministries and we know He will do it again! We never quit.

Father, I remember times that You have done something in my ministry through hardship. I may not understand what You are doing now, but I won't give up or quit.

When No One is Looking

"The LORD detests people with crooked hearts,
but he delights in those with integrity."
Proverbs 11:20

Integrity is doing what is right because it is right. We all pretty much understand this concept. But do we do it? Really? There are many areas that we are great at applying integrity and other areas we let slide, just a little. Most often we let things go a little astray in areas we don't think are important. Note that God did not say He detests people with EVIL hearts; He detests people with CROOKED hearts—hearts that are just a little off.

Here are some common examples we get a little crooked as musicians. We need to cause a stir about out music, but in an attempt to create that stir, do we exaggerate our numbers? How many people really showed up at your last concert? How many CDs have you actually sold (not just given away)? What about our taxes? Have you filed them correctly, including all your music income? Did you collect and pay sales taxes for merchandise sold? Do you have receipts for ALL your expenses? Are you actually endorsed by the company your press kits says you are, or do you just use their products? Were you on time for the last band practice? The list is endless because there are endless opportunities to demonstrate integrity, or not.

Integrity does not just happen; it requires looking at ourselves and areas of our lives that no one else sees. Integrity is going to cost you. It will cost money and time, and require humility. But God delights in our integrity. How far would you go to make God happy? What would you be willing to do? God's blessings are so critical to me that I would rather pay the price for integrity in every area than risk losing His favor.

Father, I want to have integrity in EVERY area of my life.
Reveal the places that I need to improve and I will do it.

When All is Said and Done

"Let everything that breathes sing praises to the LORD!
Praise the LORD!"

Psalm 150:6

So much of what we do as musicians involves singing praise. We would not want it to be any other way; we love to praise the Lord with music! It is wonderful to know that God wants us to praise Him. Sometimes the will of God might be hard to follow, but doing this one thing brings joy our hearts.

It is interesting that this is the last chapter, the last verse of the entirety of Psalms and "Praise the Lord" is repeated twice, as if to say, "When all is said and done, what is important is to praise the Lord." The book of Psalms encompasses the human condition: the good, the bad, and the ugly. This book explores David's heart as he lives through his life's circumstances, which can often be similar to ours. At the end and in the midst of all the ups and downs, victories and defeats, joys and suffering, we see the theme repeated over and over again—praise the Lord.

Here is a response that is always right—praise the Lord! Are you at a dead end in your life? Praise the Lord. Is your ministry full and prosperous? Praise the Lord! Do you know exactly what God wants you to do, or not have a clue? Praise the Lord! Are you hurting? Praise the Lord! Do you have abundance to give? Praise the Lord! Praise the Lord in the midst of it all and when all is said and one. Fill you heart with praise; let it overflow through your lips and lead others to do the same. Fulfill your call as a Christian musician with praise!

Father, You are so worthy of my praise. And when all is said and done I still praise You! Thank you for the calling to lead others in Your praise. This call is such a blessing and honor to me. I will do what is important. I will praise You every day, in the midst of whatever the day holds.

September 20
Follow the Regulations

"David assigned the following men to lead the music at the house of the LORD after the Ark was placed there. They ministered with music at the Tabernacle until Solomon built the Temple of the LORD in Jerusalem. They carried out their work, following all the regulations handed down to them."
1 Chronicles 6:31-32

Christian musicians are by nature creative, "out of the box" type people. We love freedom to express our faith through music, and worship music has enjoyed immense popularity because of our creativity. Unfortunately, we tend to not do as well when it comes to following the rules. We want to know "Why?" and "Who says so?" and even, "Are you sure that applies to us?" While those are not wrong questions, they can be asked at inappropriate times and places with a tone of rebellion. Many Christian pastors and leaders bristle at the thought of working with musicians. Some of these leaders prefer to marginalize our ministry because of our attitudes.

Yet, this verse depicts a group of people that were appointed as musicians—they did not get to choose the job. Then they were given regulations to follow. Most likely, more rules and "ways of doing things" were added as time went on. How would we respond in this situation? This verse says they carried out their work and followed the regulations. Do we?

Some common regulations musicians today struggle with include the volume of our instruments, what we wear on stage, arriving on time, playing the length of time allotted, and cleaning up after ourselves afterwards. How are you doing with the regulations imposed on your creativity? Can you learn to be creative and follow the regulations?

Father, I will follow the rules, not because I always agree with the rules, but because You ask me to follow them.

September 21

Faith, Hope & Love

"As we pray to our God and Father about you, we think of your faithful work, your loving deeds, and the enduring hope you have because of our Lord Jesus Christ."

1 Thessalonians 1:2

Faithful work, loving deeds and enduring hope are qualities we all want to have. We want to be known and remembered as faithful, loving, and hope-filled people. In our work as Christian music ministers we have the opportunity to demonstrate faith, hope, and love daily.

For musicians, faithful work means doing our music with excellence. We write quality lyrics, handle our business with Godly ethics, and are diligent at becoming increasingly more skilled at playing our instruments. We produce the highest quality products possible. We work for the Lord, so we work hard. This faithful work is an example to everyone around us.

Loving deeds happen as we work with other people. We truly care about our band mates, we treat our business associates with respect and integrity, and we encourage and evangelize our fans. This love is characterized by actions, not just feeling.

Hope gives us the motivation to be faithful in our work and do loving deeds. We have hope that lasts for more than just a moment. Our hope is enduring because it is based on the faithfulness and love of Jesus, not on the circumstances of life.

Christian music ministers desire that people will see their faithful work and experience their loving deeds, so their hearts will open to the message of hope found in Jesus. We can be assured that as we grow in faithful work, loving deeds, and enduring hope, our ministries will grow.

Father, thank You for the opportunity to demonstrate faith, hope and love in my ministry. Show me how to grow in each of these things every day.

September 22
Honor Your Leaders

"Dear brothers and sisters, honor those who are your leaders in the Lord's work. They work hard among you and give you spiritual guidance. Show them great respect and wholehearted love because of their work. And live peacefully with each other."

1 Thessalonians 5:12

Most of us have been taught to respect authorities because we will reap bad consequences if we don't. For example, we are very polite to the officer when stopped for a traffic violation in the hopes of receiving a less expensive ticket. We have learned to be respectful of the judge if we are in court because we could receive a judgment against us. But are we as respectful when there are no negative consequences?

The leaders that give us advice and help us spiritually with our music ministries deserve far more respect than any judge or police officer. Do we show it? How do we demonstrate our wholehearted love for them? There is no formula. Many spiritual leaders do not want to be called by a title, others truly do not want your money, and still others do not want you to raise them up in front of other people. Wholehearted love and respect is based on relationship. Through that relationship you will come to know what your leader feels is respectful, what he needs, and how you can be a blessing to him.

Perhaps the greatest form of respect you can give to a leader is to take the time to learn how to express your wholehearted love for them in the way that means the most to them. Do not be a person who only takes from them. Do not be the person that uses them to advance your ministry and then abandons them. Honoring your leaders with genuine relationship is the key to wholehearted love and respect.

Father, You have put leaders in my life to help me. Show me ways to help them, to demonstrate love and respect to them.

September 23
Greatness by Comparison

"After they arrived at Capernaum and settled in a house, Jesus asked his disciples, 'What were you discussing out on the road?' But they didn't answer, because they had been arguing about which of them was the greatest."

Mark 9:33-34

We would not want our fans to know, but we all have private competitions going on in the band and with other bands. Who do the fans like best? Who gave the best performance at the last show? Who writes the best liked songs? Who has the most industry contacts? Who sold the most tickets to the show? It is an endless comparison of ourselves to each other.

We want to excel at our ministry. We can show our significance by getting enough "best of" comparisons under our name. We validate our self worth by being the best. We prove our importance to others by being on top.

Fortunately, Jesus sees past all our comparisons. He knows our hearts, our minds, and our motivations. All of our self delusions and tactics to keep others from knowing the truth about us are crystal clear to Him. Competitions and comparisons do not sway Him. Jesus knows who we really are, knows our true value and worth, and is still our biggest fan. He cheers us on towards truly being great, not just appearing to be great.

People who only appear to be great do ministry only when everyone can see them. People who are great look for the overlooked, the ones who are not being served, and serve them. People who are only called leaders make sure that they win the competitions to be best. People who are leaders do the work of the ministry whenever and however to whomever they can. Be great by doing great ministry, not by comparison.

Father, change my heart to focus on doing what is truly great ministry in Your eyes. Show me what that is each day.

September 24
Words of Healing

"Some people make cutting remarks,
but the words of the wise bring healing."
Proverbs 12:18

How you say something is almost as important as what you say. Think about all the different ways you can say, "OK fine." In context, they can be words of affirmation or anger. A sarcastic tone can use the same words to cut into a heart.

The ability to speak using affirming words in a tone that is not abrasive is one mark of a great minister. People are drawn to people who build them up. We naturally shy away from those whose words sting. So, to become effective ministers, to draw people closer to Jesus, we must learn good communication.

Good communication nurtures hearts and minds. Cutting remarks destroy. Good communication builds trust in those you work with and lead. Lack of communication brings confusion and competition. Good communication instills confidence through encouragement and defined expectations. Harsh language causes hurt and promotes fear.

How is your communication? One way to gauge how well you are doing is to look at the people around you. People want to be around those whose words bring healing. Do people want to be around you? Are they growing in trust and confidence in your relationship? Are past hurts being healed? Do they want to continue working with you in the future? Most importantly, are they growing closer to Jesus?

What we say and how we say it affects how people view us as Christians. Our harsh words, cutting remarks, and even lack of communication can keep people from growing in their faith. Let us be wise and speak words in a way that builds up and heals.

Father, show me how my words are affecting the people around me. Teach me how to speak with wisdom and healing.

September 25
My Heart's Condition

"Search me, O God, and know my heart;
test me and know my anxious thoughts.
Point out anything in me that offends you,
and lead me along the path of everlasting life."
Psalm 139:23-24

Christian music ministers have many tasks that must be done to keep up with both music and ministry. Rapid changes in popular music styles, technology, and ministry expectations demand our full attention. The work can be time consuming and exhausting. It becomes easy to lose focus.

The tasks must be set aside periodically so we can get back to basics. Us and God—it does not get much more basic. We want to please God, but we often get so busy in attempting to do so that we forget what it is that truly pleases Him. Setting aside our ministry activities to get our own house in order is a sure way to stay on track. In the quietness of inactivity we can examine our own heart and rediscover God's profound love for us. We are reminded that His love for us is not based on what we do, but on Whose we are. Only after we have quieted ourselves in His love can we accurately reassess and reevaluate our lives and our ministries. In the quietness we can hear Him. We may find things that offend God which we were completely unaware of. We may need to change our direction. We may also find that God is more pleased with us than we imagined. Either way, we want to expose our hearts condition so we can be led by God.

Taking time away from ministry to hear from God about the condition of our hearts is the first step toward building a better life and ministry. Changing our hearts and our actions to come in line with Him is next. Please God and then do ministry.

Father, when I get too busy working for You to hear from You, call me back. Remind me to set my heart on You.

September 26
A Time

> *"For everything there is a season,*
> *a time for every activity under heaven."*
> *Ecclesiastes 3:1*

Fall is the busiest time of year for musicians. Our gig calendar is at its peak, we should be writing new music for the winter's recording project, starting to wrap up this year's business, and strategizing for the new year. Add in our families and church life and it is not surprising we feel a time crunch. Unfortunately, life does not slow down until after the holidays.

The Bible does not promise that we will have time to get everything accomplished that is on our to-do list each day. It does not say that there is time for everything. This verse does say that there is A time for everything. In other words, there are seasons of time for each thing. We cannot possibly hope to do all the tasks involved with music ministry at once. But we can shift the focus of which things are most important to accomplish in any given season. We can do some tasks minimally or even let some tasks go until it is their season.

When we feel overwhelmed with the amount of work we need to accomplish, we need to remember that God has a plan for our ministries. Part of that plan is timing. We can relax in knowing that God's plan and timing of that plan are perfect. No amount of rushing or overworking can hasten the outcome of His plan for us. Yes, we need to be diligent at our work, but we do not need to be stressed and overworked. When the stress is getting to us, we need to check our trust level in God's plan and timing. Flowing with what God is doing, no more and no less, requires trust in His plan for our ministries. Allowing God to plan our days and our season's results in us accomplishing God's purposes right on time!

Father, teach me how to walk in Your timing.

September 27
Ask the Lord

"And again David asked the LORD what to do. 'Do not attack them straight on,' the LORD replied. 'Instead, circle around behind and attack them near the poplar trees.'"

2 Samuel 5:23

The first time the Philistines attacked David in Jerusalem he asked the Lord what to do. God gave him the plan and David did it. Of course, he won the battle. When the Philistines attacked Jerusalem the second time David could have assumed that he should do the same thing again. But, he was wise enough to ask the Lord again. This time, the Lord gave him a completely different plan. David did the new plan and he won the battle. Would he have won the second time by acting on the first plan? We will never know because David wisely refused to act without hearing from God first.

Being in a Christian band and making decisions to lead a ministry are not uncharted waters. We have many Godly examples of people that have gone before us doing similar work. There are plans available to help you do the work of the ministry more easily and effectively. But, there is a huge difference between wise counsel and God's counsel. Wise counsel from people with experience is a good thing; it can help us along the way. God's counsel trumps all else. In the end, even if we had heard from God Himself about how to do a certain thing the first time, we need to ask God about His way to do things each time.

David was one of the most successful kings in history; he was a man after God's own heart. Why? It was not because he was the most perfect person ever. He messed up more than most of us ever will. But, he loved God passionately and acted on that love by spending time seeking out God's plan in each situation.

Father, remind me to rely on Your plan for my ministry more than wise counsel or the way it has been done in the past.

September 28
Waiting with Hope

"Let all that I am wait quietly before God,
for my hope is in him."

Psalm 62:5

"Are we there yet?" "When are we going to be there?" "Now are we there?" Waiting quietly is not usually associated with children (and some band members), especially when they are confined in the car. Sometimes this obnoxious behavior is simply meant to annoy, but more often it is expressing impatience, boredom, and uncertainty that the ordeal of confinement will be over as soon as possible. Do we act like this towards God when life is not progressing as fast as we would like?

Waiting quietly requires trust that God is able to do all we need and hope that He will do it. Waiting quietly demonstrates that we know God will do whatever is best for us in any given situation. When it comes to waiting, most of us talk the talk but few of us are good at actually doing it. We tend to run ahead and try to make things happen, leaving God and His plan behind. When we run ahead in ministry, the effects can be just as devastating as they are in our personal lives.

God orders and orchestrates the steps of our ministries. The wise leader will get His direction not only on what to do but how and when to do it. God's timing will often require waiting—waiting until the time is perfect for us to proceed. Of course we can trust Him and put our hope in Him to do what is best for us. He is the creator of the universe so He is able, and the God who loves us enough to die for us so He is willing. Let us put away childish attitudes and demonstrate our trust by waiting in hope. Let us remain faithful to our calling, working out our ministries while we wait in quiet confidence for the next step.

Father, wait is a four letter word. Help me to redefine it in my thinking, to put it in the same category as love.

September 29
Permeate With Yeast

"Jesus also used this illustration: 'The Kingdom of Heaven is like the yeast a woman used in making bread. Even though she put only a little yeast in three measures of flour, it permeated every part of the dough.'"

Matthew 13:33

Does your ministry permeate the lives of people? Do your song lyrics reach deep into a person's heart? Does the example of your life cause people to rethink theirs? If not, you may need a little more yeast—the kingdom of heaven.

If you mix flour and yeast in a bowl, nothing happens. The flour may be good, the yeast may be good, but no change occurs until the yeast is first dissolved in water and then mixed with the flour. Oil and a little honey can then be added to make excellent bread. The process requires paying attention to the yeast at all times—it must be kept at the proper temperature and fed with the flour, sugar, and oil in the right proportions.

Often, the music industry is focused on being more effective using tools like social media, broader distribution, radio airplay, etc. All these tools can be good because they expose people to your music. They can also be time consuming. But, they do not cause your ministry to permeate the hearts of people. To change hearts, to bring people closer to Jesus, you must have experienced the kingdom of heaven. That experience needs to be continually nurtured, fed with the water of life and the oil of the spirit. Without a continual heavenly relationship our ministries fall short and seem shallow, the yeast dies.

Perhaps we do not need to focus on more tools or training to grow our ministries. Perhaps what we need is more relationship and experience with our Father in heaven.

Father, make me thirsty for You. When my thirst has been quenched, overflow that power into my ministry.

September 30
Faith Expressing Itself

"For when we place our faith in Christ Jesus, there is no benefit in being circumcised or being uncircumcised. What is important is faith expressing itself in love."

Galatians 5:6

Our faith is not a specific set of rules that we must follow to be accepted. That is one of the things that set Christianity apart from every other religion. Yet, many times we think life's decisions would be so much easier to make if we had a rulebook. "As long as you play by the rules you go to heaven" sounds good, but as the Old Testament demonstrated, it just does not work out so well. The Christians one "rule" is love. There is not an advantage in following any other rules. We are free from rulebooks as long as walk in love! So, how's your love walk?

Many times, when our love walk is not so good we are actually suffering from a faith deficiency. It is easy to demonstrate love for our neighbors when our lives are going well. But when we are in need or crisis, love does not come naturally or as easily. Why? Because love for our neighbor is not a feeling, it is an expression of our faith in God. When our faith is being stretched to the limits the expression of our faith, our love, gets a little thin as well.

Understanding this concept can increase our patience with our band mates. Has someone snapped at you? Maybe their faith is being stretched at that moment. Have you been treated poorly by a band member? Maybe they are in a faith crisis. Rather than throwing the rulebook at them, telling them how they should have acted, we can give them grace to grow. Perhaps we can even help them grow by responding to them in love. We could help by walking alongside them while their faith is growing.

Father, show me how to express my faith with love. Deepen my faith so that my expressions of love will grow.

October 1
Rest Renews

> *"The LORD is my shepherd;*
> *I have all that I need.*
> *He lets me rest in green meadows;*
> *he leads me beside peaceful streams.*
> *He renews my strength.*
> *He guides me along right paths,*
> *bringing honor to his name."*
>
> Psalm 23:1-3

We frequently hear this verse at funerals because of the "walking through the valley of death" portion that comes later. However, these verses were not written to the dead but to the living. We have a shepherd who makes sure we are well taken care of because His reputation is on the line. When people look at us, especially as leaders in ministry, they see His ambassadors.

When we follow His guidance, along the paths that He has chosen for us, we will experience periods of rest. Most leaders do not enjoy being idle; we tend to push through, not realizing that we are actually resisting God. Rest is part of renewing our strength. When we are led to rest, it is not punishment for our frailty or lack of endurance. We are being given something good. Stop for a moment and picture yourself lying on your back in a meadow as a gentle stream gurgles nearby. The clouds are lazily floating past and an occasional butterfly flits by. This is the kind of peace of mind and rest that God is describing. It renews our spirits as well as your bodies.

Everyone needs rest to renew their strength. Christian music ministers are not exempt. In fact, because of our crazy schedules, demanding fans, and emotional temperaments, we probably need more rest than most people. God leads us to rest so that we may represent Him well, bringing honor to His name.

Father, help me be obedient when You lead me to rest.

October 2
Never Stop Producing Fruit

"But blessed are those who trust in the LORD
and have made the LORD their hope and confidence.
They are like trees planted along a riverbank,
with roots that reach deep into the water.
Such trees are not bothered by the heat
or worried by long months of drought.
Their leaves stay green,
and they never stop producing fruit."
Jeremiah 17:7-8

Musicians typically spend most of the summer and fall being extremely busy touring and much of the winter songwriting and recording. No matter what activities we are doing, we should always be producing fruit. But how do we do that? It's human nature to get discouraged during slow times and setbacks, and we slack off in our music and our ministries. When we are too busy, we worry about completing all the necessary tasks and often decrease our time spent alone with God. Musicians constantly struggle to produce the fruit that comes maintaining the balance between keeping ourselves strong and helping others during both busy seasons and slow times.

The answer to the struggle of consistently producing fruit in our lives is found in the beginning of these verses: trust in the Lord, make the Lord our hope, and have confidence in Him. Trust, hope, and confidence in the Lord allow us to work consistently to produce fruit because we are not reliant on outside sources to motivate us.

Has your fruit production slowed down? Is your harvest as large as it should be? Are you able to produce fruit even during the dry, slow times? If not, check your trust, hope, and confidence in the Lord; it may need to grow a little.

Father, increase my trust, hope, and confidence in You.

October 3
God's Business Manager

"To those who use well what they are given, even more will be given, and they will have an abundance. But from those who do nothing, even what little they have will be taken away."
Matthew 25:29

Christian music ministers are stewards of their talents and their time. There is no boss checking up on our daily progress, no time clocks to punch. We are all given the same 24-hour period of time to use our talents. What differentiates us is how well we use our talents each day. An excellent steward uses their available time, talents, and resources to advance the kingdom of God every day. A poor steward finds excuses to cover up doing very little due to fear and/or laziness.

In every stewardship relationship there are two people involved: the master and the steward. The master gives the resources to the steward; the steward manages those resources. Eventually the master asks the steward to show him how much profit was earned. The steward is rewarded or not based on his performance with the master's resources. We see this in our world every day in businesses and their managers.

How would you be rated if you were God's business manager? The parable of the three stewards clearly demonstrates that we are not all given the same resources and talents. But, we are expected to use what we have well. Have you managed the talents, resources, and time He has given you to make a profit for Him? Is the kingdom of God better off because of you today? If so, you can expect that God will reward you with more resources. If not, don't get discouraged. The past is past; ask for forgiveness and move forward to doing better today. You too will be rewarded as you work towards being a great steward.

Father, show me how to be a better steward of the time, talents, and resources You have given to me.

October 4
God's True Riches

"I know about your suffering and your poverty—but you are rich!"

Revelation 2:9a

The church in Smyrna was poor and was about to be persecuted beyond what they had already experienced. Later we read that the church at Laodicea is described as being wretched and miserable and poor and blind and naked. Yet they had an abundance of physical wealth and were not being persecuted at all. In God's eyes are the rich poor and the poor rich? Not necessarily. Is persecution, or lack thereof, a sign of God's approval or disapproval? No. We know this to be true because of numerous other scriptures; but we do not always act like we believe it. We still see abundance and an easy life as signs of God's approval, while difficult times and poverty are often used as evidence that there must be sin in our lives. In our minds, we know that God does not hate us when things are not going our way and that God does not love us more when life is easier. But, in our hearts we tend to treat others as if that were true.

We would rather get advice for our ministries from wealthy, successful people. Why? Because they seem to have a proven track record and we want to duplicate their success. At the time, it certainly would have seemed better to get advice from people in Laodicea than Smyrna. But Smyrna had God's true riches: hearts that were completely in love with Him and each other, combined with the strength of character to follow through on that love no matter what the circumstances. We need to actively seek out people who have God's true riches, regardless of their social and economic status. We need to confer with them so we can duplicate God's true riches in our lives and ministries.

Father, give me discernment in whom I choose as advisors. Teach me to look for and value Your true riches in a person's heart and life before I try to be like them.

October 5
Heart Music

"Singing psalms and hymns and spiritual songs among yourselves, and making music to the Lord in your hearts."
Ephesians 5:19

God is very concerned about the condition of our hearts. In fact, He says that our words and deeds come from the overflow of what is in our hearts. If God has our hearts, He has all of us. That is why we are told to worship Him with music in our hearts. Many believers do this throughout their day. They sing songs in their hearts that they have heard in church, on the radio, at concerts, on their mp3 player, and wherever Christian music is available. There is a constant search for new music that connects their hearts to God.

Have you ever considered that the songs you write today might become someone else's heart music? You are not simply a secular musician trying to write a marketable song or express yourself artistically. You are not only a songwriting technician, trying to craft the highest quality music. You are writing music that will change people's hearts, minds, words, and actions. When a Christian music minister writes any song, there is always a potential for that song to impact someone's life for eternity. The song does not have to hit the charts or be performed by a famous band to change a life. The song you have inside you, the songs you will write in the near future, and all the songs you have already written are your heart's music to God. Whenever you share your music, you are sharing the opportunity for the audience to get closer to God through the music. What an amazing gift and responsibility our Lord has given us! We can work towards crafting the best songs possible, but ultimately our goal is to connect people to God using the music in their hearts.

Father, thank You for the gift of music! Help me to use this gift in a way that blesses other people and honors You.

Boldness or Safety

"And now, O Lord, hear their threats, and give us, your servants, great boldness in preaching your word."

Acts 4:29

Peter and John were being persecuted by the Jewish council. They had been arrested and questioned by Jewish rulers, elders, and teachers. After they had been threatened and released, Peter and John went back to the church. This verse is part of the church's prayer upon hearing what had happened. Isn't it interesting that they did not pray for the safety of the church or for Peter and John? Instead they asked for boldness.

Most Christian musicians are not persecuted or thrown in jail like Peter and John. But we do face our share of adversities, for example vehicles breaking down, constant money problems, equipment needing repair, or living in the constant judgment of others. We struggle, so we pray for safety, conflict resolution, and provision. What would happen if we did not pray for safe travels as we are touring? What would God do if we asked for the advancement of His kingdom above all else, including our own personal safety, provision for the needs of our ministry, or a favorable reputation? What if we asked God for boldness in every circumstance instead of asking Him to change the circumstances?

Our brothers around the world risk their lives daily just to get a Bible to someone. They endure hardships that do not seem real to us because we will likely never experience that level of adversity. Nevertheless, we can have the same focus, the same drive to risk it all to bring someone closer to Jesus. We must take our eyes off the hardships we face. We must remember why we are doing music ministry. We must remember that souls are at stake. Like Peter and John, we must have boldness.

Father, give me boldness. I leave my safety, provision and reputation up to You as I ask for more souls in Your kingdom.

October 7
Doing Life in Harmony

"May God, who gives this patience and encouragement, help you live in complete harmony with each other, as is fitting for followers of Christ Jesus. Then all of you can join together with one voice, giving praise and glory to God, the Father of our Lord Jesus Christ."

Romans 15:5-6

We live life through our own eyes, with our own perspective. Often, when we are going through extreme times, whether they are difficult or joyful or full of change or monotonous, ours are the only experiences we can truly see. Too many times, we are overwhelmed by the needs and the work of our ministry. What we can see is what would help our ministry grow. Our intentions are good—to grow our ministry so that we can help more people in the future. But the temptation is to plug other people into our perspective, to get them to help our ministry, rather than to share their lives by experiencing their perspective.

Some people need to step up and be a part of our ministry in order to grow. Others need us to simply "do life," to share the experiences of our lives, with them. Still others need us to temporarily set aside our own perspectives and reach out into their world. When we are self-absorbed, especially by our ministry, we cannot live in harmony with everyone because the only perspective we see is our own. Although we would never say we believe it, we are acting like joining together with one voice means everyone being part of our ministry. In effect, we are demonstrating that we believe our organization is more important than people. Sharing or even setting aside our lives when our own ministry needs seem overwhelming is difficult. But sharing the encouragement and patience that comes from God in the midst of our need is often the most effective ministry.

Father, You know that I believe people are more important than my ministry or music. Help me to live what I believe.

October 8

Comfort Others

"He comforts us in all our troubles so that we can comfort others. When they are troubled, we will be able to give them the same comfort God has given us."

2 Corinthians 1:4

Every human being experiences trouble from time to time. In the day of trouble, we feel overwhelmed and alone. God has sent us His Holy Spirit to comfort us in our troubles, but He has also given us each other. If we experienced trouble for no other reason than to be able to comfort someone else, it would be enough reason to go through trouble. It seems that Christian leaders experience more times of trouble than most people, especially during their years of training. Could it be that God allows these times not only to strengthen us, but to give us the ability to share comfort with others?

A story has often been told of a Christian woman who was freezing in an unheated prison. An anti-Christian woman who had been very outspoken against God was sharing the cell and was also freezing. The Christian woman reached out and held the anti-Christian, sharing body heat and warmth, while she prayed to God for heat for both of them. In the morning when the guards checked the cell, expecting to find both women frozen separately on their beds, both women were warm and praying together. How did that conversion take place? The Christian shared in the suffering and comforted the anti-Christian.

Would you, as a Christian minister, share both suffering and comfort with your enemy as well as your brethren? Notice this verse did not define the word "others" as other Christians or people who attend your church. Are you willing to endure trouble now in the hope that you will be able to comfort an enemy later?

Father, give me courage in times of trouble to be vulnerable enough to share both the trouble and comfort with others.

October 9
Can't Stop Talking

"We cannot stop telling about everything we have seen and heard."

Acts 4:20

What do you talk about? What have you seen and heard? What is it that you cannot stop talking about? Peter and John could not stop talking about all they had seen Jesus do and all the Holy Spirit had done through them. They understood what it all meant—freedom from the slavery of sin and life in the New Covenant. This was so exciting that they simply could not stop talking about it. Their religious leaders ordered them to stop; they couldn't. Later, their government ordered them to stop; they wouldn't. How could they stop when they themselves were living proof that God loved us and wanted to have relationship with us? They were compelled to share the good news and their daily experience with God proved what they said was true.

Does your experience with Jesus compel you to talk about Him? Witnessing by rote is not effective. People do not want to be sold a product; they want to hear what is real. People want to hear the story of a life full of genuine experiences. Do you want to compel your fans to be closer to Jesus? Tell the stories of your experiences with Him. Many of us feel that our life stories are not compelling because they do not contain the stuff movies are made of: dramatic conversions, miracles etc. While the drama is certainly entertaining, it is not real to most people. Your fans can relate to your story because many of them will have lived similar experiences and circumstances. Pause for a moment and consider your experiences with God lately. That "small thing" you learned or did or triumphed over may be exactly the story someone else needs to hear. What have you experienced with Jesus lately? What do you have to talk about?

Father, thank You for being involved in my life. Compel me to openly talk about the story of You in my life.

October 10
The Evil Within

> *"You who love the LORD, hate evil!*
> *He protects the lives of his godly people*
> *and rescues them from the power of the wicked."*
> Psalm 97:10

We see evil around us. It is so easy to spot sin in other people. It is easy to hate their sin, especially when it affects us. It is not so easy to see our own evil, and when we do see it we often give ourselves a pass. We know the troubles of our own lives so we use them as excuses for why we are the exception in any particular instance involving sin. For example, we are running late getting to a gig. Loading up just did not go smoothly and now we need to make up the time. So, we drive way over the speed limit. It is easy to give ourselves permission to do so because we know the circumstances leading up to the sin. But when we see someone else passing us, we usually have some choice words about them. We don't know; maybe they are speeding because they are rushing someone to the hospital.

If we want to be protected, if we want to be rescued, we need to live Godly and hate evil—not just sin in other people, not just big sin, not just social injustices or war. We need to hate and fight against the evil within ourselves. Most often, this evil surfaces in our own lives in smaller, more socially acceptable ways. So, we give ourselves permission to overlook it. Do we declare all our income on our taxes? Do we give money back when it is given to us incorrectly? Do we talk about other bands in a less than kind way? The list of the ungodly things we do is endless. But let us watch ourselves, catch ourselves in the act, and change our behavior to become more and more Godly. Let us be living examples of Christ on earth.

Father, make the areas that I accept sin very real to me. Show me what I do that is not like Jesus and help me change.

October 11
The Fire of God

> *"I will bring that group through the fire*
>   *and make them pure.*
> *I will refine them like silver*
>   *and purify them like gold.*
> *They will call on my name,*
>   *and I will answer them.*
> *I will say, 'These are my people,'*
>   *and they will say, 'The LORD is our God.'"*
> *Zechariah 13:9*

This verse is part of a prophecy written to a specific group of Jews. But, they also set a pattern of refinement that most Christian leaders go through. We sometimes tend to look at other Christians who have life much easier than we do. The circumstances of their lives often illustrate God's protection, goodness, and blessing much more so than our own. But upon closer examination of their lives, we see that most of them are not called to be leaders.

Leaders are held to a higher standard and so are refined and tested more often and more deeply. No one enjoys refinement. If we could get away from the heat of the fire, we would get out of the kitchen so to speak. But the extra hot refiner's fire is what we signed up for when we accepted the call to be a Christian music minister. None of us are exempt. We do not have control of when we will face the fire or what shape the circumstances will take. The only things we can control are our actions and reactions, what we think, say, and do. We can choose to behave in ways that honor God or that compromise our ministry. The fire is not pleasant, but we can thank God that He chose us to go through it. There is no better way to gain the depth and maturity needed to lead people closer to Jesus.

Father, give me courage when the fire gets hot. Help me see Your love in the flames and learn to honor You through them.

The Fires of Destruction

"If you are burning thornbushes and the fire gets out of control and spreads into another person's field, destroying the sheaves or the uncut grain or the whole crop, the one who started the fire must pay for the lost crop."

Exodus 22:6

Bands are frequently asked to give recommendations about other bands. What you say, whom you say it to, when you say it, and how you say it can help or hinder another band from getting a gig. What you say (or infer) about another ministry can be just as destructive as a fire to crops.

Music ministry is largely based on reputation, both with fans and industry professionals. Unfortunately, there are more bands than there are gigs, so music ministry is also very competitive. In an effort to make themselves feel good, build themselves up in the eyes of others, and get ahead in the industry, some band members (intentionally or not) consistently point out the flaws, weaknesses, and imperfections of other band ministries. In effect, they start the fire of a negative reputation for the other band(s). Worse yet, some bands befriend and network with other bands in an effort to get more shows and then share negative information gained from the relationship with other people. Most of us would say we never do or have done this. Most of us would be wrong. We simply do not like to think of ourselves in that light. Be careful; evaluate what you say before you say it. Here is a good test: What would you say differently if you had to pay restitution for lost income to every ministry you talked about? Instead of constantly "giving our honest opinions" let us join together as music ministers to build each other up and support each of our ministries.

Father, forgive me for lighting fires of strife and poor reputations for Your bands and music ministers.

October 13

What About Him?

"Peter turned around and saw behind them the disciple Jesus loved—the one who had leaned over to Jesus during supper and asked, 'Lord, who will betray you?' Peter asked Jesus, 'What about him, Lord?' Jesus replied, 'If I want him to remain alive until I return, what is that to you? As for you, follow me.'"

John 21:20-22

"What about him?" is not a question that most of us ask in such an obvious manner. But, most of us do ask it. Whenever we look at anything someone else has or has achieved and wonder why we do not have the same amount of blessing in our lives, we are asking "What about him?" Just prior to these verses are the "Do you love Me? Then feed my sheep" verses. The order is not coincidental. When we are busy feeding God's sheep, doing the work of the ministry, we become acutely aware of those who are doing similar work. Inevitably we compare our ministries to theirs, our lives to theirs, and our measure of success to theirs. If they have anything that seems better than what we have, in our humanness we begin to question how we can get it too. We have taken the first step toward the downward spiral by thinking "Is he getting something more or better than me?" "Why should he get something more or better than me?" "What do I have to do to get what he has?" In effect we believe he has something more so we are asking, "God, do You love him more than me?" Look at Jesus' response: "What is that to you? You follow me."

When we compare ourselves to others, we often forget that God created each of us to be one of a kind. What He does for anyone else is not going to be best for us. He set aside work for each of us to do that only we can do. He loves each of us as we need to be loved and blesses each of us individually.

Father, thank You that I am one of a kind, especially loved by You. Thank You for giving me what is best for me.

October 14

Our Ministry or God's?

"I am the LORD; that is my name!
I will not give my glory to anyone else,
*   nor share my praise with carved idols."*
*   Isaiah 42:8*

One of the most deadly temptations we can fall in to is to take some of God's glory for ourselves. He has clearly said He will not share the glory. But the music industry is designed to create "rock stars," people who must continually be the center of attention to sell their music. All the crazy lifestyles, the publicity stunts, and the marketing are designed to do one thing: get the public's attention so they will buy the artist's music. We generally accept that this strategy is not God's plan for Christian music ministers. Instead, we pray that God will manifest Himself so powerfully through our ministries that people will be drawn. Our mistake is that we want God to work through our ministries rather than us serving in God's ministry. The difference is subtle, but it is there. In effect, we want ministry on our terms. We want God to place His power at our disposal, to use when we see the need and however we think is best to fulfill those needs. Although we are working to advance the kingdom, we want to advance the kingdom in the way we think is best. We still want to call the shots, to be in charge. When we are in charge, some of the glory that should be going to God falls to us. People see what a great man or woman of God we are instead of seeing God.

God will not share His glory with anyone, even His children. He has given us the honor and privilege of serving in His ministry to bring about His will in the world. We can add to His glory by doing so wholeheartedly and faithfully.

Father, expose my heart. Show me areas that I take away from Your glory and teach me how to correct them. I want to bring glory to You by being Your servant, not a rock star.

October 15

Made in the Image of God

"But no one can tame the tongue. It is restless and evil, full of deadly poison. Sometimes it praises our Lord and Father, and sometimes it curses those who have been made in the image of God."

James 3:8-9

We have all done it, probably more than once: stepped off the stage after playing worship to God and said something less than kind about a band member. Perhaps the drummer started the tempo wrong, or the guitar player played a verse in the wrong key, or maybe the lead singer talked and sang right over your solo. There is a way, a time, and a place to critique the performance with the honest intent of improving. There is also a way to say the same things but tear people down, often just to make sure people know that it was not us that messed up.

Evaluation and critique is necessary for us to become more skilled musicians. Music competitions are held all over the world covering every genre of music to help us hone our skills. But cursing someone, tearing them down in any way is not the same thing. The difference may be as subtle as your tone of voice, when the critique is given, who is around to hear the comments, or even if the recipient wants to know your opinion. Those circumstances can be difficult to always get right. But we can always be sure of our intent—are we seeking to honor our brother and help him improve, or are we seeking to build ourselves up at the expense of our brother?

Before you speak, ask yourself, "If Jesus had just made the same mistakes on stage would I handle the situation in this way?" Ultimately, your brother is made in the image of God. Although he is not perfect, like God, he should be treated the same as you would treat Jesus.

Father, everyone makes mistakes on stage, including myself. Cause me to remember that we are all made in Your image. Help me to treat every musician as well as I would treat You.

October 16
Sacrifices with Shouts of Joy

"For he will conceal me there when troubles come;
*   he will hide me in his sanctuary.*
He will place me out of reach on a high rock.
Then I will hold my head high
*   above my enemies who surround me.*
At his sanctuary I will offer sacrifices with shouts of joy,
*   singing and praising the LORD with music."*
                                        Psalm 27:5-6

In the Old Testament, sacrifices were taken from the possessions of the household and given to the priests at the sanctuary. Most often, these sacrifices were food: animals or grains. People took food from their own storehouse—in effect, food off their families own tables to sacrifice to God. Then, they were so happy to do so that they shouted and sang with joy.

How do our lives compare? We frequently hear that we live in the wealthiest country in the world; we have more than 85% of the world's wealth. Yet, we have unpaid bills and know that it will take more resources to expand our ministries. These two realities just don't seem to be able to both be true.

Look at the trust, the absolute confidence that God will protect in verse 5. From this trust springs confidence of standing against an enemy, even as the enemy has surrounded them. It is from this position of being surrounded but trusting in God that sacrifices are given with joy, not from the position of final victory. Can we look at our sacrifices to God and determine our level of trust in Him? What if we give begrudgingly, without joy? Or don't sacrifice at all? What if we plan to give when we have more—more time, more money, and more people to help, but not now? Can we sacrifice our lives today, who we are, everything we have, all that we want, with songs of joy?

Father, my hearts cry is that You would help me to trust You.

October 17
Succeed with Good Counsel

"Plans succeed through good counsel;
don't go to war without wise advice."
Proverbs 20:18

It has been said that music careers can be made because of who you know. The right people can open the right doors. But once the door is opened you have to be able to walk through and stand in the next room. No one can do that for you; if you are not prepared and ready you will fail. We have all seen the promising artist that is not around the following year and the one hit wonders that never get past the first hit song. Often this occurs simply because they were not ready for the next step. But, good counsel can help prepare you for your next step as an artist.

The music ministry has so many different aspects that no one person can master all of them. Consider just some of the jobs a musician needs to accomplish: booking live shows, web site design and maintenance, bookkeeping for a small business, song publishing and copyrights, album cover design, stage sound and lighting; the list is almost endless. Many of these tasks can and should be hired out—but who do you hire and when? How much should they be paid? Even the most basic questions about running a music ministry can be overwhelming without help and insight from mentors.

Success comes with the humility of being able to ask for help and advice. There are many resources available now, both online and in person. These resources can keep you from wasting time and money and damaging relationships. Even asking for help has been made easier with Google and the privacy of messaging. There just is no good reason to go without wise counsel.

Father, reveal the people I need to ask to help me become the music minister You want me to be. Give me the courage to ask for help and discernment to apply the best advice.

October 18
No Other Responsibilities

"The musicians, all prominent Levites, lived at the Temple. They were exempt from other responsibilities since they were on duty at all hours."

1 Chronicles 9:33

We have all seen "the guy"—the one who runs around doing everything; if you have a question you ask him. Often the guy has a true servant's heart and is genuinely fulfilling a valuable function. But he is unable to focus on doing one job really well because he is divided among many tasks. If you need his help you usually have to spend quite a bit of time finding him, then wait until he is finished doing his current task before you can get his attention. He will help as soon as he can get time.

Music ministers should not be "the guy." We must stay focused on the one task we have been called to do: use music to bring people closer to Jesus. If we are running around the building putting out all the little fires that come up on any given day, we will not be focused on people. Sometimes we tend to choose the small tasks, the busy work, over people because it is so much easier to deal with electrical issues for example than another hurting person. People are messy—they show up at inconvenient times with issues that we do not have the power to fix. They can make us feel stupid and inadequate. But ministry is not about us or how we feel, nor is it about making our lives easy and convenient. As ministers, we are called to be available to do whatever we can to help whenever the need arises. That means NOT doing all the other things that can get in the way of loving people to Jesus.

Father, I want to be the most influential minister possible. I want to be available to love people and help wherever I can. Help me to stay focused on the important parts of the ministry and not get caught up in the many distractions. Remind me throughout today to put people first.

October 19
Shamelessness Gets Results

"Suppose you went to a friend's house at midnight, wanting to borrow three loaves of bread. You say to him, 'A friend of mine has just arrived for a visit, and I have nothing for him to eat.' And suppose he calls out from his bedroom, 'Don't bother me. The door is locked for the night, and my family and I are all in bed. I can't help you.' But I tell you this— though he won't do it for friendship's sake, if you keep knocking long enough, he will get up and give you whatever you need because of your shameless persistence."

Luke 11:5b-8

Shameless persistence—who among us is guilty of that? Not many. Who among us is shamelessly persistent for someone else? Would you hound people time and time again, not for the benefit of yourself or your own ministry, but to help someone else? Who constantly brings other people and their needs to the throne of God as a higher priority than our needs?

Why did the friend arrive at midnight? Was there a crisis that demanded the late arrival after an extremely long day's journey? Notice that the person doing the asking is awake at midnight to let his friend into his own house. He did not tell his friend to come back tomorrow when his family was awake. He tried to meet the needs of his friend, but it is not enough. So, out of love for his friend we see his shameless persistence.

Most of the time in music ministry we do not have enough resources for our own ministry. We get so caught up in promoting our music that we often overlook the people closest to us. We know we just don't have the resources to meet their needs. What would happen if just for a few moments each day we completely focused on meeting someone else's need? What would happen if we were so shameless that we actually did whatever it takes to get their need met? What would happen, if for a few moments each day, we were shamelessly persistent for someone else?

Father, help me to set aside concern about what other people think of my ministry. Teach me to be shamelessly persistent.

October 20
Friends and Brothers

> *"A friend is always loyal,*
> *and a brother is born to help in time of need."*
> Proverbs 17:17

It has been said that the greatest impact your band's ministry will have is on the band members themselves. The effect, the ministry you have to each other, is evident immediately to even the most casual observer and will shape your lives for years to come. Is that impact positive or hurtful? Years from now, when you look back on your lives, how will you remember this time? How will your band mates, your friends and brothers, see it? Will they remember you as the person who helped them become more Christ-like, or the person that tore them down when things got tough?

Occasionally we think about questions like these, but we do not usually purposely let that thinking affect our daily lives. It is easy to blow up when the moment is stressful. It is not so easy to think about how that might affect our brother and change our actions. It is easy to be busy or keep our distance just a little when a band member is going through something messy. It is much more difficult to be closer and more available; to walk through the mess with your friend. You will get dirty and other people will probably see the dirt and misinterpret it as your own.

What if a band member does not set up correctly or on time, sound check is a mess, stress levels rise, the show starts late, or the performance is not the best? How's your attitude when you walk off stage? Do you further compromise the ministry or do you help your band mate? Do you go on to minister to the fans together? Everyone makes mistakes from time to time. A friend is loyal and a brother helps even through those times.

Father, remind me to imagine who my friends have the potential to become so I can truly love them. Show me new ways to express my love for them today.

October 21

Be an Example

"Don't let anyone think less of you because you are young. Be an example to all believers in what you say, in the way you live, in your love, your faith, and your purity."

1 Timothy 4:12

We all hate it when people look down on us. We particularly hate it when people we look up to do not respect us. Most of the time we do not ask ourselves why they choose not to see us as equals. It is much easier to blame them than to look at ourselves. But if they are people we respect, maybe we should consider that they might see something wrong with our lives.

In this verse we see that Paul did not consider being young as an excuse for other people to look down on Timothy. But we also see that being young is not an excuse to live a compromised life. A person worthy of respect is a person who is a good example to everyone around them. Is that you? Have you controlled your tongue? Does the way you live remind other people of Jesus? Are you always loving toward others? How does your faith hold up during stressful times? Are your thoughts and your actions pure? If someone else lived their life the same way you do, would you have reason to look down on them? Would you want other people to be just like you are right now?

Being an example, a role model, comes with the ministry of being a Christian musician. People will tend to idolize you just because you are on stage. Is your life on and off stage one they should copy? If so, you will most likely gain the respect of leaders around you. It may take time to demonstrate a consistent Christian life, but eventually they will have to admit that you are a good example.

Father, show me areas in my life that I am not a good example, then help me to fix them. I am Your music minister and I will strive to live up to that calling.

Doing what is Good

"So let's not get tired of doing what is good. At just the right time we will reap a harvest of blessing if we don't give up."
Galatians 6:9

The Greek word used in this verse for tired means to relax so completely and for so long that we gradually lose strength; the soul is also inferred in this particular usage. So, when it comes to doing what is good we are being told not to relax our soul because it makes our soul weak. This sounds like we should be doing a daily workout so we do not become weak.

How do we inspire ourselves during the difficult physical workout times? We picture our bodies looking better and feeling healthier. The same is true with doing good. How do we inspire ourselves to do good when we don't want to? We picture the harvest of blessing that comes with not giving up.

What is this harvest of blessing? We can't look forward to it if we can't define it. Certainly there will be rewards in heaven for how we live our lives here on earth. But there are also blessings on earth. For each act of doing good these blessings will look different. But with each act there will be a response, an outcome. For example, if your band donates playing a show to help raise money for a cause, you can focus on several outcomes: the money raised, the encouragement you gave to the organizers, and the ministry you were able to do with the audience. This harvest of blessing is the physical result of how you impact the world to bring people closer to Jesus. The key to not getting tired in your soul is to stay focused on the blessing rather than the cost of doing good. This cost can be money and/or all the work you have to do to make it happen.

Stay focused! Stay strong! Don't give up! Do good!

Father, I'm going to do good. Inspire me to go farther, to push through to do more than I ever have before. I WILL do it.

October 23
Wounds, Kisses, & Truth

"Wounds from a sincere friend
are better than many kisses from an enemy."
Proverbs 27:6

Musicians are flattered constantly. Some compliments are sincere; others are said because someone wants something. After a while we expect and get used to hearing a barrage of compliments. They do not have a huge impact on us until they come from someone we feel is important. Then, a compliment can sway our thinking. For example, an A&R rep from a large, well-respected label compliments your band. You were planning to stay an Indie forever, but now suddenly you have something to consider. A family member could have said exactly the same thing without much impact.

But how do we react when someone has a criticism? One negative comment from anyone can send us into a tailspin. We can take the comment to extreme and allow it to overshadow our day. Or, sometimes we put it back on the person who made the comment saying, "They're just jealous." But how often do we consider the source of the criticism? When can we trust that the negative comment was given by a person sincerely trying to help? Do we give the "bad" comments from a qualified person the same weight as the "good" comments?

Whether we receive wounds or kisses, we need to first consider the source. It's not whether a comment is "good" or "bad" that is important. What is important is if the criticism or compliment is true. If it comes from a trusted friend, we can consider making appropriate changes. If it comes from anyone else, we need to take all comments with a grain of salt.

Father, help me to remember to seek truth and to value those who give it. I want to be influenced by good friends even if it hurts because I know they want me to be like You.

Do As I Have Done

"And since I, your Lord and Teacher, have washed your feet, you ought to wash each other's feet. I have given you an example to follow. Do as I have done to you. I tell you the truth, slaves are not greater than their master. Nor is the messenger more important than the one who sends the message. Now that you know these things, God will bless you for doing them."

John 13:14-17

Historically, foot washing has primarily been done for three reasons: the actual cleaning off of dirt, ceremonial cleaning with water before participating in another ceremony (such as being anointed with oil), and the preparation for a special act of religious service (such as serving in the temple). It is interesting that when Jesus washed the disciples' feet here, He was symbolically doing all three things. The disciples were cleansed of their sins, being prepared for the anointing of the Holy Spirit, and being dedicated to serving the church.

Then, Jesus tells us to do the same thing. Are we willing? If we say we are willing, are we doing it in our daily life by serving others? How are we helping the people closest to us—our family, band mates, and friends— to overcome sin? How are we helping them to be more Christ-like? How are we helping them to serve in ministry? How are we laying down our lives for them?

Jesus had the most important ministry of anyone on earth, ever. He clearly shows us in this verse that He was not above washing feet. He was sent to serve and to demonstrate service, so that we would do the same. There is no room for our egos, no room for the "importance" of our ministry as an excuse. Our call is to serve just as He served.

Father, I choose to be just like Jesus. Show me ways I can better serve the people around me. I want to inspire them to be like me as I am like Jesus.

October 25
Take an Interest in Others

"Then make me truly happy by agreeing wholeheartedly with each other, loving one another, and working together with one mind and purpose. Don't be selfish; don't try to impress others. Be humble, thinking of others as better than yourselves. Don't look out only for your own interests, but take an interest in others, too."

Philippians 2:3-4

These verses sum up the difference between being in a band and being a music ministry. Bands need to be ambitious and draw attention to themselves. Each musician in the band must strive to be the best and let everyone know why he is the best by talking about their music experience and gear. Music ministries need to draw attention to Jesus and the importance of His message. Each member of the band must talk about how being a Christian has affected their lives in order to accomplish their mission of drawing people closer to Jesus.

The mission of bringing people closer to Jesus unites each member of a Christian music ministry. When we have a clear focus on what we are called to do, it is easier to work together with one mind, one goal. We keep our egos in check as we strive together to find the best methods and tools to connect with people. But egos tend to flare up when we lose sight of our calling. We become selfish, wanting to be the center of attention and to receive accolades for our talent. It's only human. But if we are wise, we will recognize this behavior in ourselves and refocus before we hurt other people. It is much easier to take an interest in others when we are not busy promoting ourselves.

Father, show me how to set aside my ambitions so that I can work in love with one purpose with my band mates. Keep us focused on our calling to love others to You. We want serve You and love people more than we want to be famous.

October 26
Songs of Joy in the Wilderness

"You satisfy me more than the richest feast.
I will praise you with songs of joy."
                                    Psalm 63:5

This psalm was written when David was in the wilderness. Verse one describes it as "a parched and weary land where there is no water." All too often, spiritual thirst and weariness are a part of our lives in the music ministry. The strain of people constantly expecting to receive from us when our own needs have not been met can be exhausting. Yet, we are expected to minister to others from this dry desert place. How can we help anyone when we are the ones who need encouragement and joy?

The key for David is to shift his focus from the dryness and weariness of the desert to the love, power, and glory of God. This is such an easy concept, but most difficult to apply consistently in our lives. Often we get so far off track that we must completely stop what we are doing just to refocus. This battle can make us wearier than the desert. Then, as we look at our failure to keep our eyes on God, we can become disappointed with ourselves, and the downward spiral continues. But look at how David keeps his focus and his strength—praise with songs of joy, in the midst of the desert. Songs of joy, full of praise to God before leaving the wilderness desert keeps our focus on God so we can draw our strength from Him. Consistent songs of joy in the wilderness keeps us consistently strong and focused so we can minister to other people consistently. The joy of the Lord is our strength, no matter where we are in life.

Father, I want to do Your will in my ministry, but sometimes it is too hard and I get so tired. Remind me, especially in those times, to sing songs of praise to You from my heart. Thank You for giving me Your love and the tools I need to stay focused on You so I can have the strength to love others.

October 27

A Good Reputation

"Choose a good reputation over great riches;
being held in high esteem is better than silver or gold."
Proverbs 22:1

Your ministry's reputation is vital. Building a good reputation will get better shows and trust from everyone around you. A bad reputation makes ministry extremely difficult. But not all reputations are true representations of the ministry involved.

Some bands are viewed as "being all about the money" because they limit the number of free shows they play. Other bands are seen as amateur because they play mostly free shows. Some ministries have a very large merchandise table and hear comments about how they give their merchandise away. Other bands do not have a merchandise area. They hear about how they would not have to charge so much for shows if they would have more merchandise. So, what's a band to do?

Reputations are made by what other people think and then say. Most importantly, a ministry needs to be concerned about what God thinks. If you are convinced that your ministry is handling money the way God wants, you will be able to say so (kindly, in love) when questions or negative comments occur. No ministry will be able to meet everyone's ideas about how a ministry should handle money. But, communication about why you do what you do is key to establishing a good reputation. Instead of bristling at the next negative comment you hear about your band and money, use the opportunity to build a good reputation by communicating why you handle things the way you do. If you are truly choosing to do things God's way rather than seeking riches, you will eventually gain a good reputation.

Father, show us how we can handle our ministry's money Your way. As we communicate in love about money, give us favor with people and a good reputation.

October 28
Belief and Contempt

"And the LORD said to Moses, 'How long will these people treat me with contempt? Will they never believe me, even after all the miraculous signs I have done among them?'"

Numbers 14:11

Treating God with contempt—can you imagine doing that? This particular situation occurred when the spies came back from scouting out the Promised Land. The people complained and chose not to believe that God would do what He promised to do. Taking over the Promised Land seemed too much and too hard.

When we complain and choose not to believe and act on what God has called us to do, we cut ourselves a whole lot of slack. We say things like, "It's just not possible in today's culture" or "We do not have enough money to make that happen." Sometimes we even cover our laziness and unbelief with complaints like, "We tried but things just did not go our way," when we really have not been faithful to do God's work in God's way and in God's time. Of course we will have times of weakness, but when we consistently do not act on what God has called us to do, we show contempt for God. We can couch it in spiritual talk or even blame our leaders, but in our hearts we know we are not living up to our full potential in Christ. Like the Jews, we often give ourselves permission to behave this way.

How would our ministry be different if we viewed every time we did not act on belief in God's promises and calling to us as showing contempt for God? God wants to bring us into the Promised Land. He wants us to reach our full ministry potential. God desires to work powerfully through us to show the world His love. But in order for us to accomplish that, we must believe that He will work actively in our ministry to do what looks impossible.

Father, teach me how to believe You to do more through me. Bring me to a place where You can work mightily through me.

October 29
God's Wisdom and Plan

"If you need wisdom, ask our generous God, and he will give it to you. He will not rebuke you for asking."
                                                                    James 1:5

The music industry has undergone radical changes in the past ten years. We now have more choices than ever before. Not all of these changes and choices are clearly good or bad. But, most of them can benefit some ministries and musicians at the right time. The exact same choice made at the wrong time or with the wrong people can be devastating to a music ministry or end a musician's career. These days there is no one right way and no one who can tell you the steps that will definitely lead to success every time. But we have a God who knows and who will show us what to do, when to do it, and how to do it.

There is no shame in asking for help. Wise counsel from other people is priceless. Wisdom from God is essential. He has a lot to say to us, if we make the time to listen. When we listen, we must listen for what He wants to say—not what we want to hear. Asking God to bless the plans we have already made is not listening. Asking God what His plans are and then aligning ourselves with that plan is wisdom.

Seeking out and applying God's wisdom for our music ministries has always been and always will the recipe for success. The tools we have available to use will constantly change. We need to keep up to date with knowledge of the most current options. But we need to ask God for wisdom in which choices to make, when to execute the decisions, and how to apply them. When we follow God's plan we will have God's success in our ministries and lives.

Father, HELP! I NEED Your wisdom today. Show me Your plan and I will follow it. Show me my plans that I need to abandon and I will abandon them to walk in Your wisdom.

October 30
Believe for Small Things

"'What do you mean, 'If I can?' Jesus asked.
'Anything is possible if a person believes.'"

Mark 9:23

The context of this verse is miraculous deliverance of a demon from a deaf and mute boy. So, we usually associate this saying with the big problems in life. But, most of life is lived in small moments that make up days which turn into weeks. What I do or don't do in this moment today impacts the rest of my life. Can I believe for this small moment today?

For example, if I set a goal to write a new song each week and it's the end of the week; I have not written a song and I don't feel like it, I don't have any inspiration. Can I believe that if I sit down with my guitar, paper, and pencil that God will help? That song could be one that changes my life and many other lives for years to come. Can I dare to believe for that kind of creative inspiration and impact? Can I believe enough to start doing it?

Belief in God to work through us can be a real challenge. We are never talented enough, have enough money, or have the right connections. It is easy to focus on our lack. But belief gives us the ability to go beyond ourselves—beyond what we can accomplish with what we have. Belief allows us to see life through God's eyes and gives us the courage to reach our full ministry potential. Most often this potential is not reached in one giant step, but in small choices every day that add up to great impact. Our influence on the world can be diminished simply by not doing the small things. Yet, when we choose to believe for and consistently do the small things we can change the world.

Father, I want to impact and change the world around me. As the father of the demon possessed boy said, "I believe in You; help me overcome my unbelief." Show me what I need to believe You for and then do with Your strength and courage.

October 31

Not As Expected

"'Why are you frightened?' he asked. 'Why are your hearts filled with doubt? Look at my hands. Look at my feet. You can see that it's really me. Touch me and make sure that I am not a ghost, because ghosts don't have bodies, as you see that I do.' As he spoke, he showed them his hands and his feet."

Luke 24:38-40

We have expectations of God and how He works in our lives. Jesus showed up in a way that was so unexpected in these verses that the disciples found it easier to believe in ghosts than to believe He actually showed up. Today with our 20/20 hindsight, we look back on the disciples and are amazed at how silly they were, not truly realizing how much like them we are. How many opportunities have we missed out on because we could not believe God was in it?

We tend to define our ministry by the position we hold. We say, "I am a bass player or drummer and I play this particular genre of music." But could God empower a bass player to become an author or a pastor? Would God ask an entire band to play a radically different genre of music than they know how to do? Would we recognize His call to change genres if He asked? We also tend to think that God will work in specific ways in our ministries. People around us, both fans and friends, are influenced to grow closer to Jesus through relationship with us. But what if we arrived at a venue to find ten fans we have never met asking to receive Jesus before we even unload our gear? Would we believe and pray with them? God does not like to be put in a box. He works in our lives and ministries in unexpected ways on purpose, to keep us from relying on Him rather than on the "way it is always done." Because we know God, we should expect the unexpected and rejoice in the unusual.

Father, surprise me today with something new about You.

November 1
Thank God Publically

*"Then I will thank you in front of the great assembly.
I will praise you before all the people."*

Psalm 35:18

This psalm was written during a time of attacks against David. The entire psalm is asking God to rise up against David's enemies and defeat them, to give David the victory. Then, David talks about thanking God publically for all He has done.

We may not have people threatening to kill us like David did. But we all have challenges, areas in our lives where we just can't seem to win no matter how hard we try. We cry out to God to help us, hoping for a sudden miracle and wishing it would just all go away. Most often, as in David's life, there is not a sudden miracle. Circumstances usually change over time—one small step at a time. When we read the story of David's life we generally do not take in to account how many years each stage took: how long he was hiding in caves, or how long he ran from Saul before he actually became king. We read it in a matter of minutes, so the years go by quickly. We apply that same mentality to our own lives. Because we do not see instantaneous victory, we often do not thank God for what He has done. Take a moment and compare your life now to your life a year ago, five years ago, and ten years ago. Have you experienced changes? Do you see long term victories that you may not have noticed in the moment? Thank God publically for them.

It is easy to be thankful for the large miracles. They make exciting stories to tell on stage. But most people cannot relate to that kind of drama in their lives. We can lead them by thanking God publically for the long term changes and growth in our own lives and inspiring them to do the same.

Father, I want to see everything You have done for me. I will thank You publically and I will inspire people to do the same.

November 2
Working for God

"Work willingly at whatever you do, as though you were working for the Lord rather than for people. Remember that the Lord will give you an inheritance as your reward, and that the Master you are serving is Christ."
Colossians 3:23-24

There seems to be a common misconception that Christian musicians are lazy. We sleep until noon, socialize every evening, stay up all hours of the night, and we eat whatever is given to us free at shows. To some people it looks like we just drive around the country having a good time wherever we go and expect someone else to pay for it. We are judged on perceptions.

But is that really what happens? A real Christian music minister is bent on using their talents to bring people closer to Jesus. This means playing late night shows and working long days. Look at the amount of work on days we have gigs: we load up, drive to the venue, set up, play, minister to fans, tear down, drive home, and unload. We often do not get enough money to pay for gas, let alone buy food and gear. So, what looks lazy may be very hard work if you see the whole picture. In between gigs we have songwriting, practice, recording and all the tasks of small business management. We don't get paid for any of that work. Fortunately, God sees the whole picture.

Are you working hard for ministry? It probably won't look like the typical 9-5 job, but it does not have to. God didn't say, "Get a career and a cubicle." He did say, "Work... as if you were working for the Lord." Then, if we work for God, look what we are promised—an inheritance as our reward. So, don't let other people's perceptions mar your self-image or diminish the value of your ministry; see your work as God sees it.

Father, show me if I am being lazy. But also let me see my music ministry as You see it—with value and importance.

November 3
Don't Yank the Dog's Ears

*"Interfering in someone else's argument
is as foolish as yanking a dog's ears."*
Proverbs 26:17

What happens when you yank on a dog's ears? Most likely, you will be bitten. There is not much room for options or negotiations. You yank, you get hurt. Interfering in some else's argument will produce the same results. It will not end well.

Christian musicians often hear about quarrels, especially within a church. Somehow, people think it's OK to unload on a visiting musician and try to win allies for their side of the quarrel. How can we respond? We all know that the Biblical answer is to tell the person to go to their brother and work it out. Unfortunately, the gossiper often frames this situation in a way that it appears they need your help.

So, how do you know when to help? Does the quarrel involve you directly? If not, ask yourself if the dog will thank you for yanking his ears in this situation. If you were the offending party, would you want to have someone else involved? Don't be manipulated by someone that wants you on their side. Remind the person of Matthew 18:14-16: "If another believer sins against you, go privately and point out the offense. If the other person listens and confesses it, you have won that person back. But if you are unsuccessful, take one or two others with you and go back again, so that everything you say may be confirmed by two or three witnesses." Suggest that if they have already tried to solve the problem that their next step should be to meet with someone in leadership at their church, but not to spread the quarrel by talking to anyone else.

Father, forgive me for the times I have gotten involved in other people's quarrels. When the situation arises again, remind me of Your guidelines for handling disputes.

November 4
Make His Praise Known

"Sing to the LORD, for he has done wonderful things.
Make known his praise around the world."
Isaiah 12:5

A Christian music minister has one goal: to use music to bring people closer to Jesus. This goal changes the way a musician presents himself and his music to the world. The message becomes more important than the music.

Music can be a very effective tool to further the gospel message. But, like all tools, we must do the maintenance required to keep it performing at its peak. As musicians we spend hours practicing our instruments, crafting the best songs, maintaining our equipment, protecting our copyrights, etc., and rightfully so. We need to be experts at using well-kept tools, and being an expert takes a huge investment of time. But let's never forget WHY we invest the time.

Secular musicians market and brag about their skills and their instruments—where they have played, who they have played with, their education, and the best gear. Christian music ministers brag about what God has done. Very often Christian music ministers are just as talented, have similar equipment, and comparable music education and experience. But what the Lord has done makes all those things pale in comparison. The most effective music ministers build their entire ministry around God's message. From their press kits to their stage presentation, everything is designed for one purpose: to praise God for what He has done. Telling people about Jesus becomes such as overwhelming goal that becoming famous is no longer an issue. Fame is just a larger platform, another tool that can be used to love people to Christ.

Father, help me to be single minded. I want to stay focused on WHY I do music ministry: to tell the world about You.

November 5
Servant Leaders

"But Jesus called them together and said, 'You know that the rulers in this world lord it over their people, and officials flaunt their authority over those under them. But among you it will be different. Whoever wants to be a leader among you must be your servant, and whoever wants to be first among you must become your slave.'"

Matthew 20:25-27

Servants, leaders, and slaves: what is the difference? Does this passage mean that our spiritual leaders should be required to scrub the church toilets? Since music ministers are not pastors, maybe we should be doing the not-so-nasty jobs like stacking the chairs, and everyone else gets to go home early? No. This passage is not describing a reversed hierarchy. In fact it is completely throwing out the idea of who does which job based on religious hierarchy. Instead, what we do is based on love for each other and advancing the kingdom together.

So, let us say you are playing at a church and the janitor has not cleaned the bathrooms yet because he is ministering to someone. As a music minister, what should you do? That's right—you set up for the gig and then clean the bathrooms. It's not about who gets to talk and who gets to clean. It's about getting the ministry done. To demonstrate your love for the janitor and the person he is helping, you want to give them as much time together as possible. So, you minister by cleaning the bathroom once the work only you can do is done. In God's eyes, cleaning is not more or less prestigious than playing on stage or being the person who does one-on-one ministry. As music ministers we put ministry first, so we must have the attitude of helping wherever, whenever, and however we can. No prima donna rock star attitudes allowed.

Father, my prayer today is simple—convict me as needed.

Wisdom, Understanding & Knowledge

"For the LORD grants wisdom!
From his mouth come knowledge and understanding."
Proverbs 2:6

There are three Greek words that can be translated as wisdom. One is sophia, meaning "insight into the true nature of things." The word phronesis has to do with "understanding or a right use of the mind." Sunesis is the "critical faculty"—"understanding, intelligence." In other words, phronesis and sunesis occur when we apply sophia.

Three Greek nouns can mean understanding: nous which means "the mind" or "the seat of reflective consciousness" (this includes feeling, perception, understanding, judging, and determining); dianoia which means "a thinking through or over" (meditation or reflecting); and sunesis.

There are two Greek nouns for our word knowledge: gnosis which means "a seeking to know" (an enquiry or investigation); and epignosis which is "an exact or full knowledge, discernment or recognition."

Thank God that He is willing to give us all these things! There are so many choices to make in our music careers that affect our ministries: label or indie, press kit contents, web site design, who to hire as a manger, and even how many t-shirts to order. But our God is willing to help us with every decision if we seek Him and His wisdom, understanding, and knowledge. God wants to take an active role in guiding our ministry and lives.

Father, thank You for giving me wisdom, understanding and knowledge. Remind me to seek Your guidance daily as I make each decision, so my ministry can be done Your way. I want to be successful by Your definition of success.

November 7

He Rejoices Over You

"For the LORD your God is living among you.
He is a mighty savior.
He will take delight in you with gladness.
With his love, he will calm all your fears.
He will rejoice over you with joyful songs."
Zephaniah 3:17

We do not work hard enough. We do not have the right look. We are not talented enough. We are too tall, too short, too skinny, or too fat. We are not business savvy. Our hair just is not right. Our music is not popular right now—not new and cutting edge. The list can be endless—somehow we just do not measure up for potential success in the music industry.

But God sees us differently. He rejoices over us! He sings songs about us! Can you even believe that we make Him happy? That right, God delights in us! If you walked in to the President of the United States' office, do you think he would be happy or delighted to see you? Probably not, because he does not even know your name or who you are. He would be polite and keep his appointment with you if possible but if something came up, he would probably not regret missing out on meeting you.

But God lives with you every day. He sees every action you take, every word you speak. He knows not only your name, but also who you are in the core of your being. We make Him happy too! Why? God loves to have relationship with us—to share in our day, hear our hearts, and help us along the way. Our perfect actions and hearts are not what make Him so happy (which is good since none of us is near perfect). God is happy just to be with us! He lives among us so He can delight in us!

Father, I have a hard time understanding that I make You happy because I see all my imperfections. Help me to see from Your perspective and to delight in our time together.

Do This... Don't Do That

"Remember, it is sin to know what you ought to do and then not do it."

James 4:17

No one claims this as their favorite verse because it takes sin out of the realm of things we should not to and into the realm of things we should be doing. Life is so much easier when we can follow the rules of "Don't do that..." and then believe we are OK. The Christian life becomes a religion of rules that are not to be broken. But what about the "Do this..."?

There are many, many times especially in the New Testament that we are told to love one another, encourage one another, and pray for each other. But we do not tend to think that NOT doing any of those things is sin. Often we are prompted by the Holy Spirit to say something or do something to help someone else. But when we don't follow the prompting, we say we "missed it" rather than calling the "not doing" sin.

The sin of not doing the "do this..." can run rampant through a ministry. We feel that something is not right but we just cannot put our finger on it. The ministry will not be as effective as it should be, people will not be responding like they should. Perhaps it is because they see a religion of "Don't do that..." without an example of a life lived in the "Do this...". Doing the good that we know we should do requires laying down our wants and desires in any given moment. But giving up our lives results in living a very full and fulfilling Christian life. More than anything, people want to live a fulfilled life with significance and purpose. When you demonstrate that life by doing the "Do this..." they will want to know more. Do you want an extraordinary ministry? Stop sinning and "Do this..."

Father, living a life of doing the good I know I ought to do is the life I want. Bring to my attention the good I should do.

November 9
Sing With Joy and Gladness

> *"Those who have been ransomed by the LORD will return.*
> *They will enter Jerusalem singing,*
> *crowned with everlasting joy.*
> *Sorrow and mourning will disappear,*
> *and they will be filled with joy and gladness."*
> Isaiah 35:10

Singing can be a sign of joy of gladness. We can frequently be caught humming a tune when we are happy. We sing together in the car when we are on a road trip. We all chant "Happy Birthday" to honor a person on their special day. Entire crowds sing at sports events. Singing seems to be a natural response to joy and gladness.

As Christians, we have more reason than anyone to be joyful. The circumstances of our life might not be all we hope for in this particular moment. But, we have been ransomed by the Lord! Imagine that you had been kidnapped and your father paid the ransom money. As a result you returned to your home and the kidnappers were hunted down. How joyful would you be? Would the not-so-perfect circumstances of your life weigh you down in that moment? No. There would be tears of joy at your return. Your entire family would celebrate.

We can live each day in that same joy by remembering that we have been ransomed by the Lord. We can be filled with gladness and joy because we know we are going home. So, of course—we sing. It is a natural reaction to our joy. Sing out, rejoice with your family, be loud, and show the world your joy at being ransomed by your Father.

Father, saying "Thank You" for ransoming me just is not enough to express what I feel. My heart overflows with joy and so I sing for You. Accept my offering of praise as an expression of my love and gratitude.

Help New Music Ministers

"We know what real love is because Jesus gave up his life for us. So we also ought to give up our lives for our brothers and sisters. If someone has enough money to live well and sees a brother or sister in need but shows no compassion—how can God's love be in that person? Dear children, let's not merely say that we love each other; let us show the truth by our actions."

1 John 3:16-18

Everyone knows we should give to the poor. We donate to food pantries and homeless shelters as we are able. We even play concerts for free that help raise money to support these worthy endeavors, as we should. But there is one more thing we can do: help support new music ministers. Remember how difficult it was when you were first starting out—the excitement mixed with trying to figure out the logistics of playing out. What did you need? Helpful, practical advice and better equipment. Now you probably have both the experience to give good advice and some extra equipment you are not using.

What can you do to encourage a new music minister? How can you demonstrate your love for your brother? Spend time showing them what you know without changing their art. The easiest place to start is to clean out your equipment. Sort out what you regularly use, what you need for parts and backup; then sell at a greatly reduced price or give away what is left. You will be such a blessing to the new music minister as you teach them how to use the equipment and talk about some things you have learned. Your time and gear is an investment in future music ministries. The demonstration of the love for your brother builds unity within the kingdom and gains rewards in heaven.

Father, show me what I can do to help new music ministers. Nothing I own is more important than Your work. Help me to mentor the next generation of music ministers.

The Value of Musicians

"I also tried to find meaning by building huge homes for myself and by planting beautiful vineyards. I made gardens and parks, filling them with all kinds of fruit trees. I built reservoirs to collect the water to irrigate my many flourishing groves. I bought slaves, both men and women, and others were born into my household. I also owned large herds and flocks, more than any of the kings who had lived in Jerusalem before me. I collected great sums of silver and gold, the treasure of many kings and provinces. I hired wonderful singers, both men and women, and had many beautiful concubines. I had everything a man could desire!"
Ecclesiastes 2:4-8

This verse contains a pretty impressive list of riches that the author of this book, who refers to himself as the Teacher, accumulated. Look what is on the list—wonderful singers! Most people believe the Teacher was Solomon, arguably the wisest man ever because he received a special gift of wisdom from God.

So, here we have the wisest man ever placing the value of musicians right up there with huge homes, impressive gardens, incredible numbers of livestock, silver and gold, and enough slaves to take care of it all. Now that is wealth! It is amazing that someone with all that money would value music and musicians so highly. We see it in the modern day as well—a president hanging out with musicians, musicians being hunted by the paparazzi, and the first part of a church service is usually music. Although music is intangible, it is highly valued not because it can make money for the musician but because it affects people. You and your music have the ability to influence and change the world around you. Your gift should be highly valued and used wisely.

Father, help me to value my gift of music as much as You do. Remind me to use my gifts to effectively to change the world.

November 12
Lions and Laziness

"The lazy person claims, 'There's a lion on the road! Yes, I'm sure there's a lion out there.'"

Proverbs 26:13

There could be a lion out there. Surely, something bad will happen eventually. If we try, it probably will not work anyway. We can come up with many reasons to quit or not start at all. Some of those reasons may even be rational, realistic fears that paralyze us. But, at some point, we must choose to trust God to take care of us when bad things happen. We must exercise our faith if we expect to have an extraordinary ministry.

Music ministry involves many potential perils: vehicles break down when we are on the road, the ministry runs out of money, and equipment falls apart at the most inopportune times. People even try to steal our equipment, songs, and ideas, not to mention the bad contracts offered. It would be easier to stay home and use all of these potential problems as reasons to stay out of music ministry. The problem with doing that is we do not get to experience the full life God has for us. We do not help anyone get closer to Jesus and we do not impact the world in any meaningful way. It is easier to be lazy, to give in to our fears.

But God has called us to live an abundant life—a life of fullness, purpose, and significance. With that calling, He gives us the ability and resources to do everything He asks. We must be courageous and never give up if we are to defeat the lion. We must exercise our faith daily to overcome our fear and laziness. There could be a lion out there, and something bad will probably happen eventually. But God is stronger than lions and greater than bad things. We need to trust God to take care of us and do the ministry we are called to do.

Father, thank You for overcoming the lions. Remind me to stay focused on doing all that You have called me to do.

November 13
Braided Cords

"A person standing alone can be attacked and defeated, but two can stand back-to-back and conquer. Three are even better, for a triple-braided cord is not easily broken."
Ecclesiastes 4:12

Being in a band is hard. Creating an extraordinary music ministry is even more difficult. But we can stack the deck in our favor with band members that are bound together like a cord. The relationships that make up this cord are precious and must be guarded with the utmost care.

We have all experienced and been trained to withstand external pressure—attacks from outside the ministry. This kind of attack causes us to close ranks and stand closer together. External pressure often makes a band partnership stronger.

So, attacks from within are the most effective way the enemy has to defeat your ministry. The ability to cause any kind of separation between band members is one of his best weapons. Our enemy is subtle; he starts small in seemingly unimportant ways—an irritation, an offhanded comment taken wrong, etc. We shake it off and go on our way, until something else happens. Then, the first offense arises to be joined with the second. Before you know it two band members aren't as close as they used to be. They just don't enjoy each other's company as much as they used to, and the joy of doing ministry together decreases. The separation begins and the enemy has won.

As Christian music ministers we say "NO!" to the enemy—"NO!" to separation from our brothers in ministry. We protect our brothers and partners and stay strong as a cord bound together. This cord will not be broken or defeated!

Father, I love my band mates. They are my brothers in arms. Cause me to act on this love at all times. Give me the courage to do whatever it takes to protect our relationships.

November 14

Singing and Praying

"Around midnight Paul and Silas were praying and singing hymns to God, and the other prisoners were listening."
Acts 16:25

What is it about singing that makes people want to listen? Surely all the prisoners in the jail would not have normally gone out of their way to hear the Gospel message, yet they were listening. We are all familiar with the events that followed: miraculously the doors to the jail flew open due to a massive earthquake that shook the jail, and the chains to every prisoner fell off. But all the prisoners stayed in the jail and the jailer's life was saved because no one escaped.

There are several amazing things that happen in this story. Many sermons have been preached on the miracles. But notice that it all started with some people singing and praying and other people listening. We can do that. The headline-making part of the story is the miraculous earthquake. But isn't the most significant part of the story the praying, singing, and listening? There would have been no earthquake otherwise. We have been conditioned to focus our attention on the headlines—the big news-making events. So, it is easy to feel that our ministry is not important unless we make the headlines. But most of the significant kingdom events happen before the news ever knows anything is going on. If you asked God, I'm pretty sure He would say the most significant part of this story was the prayer and song of Paul and Silas affecting the prisoners' hearts, causing them to listen. God simply sent the earthquake to back it up, to add weight to what they were already hearing. God cares more about people's hearts than news-making events. When we line up our focus to God's viewpoint our ministry takes on new significance.

Father, show me how You look at people's hearts and ministry. Make me aware of what is truly important.

November 15

Do Something

"So, my dear brothers and sisters, be strong and immovable. Always work enthusiastically for the Lord, for you know that nothing you do for the Lord is ever useless."
1 Corinthians 15:58

No one feels enthusiastic all the time. There are many days we do not feel like working at all, let alone working enthusiastically. So, how do we get out of bed on those less than stellar days and consistently work with enthusiasm?

The answer is found in the last part of this verse—knowing that nothing we do for the Lord is ever useless. God always uses what we do for Him. Our lives take on a new significance when we let that fact sink deep into our hearts and minds. We have significance and purpose whenever we do anything for God. Our music ministries are not useless—they are used by God. Think about that for just a moment; the creator and ruler of the universe uses whatever we do for Him!

How can we be strong and immoveable? By understanding that we have a purpose and significance. We are important and what we do matters because God uses it! Notice the verse does not say God uses the big things we do, or the things that attract attention from other people, or even the things that change the most lives. No. The verse simply says nothing we do for God is useless. It does not matter if what you do seems menial or small in comparison to what other people are doing. Do something, anything, for God and God will use it. Now that's worth getting out of bed for! Being used by God is something to get excited about! Knowing that God uses what we do for Him will cause us to be strong and immoveable and to work enthusiastically.

Father, thank You for using my ministry. Thank You for giving my life purpose and significance by using whatever I do to expand Your kingdom. I love working with You.

November 16
Huram-abi

"I am sending you a master craftsman named Huram-abi, who is extremely talented. His mother is from the tribe of Dan in Israel, and his father is from Tyre. He is skillful at making things from gold, silver, bronze, and iron, and he also works with stone and wood. He can work with purple, blue, and scarlet cloth and fine linen. He is also an engraver and can follow any design given to him. He will work with your craftsmen and those appointed by my lord David, your father."

2 Chronicles 2:13-14

Huram-abi was the man put in charge of creating all the furnishings for Solomon's temple. This was a huge creative undertaking and a prestigious position to oversee it all!

But, did you know that Huram-abi was only part Jewish? His father was a Gentile from Tyre and his mother was from the tribe of Dan. Dan was the last of the twelve tribes to receive its portion of land and they received the smallest portion; it's not the best lineage. At that time, in Jewish genealogies females were only listed if they did something really important or if land transferred through them. So, the fact that Huram-abi's mother was a Jew of the tribe of Dan did not count for much. This guy was definitely not the perfect candidate for the job as far as bloodlines go. He was recommended by a Gentile king. Yet, God chose him to be the head creative person for the temple decor.

There are many reasons we should not be chosen to be music ministers. We can easily allow these shortcomings to stifle our creativity. But God looks at our hearts, not our perfection (or lack thereof). Creativity will overflow in us as we look away from what we are not and focus on what God has called us to be.

Father, Your love for me is overwhelming. Thank You for the gift of creativity. Help me to overcome all that I am not and use my creativity to express Your love.

November 17
Quality Creative Work

"In the same way, let your good deeds shine out for all to see, so that everyone will praise your heavenly Father."
Matthew 5:16

Advice has been going around for years that if you cannot make it in the secular music industry, you should try Christian music. The inference is that musicians do not have to produce as high quality music in the Christian market as in the secular market. This should not be so. Christian work, whether it is music or not, should always be done with our very best effort because we know that people around us are watching. They equate the quality of our work with the integrity of our spiritual lives.

As Christians, and especially as Christian music ministers, our work should be done with integrity, faithfulness, punctuality, competence, good attitudes, diligence, and enthusiasm. Our lives and our ministries are under constant scrutiny by those we are trying to bring closer to Jesus. Why would we compromise that effort with by doing a mediocre job, producing low quality music?

Our inspiration is Jesus Himself! Our reason to play music is the awesome news of redemption! So, it stands to reason that our music should be the most original, the most creative, and the highest quality of any music available. Shouldn't the secular industry be coming to Christians asking how we came up with such good ideas and how we accomplished them so well?

The quality of our work should be so outstanding that people notice the difference. We do not necessarily need to produce more; we need to produce the best. In today's world, more of the same mediocrity does not call attention to itself. But a superior product, in our case amazing music, stands out. Do you want to draw attention to God with your music? Create quality.

Father, give me creative inspiration and I will put my best effort and quality work into the project.

November 18

Thoughts and Ways

"'My thoughts are nothing like your thoughts,' says the LORD. 'And my ways are far beyond anything you could imagine.'"

Isaiah 55:8

Doing what God wants us to do is not always easy. But, doing what God wants us to do, the way God wants us to do it can be even more of a challenge. God's method of accomplishing what He wants done does not always make sense to us. We like the easy way. We like the fast way. We like it to happen now. There is a certain security in believing that if we do a certain thing in the prescribed way, the results will always be the same. God likes change. God likes growth. God wants what is best for us, not necessarily what is safest, easiest, or fastest.

As musicians, the tendency is to constantly be on the lookout for the golden key—the one thing that we can do to "make it," the one person we can meet to "get us in." We focus all our hopes and efforts on THE label deal, agent, or manager. But God may have a completely different path for us to follow.

The golden key for us is actually to spend time with God. We need to clearly hear His thoughts not only on where we are going and what we are to do, but also HOW we are to accomplish His goals for us and WHEN we should take the next step. It is easy for us to hear the destination and make plans for the trip based on the path everyone else seems to have taken. Of course, we know that our trip should start immediately. Unfortunately, everyone else's roadmap may not yield the same results for us and God's timing is not always now.

True success and fulfillment comes when we do what God wants us to do, how He wants us to do it, and when He wants it done. We can only accomplish this by hearing God's thoughts and learning His ways.

Father, tell me Your ways and thoughts. I will listen.

November 19
Pursuing Fame

"But soon it was time for the Jewish Festival of Shelters, and Jesus' brothers said to him, 'Leave here and go to Judea, where your followers can see your miracles! You can't become famous if you hide like this! If you can do such wonderful things, show yourself to the world!' For even his brothers didn't believe in him. Jesus replied, 'Now is not the right time for me to go, but you can go anytime.'"

John 7:2-6

The Jewish Festival of Shelters was the biggest event of the year. Jesus' brothers were right, He needed to be present and seen if He was going to become famous. Miracles would certainly grab the crowds' attention and gain Jesus a place in the center of the big stage. From a purely marketing standpoint this was good advice. But God had other plans and it was not yet time for Jesus to become the center of attention. Jesus was wise enough to stick to God's plan in spite of a great marketing plan.

Marketing and planning our music career is not wrong; in fact we will probably not be successful without it. But the most important step is to find out God's plan for our ministry first and then build a marketing plan to achieve the greatest impact for God's plan. On the surface the difference appears subtle because we do many of the same tasks. But in God's eyes and in our hearts, the difference is quite significant. Are we pursuing fame and success in the name of doing music ministry? Or, are we pursuing God and lining our lives up in obedience to His calling? Only God and we can see into our hearts and truly answer those questions. Here is a litmus test: would you be just as happy doing music ministry in the smallest obscure, venues, never getting media attention if you knew it was God's plan for your ministry?

Father, I want You. Help me to stay focused on doing Your will and not be distracted by the tools of music ministry.

November 20

Our Responsibility

"'A farmer went out to plant his seed. As he scattered it across his field, some seed fell on a footpath, where it was stepped on, and the birds ate it. Other seed fell among rocks. It began to grow, but the plant soon wilted and died for lack of moisture. Other seed fell among thorns that grew up with it and choked out the tender plants. Still other seed fell on fertile soil. This seed grew and produced a crop that was a hundred times as much as had been planted!' When he had said this, he called out, 'Anyone with ears to hear should listen and understand.'"

Luke 8:5-8

This story has three major components: the farmer, the seed and the ground. Unfortunately, Christian music ministers often get confused as to which components we are responsible for. The seed is obviously the Word of God. We cannot change it. Just as a gardener may plant different types of seeds, carrots onions and corn for example, we can highlight different aspects of the Word of God. But the seed remains the same—seeds. The farmer is us— spreading the seed of the Word of God wherever we go. It is our responsibility to continuously spread that seed. The ground is the hearts of the people. Some ground is better than others for planting. But we are not responsible to change the ground, unless it belongs to us. Preparing the soil, the hearts of the people who will hear the Word of God, is the job of the Holy Spirit. We must be willing to allow the Holy Spirit to change us, our hearts, so that we can grow the very best crops from the Word of God in our lives. We often confuse our work to be that of preparing the ground in other people's hearts because we know the seeds will grow better in good soil. But we cannot change other people. When we try, we are usurping God's responsibility.

Father, prepare the hearts of the people that I am about to talk to. Cause them to want to get closer to You.

Crooked and Perverse People

"Do everything without complaining and arguing, so that no one can criticize you. Live clean, innocent lives as children of God, shining like bright lights in a world full of crooked and perverse people."

Philippians 2:14-15

Crooked and perverse people are not going to segregate themselves to certain geographical locations, so we must live among them daily. Usually we focus on the difficult challenge of living with them, but equally challenging is that they must live among us. Crooked and perverse things they find acceptable are often exposed by our mere presence. For example, how many times have people apologized to you after using language they are sure you do not approve of? When you are not around, their language is much more acceptable and they do not apologize for it. Our presence can put them on edge. It is no wonder crooked and perverse people find joy in criticizing us when we fail. Even our smallest failures give them an excuse to remain perverse.

Christian music ministry is a very public position in front of large numbers of people that may only meet us once. For the most part, our audience does not get to see a life consistently lived for Jesus. They only see one small snapshot of our life. What does that one small snapshot look like through their eyes? There are certainly crooked and perverse people in our audience. While we can and should tell them about our experiences with Jesus, what they will see is our actions when we are with them. Are we arguing among ourselves about the stage set up or sound? Are we complaining about the lack of pay, the amount of work, or the size of the audience? Or are we making use of every opportunity to demonstrate the love of Christ to a crooked and perverse people? What will they see and remember about us?

Father, show me my Christian walk through the eyes of my audience. Teach me how to represent You more effectively.

Covenant Power

"Each time he said, 'My grace is all you need. My power works best in weakness.' So now I am glad to boast about my weaknesses, so that the power of Christ can work through me."

2 Corinthians 12:9

Working from our own strength, doing what we do best, is easy. But doing what we do not do well, especially in public ministry where people can see us fail, will test the best of us. Do we get frustrated with ourselves? Do we get angry that we are in this situation? People notice how we handle the tough times more than when life is easy. When they see us relying on God, they are encouraged to believe that they can also rely on Him. Our actions write our testimony on the tablets of people's hearts when things are tough without ever having to speak a word.

We have a covenant relationship with God. Covenant is different from partnership, because in partnership each party is responsible for a specified amount of effort put in and benefits given out, usually 50%. In covenant, each party is 100% responsible for everything. They each put in as much as is needed and each party shares the benefits as needed. In other words, God does not put in or take out only 50%. He makes up for however much we do not have and He gives us back however much we need (and more). He does this with whatever we need, in whatever quantity we need. We are responsible to use all of our resources and He makes up the difference. So, when we are weak, when we have very few resources, He provides more than when we are strong. This concept is why it is less beneficial to us to work from our strengths. When we work from our weakness, God is at work in us. God's power is more easily seen by others when they know we could not be doing this ourselves.

Father, demonstrate Your power through my weakness today. Remind me that my weakness is part of covenant with You.

November 23
Running to Tarshish

"But Jonah got up and went in the opposite direction to get away from the LORD. He went down to the port of Joppa, where he found a ship leaving for Tarshish. He bought a ticket and went on board, hoping to escape from the LORD by sailing to Tarshish."

Jonah 1:3

There are some parts to almost every ministry that we prefer to avoid at all costs, even in the music ministry which we love. Some of us do not like to speak on stage or record, others hate anything to do with money or marketing. Unfortunately, when we choose to avoid, delay, procrastinate, or run the other direction from any portion of what God has called us to do, we experience an absence of His presence in that area. The impact of our disobedience affects the entire ministry, even the areas where we are completely obedient.

Why did Jonah run to Tarshish? Later the book of Jonah says that he knew God would change his mind. Was Jonah afraid of what people would think about him if God did not destroy Nineveh? Did he simply not want to be the bearer of bad news that did not happen? Or was he using that as an excuse because the task he was given was too much work and outside of his comfort zone? The reasons why we or Jonah choose not to do the work God has given us to do are not as important as losing the presence of God. We all know the story of the whale and the plant, how Jonah's circumstances were made very uncomfortable for him. Have you considered that these circumstances are God's way of fighting to bring Jonah into obedience and back into relationship with Him? Perhaps some of our uncomfortable circumstances are actually God fighting for us—to bring us into obedience and into closer relationship with Him.

Father, do whatever it takes to bring me closer to You. Expose my areas of disobedience and cause me to run to You.

November 24

Frustrating People

"Then he and Aaron summoned the people to come and gather at the rock. 'Listen, you rebels!' he shouted. 'Must we bring you water from this rock?'"

Numbers 20:10

What happened to Moses? Just a few chapters earlier he was pleading with God not to destroy the Israelites, now he is calling them rebels. Was he that upset at the death of Miriam? Or could it be that he had been travelling with the Israelites in the desert for nearly 40 years and the constant complaining finally wore him down? The book of Numbers is silent for most of the desert wanderings after the Israelites did not enter the Promised Land the first time. God dealt with the rebellion at Kadesh the first time and now, 20 years later, here they were back again—and this new generation of Israelites was complaining once more. It is no wonder Moses lost his temper and struck the rock instead of speaking to it. Unfortunately God did not give Moses a pass on this sin. What exactly was Moses sin? It was not being frustrated with frustrating people. It was not even having a temper tantrum. God says Moses' sin was not trusting Him enough to honor Him in front of the Israelites. That single act of lack of trust and honor kept him from going into the Promised Land.

We must pay attention to this. In our ministry we will have to interact with frustrating people. We will be expected to perform too soon after the death of a loved one. Most likely we will lose our temper because of the frustrations of ministry. Of course we should work on handling those situations better. But God seems to be far more concerned with our trust in Him and honoring Him in front of others. So concerned in fact that He will withhold the ministry we desire. As usual, God is more concerned with the condition of our hearts than the frustrations around us.

Father, help me to grow in my trust for You, especially when I am dealing with frustrating people. I want to honor You.

November 25
Dearly Loved

"One day Jesus came from Nazareth in Galilee, and John baptized him in the Jordan River. As Jesus came up out of the water, he saw the heavens splitting apart and the Holy Spirit descending on him like a dove. And a voice from heaven said, 'You are my dearly loved Son, and you bring me great joy.'"

Mark 1:9-11

When we read about this event, we focus on what God did. It was amazing, but we should also pay attention to when God did it. God told Jesus that he was dearly loved and gave Him great joy before Jesus did His primary ministry. This should be significant to us because it demonstrates that God's love for us is not based on our performance in ministry. We know this in our heads, but our hearts do not always believe it. The funny thing is that most of us do not believe God loves us more when we are doing ministry well. However, our hearts tend to believe that His love decreases when we mess up.

Before we start our day, before we have done even one thing, we have already brought God great joy. Imagine that—we make God happy! Sure, He is proud of what we do in ministry, especially when we triumph over difficult circumstances and still do the work of the ministry excellently. But what really makes Him happy is that we have chosen to belong to Him and to spend time in relationship with Him. It is not about what we do; it is about whose we are. Knowing that we are dearly loved by God and that we bring Him great joy changes the perspective on even the most dismal day. Music ministry can be tedious and difficult and we often do not do it as well as we think we should. We can dread the upcoming day and beat ourselves up over the mistakes or we can delight in the fact that God loves us so much that we make Him happy simply because we are His.

Father, change my heart to know that You love me.

November 26
Fight or Flight

"So David escaped from Saul and went to King Achish of Gath."

1 Samuel 21:10

David was a great warrior because he knew when to fight and when to run away. Yes, there are times when warriors avoid and run away from battle. Conventional warfare would say that warriors should run when they know they cannot win, so they can live to fight another day. But David learned how to stand and fight when victory looked impossible and to run when victory seemed probable. David learned to base his decision to fight or run on what God directed, not on the situation. He did not fight or run out of fear. We must learn to do the same in our ministry.

Christian music ministries do not have to play every show we can find to book. Not every show is a good fit for us. In an age when we have been taught to increase our fan base by playing every single show we can get, those ideas are difficult to believe. But, we will not lose out on ministry opportunities by turning down gigs that are not in God's plan for us to play. Shows that do not line up with our mission, what God has called us to do, will not increase our ministry. In fact, playing those shows can leave us financially and physically drained, without enough resources to do the gigs that do line up with our mission. How are we to decide when we should or should not book a show? We must be like David and inquire of God. He will give us wisdom and discernment when we ask Him. Most of the time His answers will fall in line with what we consider to be common sense—does the show line up with our mission statement? Can we cover our expenses? Does it route well with shows we already have booked? But other times God's answers will make no sense at all. Knowing when to run and when to fight by inquiring of God will always give us the best direction to attain a successful music ministry.

Father, help us to hear Your plan during the booking process.

November 27
Thankful for Opposition

"Let your roots grow down into him, and let your lives be built on him. Then your faith will grow strong in the truth you were taught, and you will overflow with thankfulness."
Colossians 2:7

We are often told to be thankful around this time of year. But we are not often told how to be thankful, especially when we do not feel thankful. In this verse we are shown that thankfulness comes after sinking our roots deeply into God, building our lives on Him and then growing strong in truth.

Music ministry and the lifestyle that goes with it are not understood by most people. Questions like, "When are you going to grow up and get a real job?" are often not spoken so loudly that it sounds like screaming. So, we have a tendency to look around the Thanksgiving table and feel intimidated by the expectations of family and friends. But when we sink our roots deeply into God and let our lives be built on Him, we find it easier to remember that we are ministers bent on pleasing God. It would be nice to meet the expectations of friends and family, but if their expectation is not for us to do all we can to live for God then we are not responsible to meet those expectations.

We can be thankful for friends and family who do not fully understand why we are living as Christian music ministers, because opposition causes us to increase our faith. To live as a Christian musician in spite of opposition we must have deep roots in God so we can explain, in love, why we are making lifestyle choices for Him. We are forced to seek out the truth about why we do what we do both in the Scriptures and in our relationship with God. This process makes our faith grow stronger.

Father, thank You for releasing me from the burden of meeting other people's expectations. Show me how You are using their expectations to grow my faith.

November 28
Effective Ministry

"The Spirit of the LORD is upon me,
  for he has anointed me to bring Good News to the poor.
He has sent me to proclaim that captives will be released,
  that the blind will see,
  that the oppressed will be set free."

                                                    Luke 4:18

What does effective ministry look like? Exactly like Jesus. We can gauge the effectiveness of our ministry by how well we live up to His own description of His ministry, doing what Jesus did. What are some signs that the Spirit of the Lord is upon us? Our ministries should do four things to look like Jesus ministry: bring good news to the poor, release captives, cause the blind to see, and set the oppressed free. How well we are doing these things will tell us how effective our ministries really are.

The size of our fan base, how much music we sell, and how many gigs we play each year is not a gauge of effective ministry. These things are important only in that they demonstrate how much ministry opportunity we experienced. Opportunity is not the same as effectiveness. For example, a band with a large audience can play in a stadium and not accomplish any on of the four things Jesus did, while an unknown band can play a small show and see several captives set free. In this case, the smaller, unknown band is the more effective ministers even though they had less opportunity.

Strive for greater and greater effectiveness and allow God to promote us to more and more opportunities. Only after we have proven ourselves faithful to the ministry God calls us to do, He will enlarge our sphere of influence, our opportunities. For our ministries to be effective, we must do what Jesus did.

Father, teach me how to be more effective and to make the most of every opportunity You provide.

November 29
Genuineness

"You yourselves are our witnesses—and so is God—that we were devout and honest and faultless toward all of you believers."

1 Thessalonians 2:10

Genuineness is one of the most valued characteristics by people today. We do not need everyone to agree with our point of view or to be just like us, but we do want people to be real. Some descriptions of genuineness are: free from pretense or hypocrisy, authentic, and not counterfeit. Notice that the word perfect does not mean genuine. For example a flawed diamond is still a genuine or real diamond. A genuine Christian does not need to be perfect, but we do need to be consistent in our walk, no matter where we are, what we are doing, or who we are with.

How genuine are we with our life and our ministry? Do we hold to two sets of standards, one for performing and one for the rest of our life? If we are genuine, why do we feel the need to become more spiritual just before walking on stage? We should always feel privileged to serve God on stage and experience a sense of holiness. But we must be careful not to take the honor of serving on stage so far that we build up walls between us and the audience. There is no spiritual hierarchy of God, then us, and then the fans. The hierarchy is simply God and then the rest of us humans. When we lose that perspective, we lose the ability to be genuine. When we believe we are somehow higher up than other people, we feel a need to hide who we really are in favor of who we think we should be. But who we are eventually comes out and then we become hypocrites. When we are genuine, our actions are consistent. We demonstrate that we are increasingly holy, devout, honest, and faultless as a result of true maturity in faith. We simply desire to share the relationship we have with God.

Father, help me to be genuine in my life and my ministry. I want to live out the mature faith You have given me.

November 30
Build Them Up in the Lord

"We should help others do what is right and build them up in the Lord."

Romans 15:2

Christian music ministers are often asked to 'help people out.' We consistently get requests to do free shows that benefit a personal cause as well as being asked to have counseling-style conversations with people in crisis. We hear many stories of how one Christian has wronged another and are asked to take sides or intervene. Helping other people to do right is quite a bit more complicated than it should be. The problem is that not everyone has the same definition for doing what is right and not every one wants to be helped in the same way. How do we decide what is the right definition and best way to approach the problem? The key is in the last half of this verse: "build them up in the Lord."

What is right is not defined by how we feel or what we think about a situation. What is right is defined by God, what He says in His Word. Sometimes we can help someone to do what is right by showing them the Word and allowing them to apply it themselves. Unfortunately, most often, people need more help.

Helping others is not usually taking care of people's problems for them. Many people would prefer us to help them in this way, but this kind of help is only a short term fix. True help builds them up in the Lord by equipping them to do what is right themselves. Often, that is much more difficult and takes much more time and effort to do. Deciding what kind of help to give can be answered by seeking the Holy Spirit's guidance about what will be most effective in building them up in the Lord. That answer will not always be comfortable for anyone involved and will definitely not always be perceived as help. But, bringing people closer to Jesus is always the motivation for our actions.

Father, help me not to respond to needs without first seeking discernment to know the best way to build people up in You.

December 1
God's Rewards

"But when you pray, go away by yourself, shut the door behind you, and pray to your Father in private. Then your Father, who sees everything, will reward you."
Matthew 6:6

Praying to be noticed—everyone knows not to do it. But because we are human, we would all like a pat on the back, an acknowledgement from someone important that we are doing well spiritually. We work hard to please God and we want it to have some noticeable effect. There is nothing wrong with wanting a reward. God seems to have wired us to respond to rewards. But we need to pay attention to whom we are seeking the reward from. Part of music ministry is to pray with the people we meet. We definitely should not shirk from this responsibility. But publically praying for people can have its own rewards in the amount of attention we can draw to ourselves. We cannot pray for people with the hope of appearing spiritual to be rewarded with more fans or being re-booked at a church. We must be careful not to lift ourselves or our ministry up with false spirituality. We must draw attention to God and what He is doing, not our ministry and what we are doing.

Praying for other people's needs is not more important than spending time alone with God. God sees both prayers and while other people thank you for praying with them, God rewards you for spending time with Him as well as for taking care of His sheep. The greater the person who gives us a reward, the more important the reward. Seek God's rewards, which are given because of deeds done privately, with pure motives. He can more than make up for any rewards that people might have given because they saw us doing something spiritual.

Father, examine my heart. Show me when my motives are not pure. I want Your rewards, not the lesser rewards from men.

December 2
River of Righteous Living

"You sing trivial songs to the sound of the harp
and fancy yourselves to be great musicians like David."
                                                    Amos 6:5

Amos is not a very popular book in the Bible because it is geared to making us look at our own lives of holiness before God. Chapter 6 talks about the future destruction of Israel due to their arrogance. A picture is painted of people who loved parties, luxury, and fame but did not take care of others. They turned "justice into poison" and "righteousness into bitterness." Amos 5:23-24 says, "Away with your noisy hymns of praise! I will not listen to the music of your harps. Instead, I want to see a mighty flood of justice, an endless river of righteous living."

So, in the midst of our concerts and worship services, how are we doing with justice and righteous living? It is not enough to NOT DO the things we should not be doing; we must DO the things of God. Often we can easily see the shortcomings in other people's lives but are blind to weaknesses in our own life. What are we actively doing personally and as a ministry to promote justice and righteousness? What more could we do? "Remember, it is sin to know what you ought to do and then not do it." (James 4:17) Have you ever repented for the sin of omission? Omission means "to leave out"; in this application it means NOT DOING all that we know we could and should do.

David was a great musician because his heart was on God and the things of God. His music was a reflection of what he did with his life. Let's also be great musicians in God's eyes because of the way we demonstrate justice and righteousness in our lives!

Father, I want to be great in Your eyes! Show me how to do better at righteousness and justice. Remind me until I actually do it. Thank You for Your love toward me, while I am working toward being all that You want me to be.

December 3
Calculating Ministry Costs

"Jesus soon saw a huge crowd of people coming to look for him. Turning to Philip, he asked, 'Where can we buy bread to feed all these people?' He was testing Philip, for he already knew what he was going to do. Philip replied, 'Even if we worked for months, we wouldn't have enough money to feed them!'"

John 6:5-7

"The gospel is free but it takes money to get it to them" has been a popular quote in the church. It is true—ministry costs money. The real problem comes when we find out that we do not have the money to do the ministry we want to do. How do we react? Many times we do not recognize that we are in this position simply so God can test our reaction. If we knew the lack of money to do ministry was a test, would we react differently?

Every ministry experiences lack of money from time to time. God allows this to give us an opportunity to grow our faith. Rather than being overwhelmed at the lack and how much it will take to meet the need, like Phillip, we may want to view these tests from God's perspective. A more appropriate response would be to first make sure that this particular ministry is what God wants to do through us. It is possible that we are trying to do something we want to do, but that He has not planned for us to do. If we are called to do it, we can then seek wisdom on how to go about doing it His way.

God has many different ways to get us the resources we need, even stretching a small amount of food to be enough for everyone. We must not turn down ministry simply because we have calculated the cost. All our ministry must be led by God and provided for by God, whether we have the money we need before we start or not.

Father, clearly direct me to do Your ministry Your way.

Fear, Pressure & Intimidation

"Meanwhile, Saul stayed at Gilgal, and his men were trembling with fear. Saul waited there seven days for Samuel, as Samuel had instructed him earlier, but Samuel still didn't come. Saul realized that his troops were rapidly slipping away. So he demanded, 'Bring me the burnt offering and the peace offerings!' And Saul sacrificed the burnt offering himself."

1 Samuel 13:7b-9

Kings were not allowed to sacrifice offerings—that was the job of priests. Saul knew it was wrong, but he did it anyway. What caused such a blatant rebellious action? Fear. Saul decided to take things into his own hands because his men were afraid. They were abandoning him. Saul was afraid that if he didn't do something quickly, he would not have enough men left to defeat the enemy. So, Saul failed God's test of faith by running ahead of God and taking control of the situation. Saul gave in to intimidation from the enemy, pressure from his men, and the fear that God might not take care of it all this time. This sounds exactly like something we would do.

Running ahead of God (not waiting for His timing) and taking situations into our own hands are two of the most common ways we use to get out of synchronicity with God. Whenever we act because we are giving in to fear, pressure, or intimidation, we are wrong because we are not acting in faith. We must not move until we have God's direction. Leading a ministry involves other people who do not always act in faith. They will pressure us to act on their fear, and even create crisis to increase the intimidation. But we must not give in. Acting on their fear will make the situation worse for them and us. Effective ministry leaders wait for God and follow Him courageously.

Father, cause my spirit to be alerted to fear, pressure and intimidation tactics from the enemy. I will follow Your lead.

December 5
Fear and Love in Creation

"Such love has no fear, because perfect love expels all fear. If we are afraid, it is for fear of punishment, and this shows that we have not fully experienced his perfect love."
1 John 4:18

Fear is a tactic of Satan, which he uses on all of us. He tells us many lies about God and how God will withhold His love if we are not perfect or do not perform perfectly every time. This fear of failure and rejection is one of the best tools Satan has to keep creative people from creating. The ability to risk it all and overcome this fear is why creative people are often so different from 'normal' people. Christian artists are free to create because we know God loves us and will be with us no matter how our creation turns out or if other people like what we created. Secular artists do not have this love relationship with God, so they often create from their own fear and perversity.

This love relationship enables Christian artists to try new methods, explore new ideas, and work with new materials in an environment without fear of punishment for failure. People may not always want to hear our new music so it might not be marketable, but God will never punish us for attempting to create something new. He will love us and be with us to participate in the creative process! He will inspire us to push our creative boundaries further and further as we lean on His love through the process. God is proud of even the works we consider to be our worst endeavors, if we were creating them in relationship with Him. He is like a parent who hangs the child's artwork on the refrigerator, even when the child paints the sky yellow and colored outside all the lines. Our creations are expressions of love in relationship.

Father, help me to be more free in the creation process. Inspire me with new ideas and ways to express them.

December 6
Successful Efforts

"And may the Lord our God show us his approval
and make our efforts successful.
Yes, make our efforts successful!"

Psalm 90:17

There is no such thing as a completely self-made successful artist. Success requires an artist to utilize a team of people to do a myriad of tasks that the artist is not skilled at doing. Most artists are not skilled at managing all these people and tasks, so they hire a manager to do it for them. But even with an excellent manager, many artists do not succeed. We sometimes assume that because an artist is Christian they will succeed. But, many Christian artists are not successful. Why? Because we do not accept God's ministry plan or definition of success and then work toward it by doing what He wants, when He wants it done, and how He wants us to do it.

The approval of God plays a critical role in our success. It is easy to define how to get God's approval—do what He says. It is much more difficult to actually do it. Even though our brains acknowledge that God's plan, God's way, and God's timing are all best, we somehow continue to struggle with doing what we want, when we want, and how we want to do it. Unfortunately, this struggle will not end as long as we are on earth. We are left with setting our hearts toward the goal of pleasing God and doing our best to attain it. Fortunately, we have a God who has lived this same struggle and understands. His approval is given despite our failures, as long as we continue to come to Him in repentance and love. We will never have perfect ministries because we will never do everything perfectly. But we can have successful ministries because God approves of our efforts.

Father, thank You for blessing my efforts and making me successful in ministry despite my failures.

December 7

I Am There

"For where two or three gather together as my followers, I am there among them."
Matthew 18:20

To the Jews, "I Am" has a very significant meaning. It encompasses the entire being of God: "I Am the alpha and omega, the beginning and the end." Studying the names of God shows us that He is Jehovah Rapha our healer, Jehovah Shalom our peace, El Shaddai the Lord of Hosts, El Elyon the Most High God, Adonai Lord and Master, Jehovah Nissi our banner, Jehovah Raah our shepherd, Jehovah Tsidkenu our righteousness, Jehovah Jireh our provider and Jehovah Mekoddishkem the one who sanctifies us. All of this and more is contained in "I Am." When God says, "I am there among them," it has a powerful meaning.

The entire being of God is among Christian music ministers whenever we gather as His followers—every gig, every practice, every recording and songwriting session. Meditating on the many aspects of God and how big He really is will radically change how we approach time spent with other Christian musicians. Our perspective rapidly changes from "What are we going to do?" to "What is it that God wants to do through us?" and "How can we best prepare ourselves to be used by Him?" The pressure of striving for successful ministry is removed, and a joyful expectation of God's hand at work arises as we consider ourselves to be simply vessels for His greatness to pour through.

There is nothing else that can be substituted for His presence. No amount of work or better equipment or connections with the right people will bring us true success. God's presence is life changing, both for music ministers and for everyone we encounter. The fullness of God's presence in the midst of us is the "formula" for successful ministry.

Father, show Yourself strongly in our midst. Let us see Your hand at work in us and affecting the people around us.

December 8
Marking and Equipping

"Jesus realized at once that healing power had gone out from him, so he turned around in the crowd and asked, 'Who touched my robe?'"

Mark 3:30

Why did Jesus insist on calling attention to this woman? She would probably have preferred a private, quiet miracle because her situation was embarrassing. Then, when she does come forward He does not do more or greater miracles for her. What He does do is to mark the moment, to establish a particular moment in time that she can point back to in the future as proof that Jesus actively worked in her life. He also equipped her with knowledge of three things that she possesses: faith, peace, and freedom. Whenever God does something in anyone's life, the enemy comes later to try to steal or pervert that work. Confirming this woman's faith, peace, and freedom and marking the moment gave her what she needed to withstand future attacks from the enemy. She could remember the conversation with Jesus when the enemy came to try to deceive her by saying that she was not really or completely healed.

When our fans experience our music, especially at live gigs, God often does a work in their lives. But hours or days later, the enemy comes to try to steal that work with lies. So, it is important for us as music ministers to follow the example of Jesus by marking the moment and to equip them with words, particularly Bible verses, they can stand on. Talking to us one-on-one after the show can mark the moment, but we need to be keenly aware that what we say must be more than thanking a fan for coming to the show. Our conversation must be full of God's words. To initiate that kind of conversation, we must be full of God's Word and paying attention to the prompting of the Spirit.

Father, help me to equip fans with Your Word to withstand the enemy as he attempts to steal what You have done.

December 9
Love Each Other

"This is my commandment: Love each other in the same way I have loved you."

John 15:12

Do you remember what it was like to be a fan before you were a performing musician? You stood in line before the show to get a good seat, closer to the band. After the show you waited in line again to buy merchandise and get an autograph. You hoped the band would somehow notice you and acknowledge you with a handshake or by talking to you for a couple minutes. If they did, the evening was something you talked about with your friends for days afterwards. Maybe you were the kid who did something crazy just to make sure you got the bands attention. Remember the good old days... before you knew about the difficulties of being in a band: loading and sound check, travelling in a small van, no money, lack of sleep and way too much pizza.

Jesus experienced many similar difficulties in ministry. While He did not have to deal with malfunctioning sound systems, He did have to meet by lakes so His voice would carry. He did not have a small van to travel in—He walked. Yet, he took time for people. He constantly loved on people personally even while He was training the disciples. There are no stories of Him ignoring people or telling someone who sincerely wanted His help to come back at a more convenient time. In fact, He went out of His way to find people to love on. Even now, as He is doing His work in heaven, He never tells you that He is too busy to talk.

Let us follow His example when we are dealing with fans at a show. Love on them the way you wanted to be loved on when you were a fan. Be patient, knowing that they do not know what you had to go through to play the show. Show them the love of Christ as He has shown it to you.

Father, remind me of how patient You have been with me. Pour out Your love through me to fans so they will know love.

December 10
With God

"For nothing is impossible with God."

Luke 1:37

Most people love this verse. Unfortunately, most of us misuse this verse. We quote it correctly, but we actually mean "For nothing is impossible." We use it to spiritualize our own big plans for the success of our ministry. All too often, Christian music ministers start out on an extended tour only to run out of money and return home early. Or, we start a recording project and are not able to finish. Then we wonder why God did not back us up. Surely, we had with faith to believe for the impossible. What went wrong? We left out two little words "with God."

Doing things "for God" is not the same as doing things "with God." When we do things for God, no matter how good or well intentioned they are, we retain a measure of control. We decide what we are going to do and how we are going to do it. God is not obligated to back up our plans, simply because we choose to believe for the impossible. This is not faith; it is an attempt to manipulate God. Doing things "with God" implies that He is there for the decisions in what to do as well as planning how to accomplish the goal. "With God" means that we are on His side, working through His plan. We do not retain control. Many actions associated with doing things for God or with God might look exactly the same. But a heart check at any moment can tell us quickly which we are currently doing. This one difference may be indiscernible to other people and we may rationalize it away because we want to do our big idea. But it means everything to God. Doing ministry with God or for God will make the difference between a successful ministry, no matter how impossible it seems, or failing with impossible dreams.

Father, show me the true motives of my heart. Convict me immediately every time I try to move forward without You.

December 11

Who Defends Your Ministry?

"They said, 'Has the LORD spoken only through Moses? Hasn't he spoken through us, too?' But the LORD heard them. (Now Moses was very humble—more humble than any other person on earth.)"

Numbers 12:2-3

Humbleness is a requirement for being an excellent Christian music minister. We know that "pride comes before the fall" because we have seen other people in ministry fall. So, we have learned to stay watchful against pride both with ourselves and using our band mates for accountability. But sometimes the jealousy and arrogance of other people causes them to talk badly about us and our ministry, no matter how humble we are.

In this verse we see Moses' key supporting people, Miriam and Aaron, trying to usurp his position as the leader of the Israelites. First they criticized his choice of a wife, using her different race as a tool to cause people to question Moses' position as the only leader. Then they came right out and tried to make themselves equal to Moses in position. If they had succeeded Moses would not have been the leader; he would have been a leader who could have been out voted whenever Aaron and Miriam joined together. This was not God's plan and Moses knew it. So, what did he do? He let God handle the situation.

True humility occurs when we allow God to be in complete control. It has often been said that the definition of humility is "power under control," but perhaps for a Christian a more accurate definition would be "power surrendered to God's control." When someone comes against us or our ministry we want to defend ourselves, strike back, and even retaliate. Most of the time, we have the power to do so by talking badly about that person. But a humble person will surrender the power to protect themselves and let God take care of the problem.

Father, thank You for being the defender of my ministry.

December 12
Rejoicing in Small

"Do not despise these small beginnings, for the LORD rejoices to see the work begin, to see the plumb line in Zerubbabel's hand."

Zechariah 4:10

Most mature Christians interpret this verse to mean that we should be OK with starting a ministry small and then building it up to be larger over time. This is a good application of the verse, but we tend to forget it when our ministries grow. As we experience more success, we want everything we do to be proportionally bigger. But small beginnings should happen within larger ministries. Every new release, every new line of merchandise, every new project we take on can start small. In fact, the most prudent path is often to start small on purpose. For example: we do not need to buy thousands of pieces of a new line of merchandise. It is much more prudent to try a very small amount first to see how well it will sell. We can apply this principle to most of our ministry. There is little harm in trying something new if we start small, growing a little at a time.

The reason that many larger ministries get stuck in a rut is that they are unwilling to experiment with anything new because they despise small beginnings. They see their ministries as large and expect everything they do to be larger and more immediately successful than their current view of their ministry. Small beginnings are viewed as being not worth their time and effort. But God looks at potential. He has a way of taking a very small opportunity and growing it into something that glorifies Him in a large way. We need to see each possibility and opportunity set before us through His eyes. Even when our ministries grow large, we must remember that God often works best through small beginnings.

Father, remind me that my ministry will never be too large to start something new that is small if it pleases You.

December 13
Uncomfortable Seasons

"For everything there is a season,
*   a time for every activity under heaven.*
A time to be born and a time to die.
A time to plant and a time to harvest.
A time to kill and a time to heal.
A time to tear down and a time to build up.
A time to cry and a time to laugh.
A time to grieve and a time to dance.
A time to scatter stones and a time to gather stones.
A time to embrace and a time to turn away.
A time to search and a time to quit searching.
A time to keep and a time to throw away.
A time to tear and a time to mend.
A time to be quiet and a time to speak.
A time to love and a time to hate.
A time for war and a time for peace."
*   Ecclesiastes 3:1-8*

Seasons in our life are not always pleasant or positive, but that does not mean they are not of God. We would be most unwise to change the direction of our ministry based on whether or not we approve of or like the current season we are in. God uses each season to bring us closer to the likeness of Jesus. He will not remove from us that which He is using to perfect us. Our challenge is to discern the season in which God has placed us and then to flow with that, rejecting all other opposition until we discern a changing of God's planned season. We may be uncomfortable, but uncomfortable is not necessarily bad. We may feel delayed in attaining our goals but delays can be yield wonderful fruit. God's season always produces the best in us.

Father, give me discernment of the seasons. Teach me to work in harmony with what You are doing in my life.

December 14
Create Income, Then Build

"Put your outdoor work in order and get your fields ready; after that, build your house."

Proverbs 24:27

For those of us who do not make our living as farmers, this sounds like a strange thing to say. Outdoor work and getting fields ready are ways that farmers produce income. They get money only after they sell the harvest. So, this verse is actually saying that we should focus on producing an income before we build our house. The full meaning of building our house is more than constructing the physical structure of the home. It includes increasing the amount of treasure, or stuff as we call it, we have in our home. The principle of this verse is to focus on creating an income before figuring out how best to spend it. Building up our home is a good thing, but creating an income is better and should come first.

Applying this principle is especially important for music ministers and ministries because our income tends to be sporadic and very small at first. It builds over time. We must focus on increasing that income in every area: performance fees, merchandise sales, royalties, etc. before we spend money on things that we want but do not directly help produce an income. Of course we all want the best gear, but if we have to choose between upgrading our gear and purchasing enough merchandise, we should choose the merchandise. The sale of that merchandise will create a profit which will help keep our ministry going and provide for new gear. The principle of focusing our resources, including our time, on creating an income first allows us to ensure financial stability and longevity of our ministry. Applying that same principle to our personal lives provides stability and sustainability for our future.

Father, give me wisdom to know how to invest time and money to create a future income for myself and my ministry.

December 15
We Never Give Up

"Therefore, since God in his mercy has given us this new way, we never give up. We reject all shameful deeds and underhanded methods. We don't try to trick anyone or distort the word of God. We tell the truth before God, and all who are honest know this."

2 Corinthians 4:1-2

Making a living as a musician is hard work. Most people struggle for years before they see enough income to support themselves. Along the way they learn to try every trick in the book, including some not so legal black hat style tactics. In the end, most give up their art and move on to a "regular" life. But Christian music ministers are not struggling and fighting for their art. We do not sacrifice our lives for music. We lay down our lives for Jesus. If we are successful at following Jesus, we are successful in God's eyes. So, we do not need to strive to make more money for ourselves and our ministries using trickery or illegal tactics. We are free to do what is right in all our business dealings. We do not need to distort the truth in our marketing to get ahead. We simply tell the truth about what God is doing through us and our ministry. While we do make the most of every opportunity, we do not need to strive to get to know the "right" people while ignoring those whom our ministry is meant to serve. We are free to do our ministry, serving in truth with integrity.

When our goal, our ministry, is to simply follow Jesus in obedience, all striving for worldly success ceases. We experience freedom to do our ministry regardless of the size of the audience, the amount of merchandise we sell, or the number of people who follow us on social media. Unlike secular musicians, those things do not determine our success. So, we never have a reason to give up! We simply keep following Jesus.

Father, reveal areas that I am striving to achieve worldly success. Change my focus to be successful in obeying You.

December 16

Repeating the Solution

"The LORD appeared to Isaac and said, 'Do not go down to Egypt; live in the land where I tell you to live.'"

Genesis 26:2

Previously Abraham had experienced famine in the land, and now there was another famine in the land. When Abraham saw famine, God told him to avoid it by moving to Egypt. Imagine what Abraham (if he was alive) could have said to Isaac: "Back in my day there was a famine and so I moved to Egypt." If he did not come right out and say it, he could have certainly implied that Isaac should do the same thing. This sounds like many of our friends and family attempting to fix our lives. But in this verse, Isaac is told to go through the famine by staying where he was in Gerar. Both men experienced a similar problem, but God had two very different solutions. This story points out the importance of hearing God's solution for our particular situation, rather than simply doing what has worked in the past. Imagine what would have happened if Abraham had stayed, or Isaac had moved? Where we live is an easy example of how this principle can affect our lives. As we lead our ministries and our families, Christian music ministers face many other kinds of decisions that will impact our current situation as well as our future.

God's solutions and instructions position us for our future. His plan will cause us to grow to be able to handle our future as well as put us in the right place at the right time to be able to move into our future. God's solutions may not always seem right to the people around us, because they will draw from their past experience to come up with an answer. It is always wonderful to hear their stories, and testimonies of what God has done for them. But ultimately, we must hear from God.

Father, continue to speak to me about Your plan and Your solutions for my life and ministry. Give me ears to hear You.

December 17

Dry Bones with Purpose

"The LORD took hold of me, and I was carried away by the Spirit of the LORD to a valley filled with bones. He led me all around among the bones that covered the valley floor. They were scattered everywhere across the ground and were completely dried out. Then he asked me, 'Son of man, can these bones become living people again?'
'O Sovereign LORD,' I replied, 'you alone know the answer to that.'"

Ezekiel 37:1-3

These verses have been commonly used to demonstrate how God can resurrect and restore dead things in our lives. It is always an encouraging message to hear, particularly when we have lost something that we really wanted. But there are also times when God chooses not to resurrect the dead things. It is critical for us to know the difference. But how can we tell if and when God well resurrect something? Just as he did for Ezekiel, He will speak and tell us what to do. God did not randomly resurrect the dry bones—He had a purpose and a plan for them.

As we approach the end of the year and are evaluating our ministry, it is important for us to discern which aspects of the ministry God wants us to continue to do, which things he wants us to let die, and which things He wants to resurrect. God absolutely can resurrect dry bones. But we also can waste much time and effort attempting to resurrect a thing simply because we want it back. We certainly do not want to waste time and effort next year trying to resurrect things that do not fit with God's purpose and plan or to continue to do things that are not going to be effective. We must clearly hear God's leading and then run in that direction with all our might, no matter how impossible or common the circumstances look.

Father, speak to me clearly about the upcoming year and the direction of my ministry. I long for Your leading.

December 18
Counting the Cost

"But don't begin until you count the cost. For who would begin construction of a building without first calculating the cost to see if there is enough money to finish it? Otherwise, you might complete only the foundation before running out of money, and then everyone would laugh at you. They would say, 'There's the person who started that building and couldn't afford to finish it!'"

Luke 14:28-30

No one likes to live on a budget. No one enjoys the self-discipline of putting off buying something they really wanted. No one looks forward to saying, "No, I can't afford to do that right now." But isn't it worse to run out of money?

Most musicians are asked to play for free more often than for payment. Free shows cost us money in travel expenses and wear and tear on our equipment. If we played every time we are asked for free, we would run out of money. It is especially hard to curtail the amount of ministry we can do for lack of money. But, that is exactly what we need to do—balance the cost of doing free shows (giving) with what we can realistically afford.

Often, shame accompanies turning down shows. Sometimes the source is within us. Sometimes, other people try to shame us because they view our denying their gig as us not believing in their good works. But there is no shame in doing what the Bible says. Rather, we should be proud that our ministry endeavors to live on a budget; doing as much as we can with what we have—but using wisdom to know when we have reached our limits. Using this wisdom, and allowing God to guide us through our finances, gives our ministries longevity.

Father, help me to see Your hand guiding my ministry through money and budgets. Remind me to be self-disciplined and patient as I walk out Your plan for my ministry and life.

December 19
Love Warriors

"'Don't be afraid!' Elisha told him. 'For there are more on our side than on theirs!'"

2 Kings 6:16

People come against Christian music ministers more frequently than other Christians simply because we are in the public eye. The reasons for the opposition are varied: jealousy, misunderstanding our motivations, incorrect doctrine about music ministry, etc. Christians tend to find one thing that they do not agree with and withdraw their support, while non-Christians feel threatened by our spiritual stance. Unfortunately, because of the variety of reasons for opposition, we are often left feeling attacked on all sides, from Christians and non-Christians alike. But this feeling is not truth. It is an emotion based on misperception. Our enemy designed this threat to keep us in a defensive posture. When we feel opposed, threatened, and attacked we are less likely to be on the offensive about sharing the love of Christ. We withhold expressing the love of God in our actions and our words, especially towards family and friends, when we are trying to protect ourselves from them.

In the story from this verse, God opened the eyes of Elijah's servant to see all the heavenly beings surrounding them. Elijah and his servant did not need to fear those who opposed them on earth because the presence and power of God was with them. We are in a similar situation; we do not always remember who is with us. If we look at those who oppose us, it is easy to fall into a protective, defensive position. When we are defensive, the losers are the people around us because they do not get to experience the love of God through us. But, we can offensively fight to express God's love to them because we know the love and power of the one whose side we are on.

Father, remind me of the strength of Your love and power working through me. I am a love warrior!

December 20
Night Watchmen

"O Jerusalem, I have posted watchmen on your walls;
they will pray day and night, continually.
Take no rest, all you who pray to the LORD."
Isaiah 62:6

One of the most misunderstood aspects of being a Christian music minister is the strange hours we keep. People who maintain more 'normal' hours do not understand why we sleep until noon and are awake at 3 am; and so, we are often judged as being lazy. The truth is that God has wired us to be able to stay up all night because that is most often when we need to do our ministry. We are not 'wrong' simply because we were created to live differently. We have the freedom to be used by God when other people are unavailable.

One of the more important things we do during the nighttime hours is to keep watch over our cities. We pray while everyone else is asleep. We are available for ministry when no one else is awake. Who do people contact at night to get help? The people they know who will probably be awake—musicians. People who need help in the middle of the night are in crisis; otherwise they would wait until morning. So, being available to pray and minister at night is important. We cannot lose sight of our calling, even in the face of judgments by people who do not understand it. We must be who God has created us to be, and be faithful to do all that He has planned for us to do. Our life is unusual but because we are willing to be unusual, God can use us in extraordinary ways to take care of His people. God did not create us to be 'average' or 'normal' or to blend in with people. He created us to love and take care of people. Our strange lifestyle puts us in a unique position to do so.

Father, help me to make good use of my nighttime hours. Send me people who need help when no one else is awake.

December 21

Favor vs. Favoritism

"But there will be glory and honor and peace from God for all who do good—for the Jew first and also for the Gentile. For God does not show favoritism."

Romans 2:10-11

Does God show us favor? Absolutely. Does God show favoritism? Never. It is amazing how just a few letters can change the meaning of a word so much. Favor means being held in high regard or a gift given out of goodwill rather than to be paid back. Favoritism means preferring one above another. Favor is a God concept; favoritism is our enemies' way of perverting favor.

We live in God's favor. But we do not always live in favorable situations. So, our enemy uses the difficult times to make us doubt God's favor. He will tell us to compare our life and ministry to someone who is in an easier or more prosperous situation. From there we assume that for some reason God has given them more favor; perhaps they worked harder, or sinned less than us. We start to believe that somehow they must be better than us, because God has given them more. But God does not show favoritism. In truth, our less-than-favorable situation is God's favor on our life. We may be in a season of discipline and training, or experiencing a time of refinement, or we may simply be in a position to experience our next season. Regardless of the reason, the person who appears to be receiving more favor is actually just in a different season than we are. Both seasons, the easy and the difficult, are God's favor—God's hand at work in our lives to bring us into His fullness. Understanding God's favor vs. favoritism allows us to set aside all comparisons between each other and our ministries. God will give us what is the very best for us, of course that is not going to look the same as what is best for someone else. God's favor is equal but not the same.

Father, thank You for the exact favor that is best for me.

December 22
Working in a Fallen World

"And to the man he said,
'Since you listened to your wife and ate from the tree
   whose fruit I commanded you not to eat,
   the ground is cursed because of you.
All your life you will struggle to scratch a living from it.
It will grow thorns and thistles for you,
   though you will eat of its grains.
By the sweat of your brow
   will you have food to eat
   until you return to the ground
   from which you were made.
For you were made from dust,
   and to dust you will return.'"

Genesis 3:17-19

Why is making a living from music so difficult? Why do we work so hard and still the money does not come in like it should? Part of the reason is that we live in a world that has been cursed. Specifically, since the fall in the garden, making a living requires very hard work. Often we will receive thorns and thistles for that work. Yes, Jesus redeemed us from the curse, but the entire world has yet to see that redemption.

The curse will sometimes impact our ministry, no matter how hard we work. So, when we do not make as much money as we hoped or needed, we cannot automatically assume that we have done something wrong or that God is leading us in a different direction. Our circumstances can be affected from three different places: our enemy, our God, and the physical world. We must exercise discernment to know which is affecting each specific situation. Then, we can make the best decisions about the future of our ministry.

Father, give me discernment to know where to work hard so that my work will be the most effective possible.

December 23
Misunderstood Actions

"Meanwhile, Jesus was in Bethany at the home of Simon, a man who had previously had leprosy. While he was eating, a woman came in with a beautiful alabaster jar of expensive perfume made from essence of nard. She broke open the jar and poured the perfume over his head."

Mark 14:3

"Wasteful," they said. "Why didn't she sell the perfume and give the money to the poor?" But that is not what Jesus said. The perfume that the woman used was perfume usually reserved to anoint the bridegroom by the bride on the wedding day. It was very expensive and considered to be part of a woman's dowry. So, the woman's actions meant that she was dedicating herself to follow Jesus at all costs, even at the cost of her future marriage. What the disciples saw was a lost opportunity to help the poor. How many times have you done something that was meant for good, but was misunderstood because someone else had a different focus on ministry? It happened in Jesus' day, it happens now, and it probably will always happen.

In this situation, we are each responsible for two things: (1) to do what we believe God is leading us to do, and (2) not to condemn other people as they do the same. Part of the test in different ministries is for us to love each other even when we do not understand each other. How many times have we heard a Christian musician condemn another ministry because what they are doing is not of God? If what they are doing is not blatant sin, how do we know what God has asked them to do? We need to love first and then if we do not agree or understand, seek to communicate. What would the disciples' response have been if they asked Mary why she was using up her perfume before condemning her in front of Jesus? Then, what would Jesus say?

Father, give me love even when I do not understand.

December 24

God Loves You

"For God loved the world so much that he gave his one and only Son, so that everyone who believes in him will not perish but have eternal life."

John 3:16

Most Christian music ministers spend all year demonstrating the love of God to other people. But many of us forget to apply the grace needed to accept that love for ourselves. Sure, we know all about it, but we have a difficult time allowing God's overwhelming love to completely take over our hearts. We see who we are with all our faults and imperfections. We know how far short all our ministry efforts have fallen. We know that we are not as good as we should be, and that we have not tried as hard as we could have. Our hearts believe that we are not now and never will be quite good enough. Even though it does not show on stage, we know how broken we really are. So, it is hard for us to allow the fullness of God's love to overwhelm us. We end up experiencing only small portions of His greatest gift to us.

We know the correct doctrine about God's love. If anyone asks, we give them the correct answers. But God is not as interested in correct doctrine and answers as He is with our hearts. He loves us—period. He loves us. He is so very proud of us dedicating our musical gifts to His use, but His love is not about what we do or do not do in ministry or music. He loves us—who we are at the very core of our being. He overwhelmingly loves who He created—you. No expectations, no contingencies, and no agenda—He loved you before you loved him and He certainly loves you now that you love Him in return. Today, take the time to come with all your brokenness and imperfections to simply be overwhelmed with the greatest gift He has to give us, His love.

Father, do not only pierce my heart with Your love today—completely overwhelm it.

December 25
What are we Talking About?

"After seeing him, the shepherds told everyone what had happened and what the angel had said to them about this child."

Luke 2:17

During the holidays family and friends often talk about their jobs, what they are doing at work, and how well their careers are doing. It is an easy conversation that does not usually raise controversy. By default, Christian music ministers tend to talk about their jobs as well—where we have been, how many new songs we have written, or funny road trip stories all come up as topics of conversation. While those conversations can be entertaining and certainly are not wrong to have, they are not the same as talking about God and our relationship with Him. Discussing what we are doing in our ministry is not telling people what God is doing through our ministry. For example, if two friends went on a road trip together, they could talk about all the things they did and saw, or they could talk about how that experience changed them and their friendship forever.

Throughout the year our friends and family may not get as much time for quality conversations with us as we would like because we are too busy. But Christmas is a time to stop our normal activities and reconnect. We need to follow the example of the shepherds—to leave our work behind and go tell everyone what God is doing. These conversations are not always safe; they require personal vulnerability and therefore personal risk. But isn't that what Christmas is all about? A vulnerable baby risked it all to have relationship with us. This year, let us determine to share what is most important with those closest to us: the love of God and what He has done.

Father, give me courage to talk about what You are doing in my life. Give me wisdom to know when these conversations are appropriate and open the hearts of the people I love.

December 26
A Good Future and Hope

"'For I know the plans I have for you,' says the LORD. 'They are plans for good and not for disaster, to give you a future and a hope.'"

Jeremiah 29:11

This is one of the most commonly read verses in the Bible. Unfortunately, common verses tend to lose their impact over time. Take a moment and reread this verse as if you had read it for the very first time. Look at what God is saying to you about your life and your ministry. It is very exciting!

God has a good plan for us—we have a good future ahead of us! If we completely believed this, what would we dare to do in ministry? What kind of future would we hope for? As this year draws to a close, we naturally look back and assess how it went. We see things we liked and things we could have done better, successes and failures in our ministry and our personal lives. While it is important to look back and then assess where we are at now, it is more important to dream of the future. Pondering the things we would like to do in the future, what we would like to be known for, and who we would like to be reveals our hearts' desires. Spend time dreaming; envision the kind of future God may have planned for your ministry. Dream beyond where you are now and the resources your currently have available. If you could do anything in ministry, what would you do?

Then, take your dreams to God. Many people have been amazed to find out that God placed that dream in their hearts as His good plan for ministry. Defining and refining those dreams leads us towards God's plan. It will take us a lifetime to walk out God's complete plan for our lives and ministry, but we can trust that His plan is good and so we have hope for a very good future.

Father, place Your plans for my future in my heart. Give me eyes to see unlimited potential of the ministry we can do together. Then, show me how to walk out our dream.

December 27
Heart's Desires

"For God is working in you, giving you the desire and the power to do what pleases him."

Philippians 2:13

Many people believe that simply because they want to do something, it must not be God's will. Some people also believe that if a task comes easy to them, God must be calling them to do something else. These beliefs cause confusion for music ministers because we love what we do and we have a gift to do music. We practice to be better at using our gift, but for the most part even practice brings us joy. Obviously, God created us and gifted us to do music. It pleases Him when do it.

Unfortunately, society often tries to get musicians to use gifts that they deem to be more practical, such as auto mechanics or data entry. We usually fail miserably at those jobs. Why? Because we are not called or gifted for them and we have no desire to do them. We do not experience God working through us when we try to do jobs that God has not called us to do. While we may have to take jobs to support our ministry, doing jobs instead of our ministry does not please God. God working through us powerfully does not require us to be miserable. Pleasing God does not mean that we set aside every desire of our heart.

As we mature in our faith and renew our minds, our hearts become more like God's heart. The closer we get to Christ, the more our hearts' desires become His heart's desires. So, for mature Christ followers, it is reasonable to use the desires of our hearts as one of several guides that help us discern God's will for our lives and ministry. We can trust Him to give us the tools we need to do what pleases Him and the desire to do it.

Father, I do not want to spend my life as an unhappy Christian, doing Your ministry without joy. Change my heart's desires to be Yours and give me my hearts desires.

December 28

It Never Ends

"If it is true that you look favorably on me, let me know your ways so I may understand you more fully and continue to enjoy your favor. And remember that this nation is your very own people."

Exodus 33:13

We can understand a person better by observing what they do. For example, when we see a lead singer warming up his voice before a show we can tell that he probably has had some vocal training and possibly hopes to make a career out of singing. Similarly, when we see any musician consistently using ear plugs we can understand that they are intentional about playing music for the rest of their lives. Just as we gain a better understanding about people and musicians by watching what they do, we can understand more about God by knowing His ways.

When we choose to take time to spend with God, we then experience Him drawing closer to us; from this we can learn that He desires to have relationship with us. This relationship is a continually growing process. We use each new thing we learn about God to from a more complete picture of Him. Eventually we can come to know not only what He thinks but how He thinks, which leads us to understand why He does things in certain ways. We grow in our understanding of God as we seek to know Him better because He says that when we seek we will find. The more we seek, the more understanding we gain and the more favor we receive. But, in the end, we never truly "arrive." We can never completely understand, never fully know God. This is the joy of our seeking, of our journey; it will never end because there is always more to know and experience. There is always a new adventure with God just up ahead.

Father, more than anything else, I want to know You. So, just like Moses I pray: let me know Your ways so I may understand You more fully and continue to enjoy Your favor.

December 29

Signs or Relationship

"Whether the cloud stayed above the Tabernacle for two days, a month, or a year, the people of Israel stayed in camp and did not move on. But as soon as it lifted, they broke camp and moved on. So they camped or traveled at the LORD's command, and they did whatever the LORD told them through Moses."

Numbers 9:22-23

The pillar of fire and the cloud made it easy for the Israelites to know where to go and when. Although we do struggle with being disobedient, most of our struggles come from not knowing for sure which way to go and when. We think that if we just had some sign, like fire or a cloud, we would find life and ministry to be much better.

What the Israelites did not have was relationship with God. So, they were led like children. Can you imagine waking up each morning without knowing if you would move your entire household that day? No warning, no time to prepare—each day you could move, or not. That is how children are treated, they live in the moment. God says, and they do (or be disciplined for not doing). But adults, friends of God, have conversations ahead of time to give them time to adjust and prepare for changes. This is part of relationship. God will speak to us and involve us in the whole process, not just the one day's event. Unfortunately we sometimes still act like children, jumping ahead and doing when we hear the first thing we want to hear. Although there will be exceptions when God wants to surprise us, most of the time God will speak to us ahead of time when a change in our direction is coming. He will allow us time and help us plan to make the change in our ministry and our lives as easy as possible. So, which is really better—a physical sign or relationship?

Father, help me to grow in maturity in my relationship with You so I can lead my ministry in Your direction and timing.

December 30
Imprisoned by God

"For the next two years, Paul lived in Rome at his own expense. He welcomed all who visited him, boldly proclaiming the Kingdom of God and teaching about the Lord Jesus Christ. And no one tried to stop him."

Acts 28:30-31

Paul lived as a prisoner under house arrest in Rome for two years. Apparently, this was God's plan all along. Paul was given several warnings about what would happen to him in Rome but he still felt that God was leading him to go there. Being confined to the house at his own expense is not what most of us would call successful ministry. Surely Paul would have preferred to be on the road on one of his missionary journeys.

Still, it could be argued that this time of being hemmed in, imprisoned, by God was Paul's most influential and successful time in ministry. During these 2 years he wrote many letters to churches at a time when there were no instructions for how to be a Christian and no New Testament. For two thousand years people have used some of those same letters in our Bible. Also during these two years, Paul testified to some of the highest government officials. When Paul stood trial there were usually many, many people present who also heard the Word of God. Most of these people would never have gone into the local church or synagogue. We do not have a record of what these people did after hearing Paul, but they had the potential to influence how the world was run. History would certainly have been different if Paul had not spoken to them. So Paul, at what could have seemed to be an inactive point in his ministry, changed the world forever. Ministry is not always about being on the road. Some of our greatest ministry times will be when God hems us in.

Father, give me discernment to know when You are hemming me in for a greater work or when the enemy is hindering me.

December 31
I Am with You Always

"Jesus came and told his disciples, 'I have been given all authority in heaven and on earth. Therefore, go and make disciples of all the nations, baptizing them in the name of the Father and the Son and the Holy Spirit. Teach these new disciples to obey all the commands I have given you. And be sure of this: I am with you always, even to the end of the age.'"

Matthew 28:18-20

As we close out this year and begin another, it is appropriate to remind ourselves once again of our goal as Christian music ministers. Our primary goal is not to play in front of as many people as possible, make a living doing full time ministry or even having a powerful impact on the world around us. All of those things are good, but God's best for us comes when we are obedient to seek out and do His will. Our goal is to bring people closer to Jesus using the tools and methods He wants, in the timing He wants, and with the right motives. Defining how close we came to attaining our goal is not found in seeing an increase in the results of our efforts. It is found in seeing how much closer we came to simple and humble obedience in following God's plan for us and our ministry. We should take the time to assess how well we did this year and determine what steps we can take to do better next year.

No matter how well we did or did not do, two things remain the same: we are called to bring people closer to Jesus, and He will always be with us to help us accomplish that mission. We must be careful not to run ahead or lag behind where God is leading us in order to achieve that mission. The only way to stay in sync with God is to consistently have fellowship with Him. As the New Year dawns, let us thank Him for all He has done in the past year and for the promise of His presence in the next year.

Father, Your active presence in my life is all that I desire.

Afterword

Thank you for taking this journey of digging deeper into ministry with The Christian Musicians Devotional. It was truly my pleasure to write it for you. I have grown closer to Jesus as a result of the two-year journey it took to create this book. Now, I am trusting God that you have grown closer to Him along the way. Please share this book with someone else who will benefit from its contents.

As always, I pray God's best for you and your ministry, and so I will leave you with this blessing which was originally given by Moses and Aaron to the people of Israel:

> *"May the LORD bless you*
> *and protect you.*
> *May the LORD smile on you*
> *and be gracious to you.*
> *May the LORD show you his favor*
> *and give you his peace."*
>
> *Numbers 6:24-26*

Contact Marie Wise

Website: ChristianBandHelp.com

E-mail: marie@ChristianBandHelp.com

Facebook: facebook.com/ChristianBandHelp

Twitter: twitter.com/ChristBandHelp

Final Notes

• Did you enjoy this book? Please consider submitting a review on Amazon.com. Reviews are very helpful to other people who might consider purchasing The Christian Musicians Devotional.

• The companion book to The Christian Musicians Devotional is **The Christian Band Handbook: Wise Guidance to Build an Extraordinary Music Ministry.** Why learn from the school of hard knocks if you don't have to? The Christian Band Handbook contains the how-to's of Christian music ministry with advice about which things Christian bands must do differently than secular bands to reach their full ministry potential. This one of a kind resource tool is available as a paperback or as an e-book (formatted for any device: Kindle, Nook, and as a PDF file) at **ChristianBandHelp.com/store/Christian-band-handbook/.**

• Be sure to check out Marie's website **ChristianBandHelp.com** for FREE lists of Christian venues, state and county fairs and Christian festivals. The website includes information about press kits, copyrights, merchandise, band business and money.

• Additional copies of The **Christian Musicians Devotional: 365 Days of Digging Deeper into Ministry** can be purchased at **ChristianBandHelp.com/store/christian-musicians-devotional.** This book is available as a paperback or e-book.

• Marie's husband, Mark, writes supernatural fiction. You can learn more about Mark at **facebook.com/markcampbellauthor.**

• The Christian Musicians Devotional is printed by CreateSpace, an Amazon company.